Warriors

ED NIELSEN

WARRIORS

2008

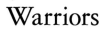

Warriors

TABLE OF CONTENTS

To Sarah —
On the occasion of our birthdays.
Happy birthday, Sis!
Love, Ed Nielsen

6-2-09

INTRODUCTION

There are two rules in war: Rule One, people are going to die. Rule Two, you can't change Rule One.—Larry Touchstone

The Vietnam War was one of the most divisive events in American history. It tore apart country, family, and friends. Some believe we entered this conflict with noble goals but the same will probably admit our implementation left much to be desired. Others felt strongly we had no business at all interfering with affairs in that part of the world. The goal of this volume is not to resurrect those debates, but rather to offer a forum to those in uniform who participated. However you feel about the debate, the efforts and sacrifices of our servicemen must be acknowledged.

World War II veterans report that when they returned from service and went into a bar, they weren't allowed to buy a drink—it was always on the house or on the tab of other patrons. Korean War veterans recall that they were usually on their own when it came to purchasing drinks and that other patrons mostly ignored them. On the other hand, some Vietnam War veterans say they were often refused service and sometimes ridiculed if not attacked by other patrons.

Our Vietnam vets did not choose to go to war in most cases. In fact, conscription was the order of the day so many went there against their will. Yet most valiantly gave their all. The total lack of appreciation for their sacrifice from some quarters still nettles many of these men. That could well account for so many Vietnam veterans being so tight-lipped about their experiences. One gentleman I approached put it this way, "I seldom talk about my time in Vietnam and on those rare occasions when I do it's only with my fellow veterans."

Others I approached seemed happy to bare their souls. Some didn't consider it a big deal at all, and others thought it therapeutic and cathartic to get their memories out in the open. To be perfectly honest, there were probably one or two vets who told me their story only because I am a personal friend. One willing vet told me, "You're the first guy who's ever asked me to talk!"

I desperately wanted to interview a retired Intelligence officer I know, but he couldn't talk to me—the things in his head are still classified! Another officer I approached was a pilot who had been shot down, captured, and spent considerable time in the Hanoi Hilton as a POW. He wanted to save his story for a book of his own, and that's great. Go for it, Scotty, and put me down for a copy.

To all who shared their thoughts and memories with me I cannot thank you enough. The events you reprised are solid gold, and I've recounted them just as you told them to me—okay, I touched up the grammar a bit and moved things around for continuity. Otherwise, these are *your* stories—I'm just the lucky narrator. I am honored and forever in your debt for allowing me to tell the world about your experiences.

I apologize for any mistreatment you may have suffered at the hands of war protestors. Please believe that time has softened their hearts and that we all have a profound respect and appreciation for what you went through for your country. May time heal all your wounds, both physical and emotional. We love you.

Ed Nielsen

PROLOGUE
I Was There Last Night

A couple of years ago someone asked me if I still thought about Vietnam. I nearly laughed in his face. How do I stop thinking about it? Every day for the last twenty-four years, I wake up with it, and go to bed with it. But this is what I said: "Yeah, I think about it. I can't quit thinking about it. I never will. But, I've learned to live with it. I'm comfortable with the memories. I've learned to stop trying to forget and learned instead to embrace them. Vietnam just doesn't scare me anymore."

A psychologist once told me that not being affected by the experience over there would be abnormal. When he told me that, it was like he'd just given me a pardon. It was as if he'd said, "Go ahead and feel something about the place, Bob. It ain't going anywhere. You're going to wear it for the rest of your life. Might as well get to know it."

A lot of my "brothers" haven't been so lucky. For them the memories are too painful, their sense of loss too great. My sister told me of a friend she has whose husband was in Vietnam. She asked this guy when he was there. Here's what he said: *"Just last night."* It took my sister a while to figure out what he was talking about. Yep, I was there. When? Why, just last night. And on my way to work this morning. Over my lunch hour. Yeah, I was there.

My sister says I'm not the same brother that went to Vietnam. My wife says I won't let people get close to me, not even her. They are probably both right.

Ask a vet about making friends in Vietnam. It was risky. Why? Because we were in the business of death, and death was with us all the time. It wasn't the death of, "If I die before I wake." This was the real thing, the kind where boys scream for their mothers. The kind that lingers in your mind and becomes more real each time you cheat it. You don't want to make a lot of friends when the possibility of dying is that real, that close. When you do, friends become a liability.

A guy named Bob Flannigan was my friend. Bob Flannigan is dead. I put him in a body bag one sunny day, April 29, 1969. We'd been talking only a few minutes before he was shot, about what we were going to do when we got back in the World. Now, here was a guy who had come in-country the same time as myself, a guy who was loveable and generous. He had blue eyes and sandy blond hair. When he talked, it was with a soft drawl. Flannigan was a hick and he knew it. That was part of his charm. He didn't care. Man, I loved that guy like the brother I never had. But, I screwed up. I got too close to him. Maybe I didn't know any better. But I broke one of the unwritten rules of war: *Don't get close to people who are going to die.* Sometimes you can't help it.

You hear vets use the term "buddy" when they refer to a guy they spent the war with. "Me and this buddy of mine..." *Friend* sounds too intimate, doesn't it? *Friend* calls up images of being close. If he's a friend, then you're going to be hurt if he dies, and war hurts enough without adding to the pain. Get close; get hurt. It's as simple as that.

In war you learn to keep people at that distance my wife talks about. You become so good at it that, twenty years after the war, you still do it without thinking. You won't allow yourself to be vulnerable again.

My wife knows two people who can get into the soft places inside me: my daughters. I know it probably bothers her that they can do this. It's not that I don't love my wife, I do. She's put up with a lot from me. She'll tell you that when she signed on for better or worse she had no idea there was going to be so much of the latter. But with my daughters it's different. My girls are mine. They'll always be my kids. Not marriage, not distance, not even death can change that. They are something on this earth that can never be taken away from me. I belong to them. Nothing can change that. I can have an ex-wife; but my girls can never have an ex-father. There's the difference.

I can still see the faces, though they all seem to have the same eyes. When I think of us I always see a line of dirty grunts sitting on a paddy dike. We're caught in the first gray silver between darkness and light. That first moment when we know we've survived another night, and the business of staying alive for one more day is about to begin. There was so much hope in that brief space of time. It's what we used to pray for. "One more day, just get me through one more day."

And I can hear our conversations as if they'd only just been spoken. I still hear the way we sounded, the hard cynical jokes, and our morbid senses of humor. We were scared to death of dying, and trying our best not to show it. I recall the smells. The odor of cordite, the way it hangs in the air after a firefight. Or the pungent stench of rice paddy mud, so different from the black dirt of Iowa. The mud of Vietnam smelled ancient, somehow, like it's always been there. And I'll never forget the way blood smells, sticky and drying on my hands. I spent a long night that way once. That memory isn't going anywhere.

I remember how the night jungle appeared almost dreamlike as the pilot of a Cessna buzzed overhead, dropping parachute flares until morning. That artificial sun would flicker and make shadows run through the jungle. Sometimes, it was worse than not being able to see what was out there. I remember once looking at the man next to me as a flare floated overhead. The shadows around his eyes were so deep it looked like his eyes were gone. I reached over and touched him on the arm; without looking at me he touched my hand. "I know man. I know." That's what he said. It was a human moment. Two guys a long way from home and scared shitless. "I know man." And at that moment he did.

God, I loved those guys. I hurt every time one of them died. We all did, despite our posturing. Despite our desire to stay disconnected, we couldn't help ourselves. I know why Tim O'Brien writes his stories. I know what gives Bruce Weigl the words to create poems so honest I cry at their horrible beauty. It's love. Love for those guys we shared the experience with.

We did our jobs like good soldiers, and we tried our best not to become as hard as our surroundings. We touched each other and said, "I know." Like a mother holding a child in the middle of a nightmare, "It's going to be all right." We tried not to lose touch with our humanity. We tried to walk that fine line. To be the good boys our parents had raised and not give into that unnamed thing we knew was inside us all.

You want to know what frightening is? It's a nineteen year-old boy who's had a sip of that power over life and death that war gives you. It's a boy who, despite all the things he's been taught, knows that he likes it. It's a nineteen-year-old who's just lost a friend, and is angry and scared and determined that some son-of-a-bitch is gonna pay. To this day, the thought of that boy can wake me from a sound sleep and leave me staring at the ceiling.

As I write this, I have a picture in front of me. It's of two young men. On their laps are tablets. One is smoking a cigarette. Both stare without expression at the camera. They're writing letters. Staying in touch with places they would rather be. Places and people they hope to see again. The picture shares space in a frame with one of my wife. She doesn't mind. She knows she's been included in special company. She knows I'll always love those guys who shared that part of my life, a part she never can. And she understands how I feel about the ones I know are out there yet. The ones who still answer the question, "When were you in Vietnam?"

"Hey, man. I was there just last night."

Robert Clark
Author of *Flowers of the Ding Ba Forest*

CHAPTER 1
ARMY SECOND LIEUTENANT BILL HOWELL
Artillery

Someone was firing at us with a mortar. He did exactly what I'd have done: fire once long, once short, split the difference, and keep doing that until the objective has been achieved, that is, a direct hit. This guy was landing short but kept walking them closer and closer. He finally fired one over my OP and, when he did that, I told the two guys in the bunker with me, "You guys need to get down and grab hold of something because he's got us bracketed and this next one is going to be close."

*B*ill's dad was in the military when Bill and his siblings were born. He was a career soldier and retired in 1966 as a command sergeant major. Naturally, his children leaned toward careers in the military. Bill graduated from high school in 1964, attended a local junior college in Lawton, OK, and then transferred to Oklahoma State University. After a year there, he was doing poorly in all courses except ROTC. Bill joined the Army in 1967, took basic training at Fort Bliss, TX, applied for and went through OCS at Fort Sill, OK. His brother went through ROTC at University of Oklahoma. Both chose Field Artillery as a result of growing up in Lawton, OK, just outside Fort Sill, the Army's Field Artillery Training Center. Bill's dad was stationed at Fort Sill when Bill was in middle school and finished his career as a National Guard advisor in nearby Oklahoma City. Bill served in Vietnam 1968-69.

During OCS, I filled out a dream sheet indicating I'd like to go to flight school and learn to be an Army aviator. I had planned to go to Fort Hood, Texas, and six months later to Fort Walters, Alabama, for helicopter school. Unfortunately, my eyes weren't 20-20. Back then, because the Vietnam buildup was just starting, they could be choosy about whom they let into flight school. In my case, since I had a refraction to correct my vision to 20-20, they had enough applicants who had perfect vision and wouldn't send me to flight school.

My brother got an ROTC commission upon graduation from OU at Norman, while I was a candidate. He came into my barracks while I was in OCS and he was already a 2LT. The whole barracks snapped to attention when someone hollered, "Attention! Officer on deck!"

When I realized who it was, I asked him what he wanted.

He said, "I need to borrow 20."

As a brand new 2LT, he loved all the commotion he caused by coming into our barracks. After he left, everybody wanted to know who that officer was. I just told them it was my poor brother.

Two days before I graduated from OCS, I got called into the Orderly Room. My battery commander said, "I've got some bad news for you. Your orders to flight school have been canceled."

I asked where I was going instead, adding that I'd like to stay at Fort Sill near my hometown. A lot of 2LTs on graduation were used as safety officers where they'd go out with firing batteries and verify that the guns were laid properly.

But they said no, you're going to the 190th Replacement Detachment in Long Binh. I knew where that was because a month prior, when we were sitting around in an auditorium and everybody was getting their orders, our class was the first class to have 2LTs go straight from OCS to Vietnam. I felt sorry for all those guys who had gotten notified a month ago that they were going to Vietnam, but now here I was, two days away from graduating, and had the same orders.

Well, the rest of my class who had orders to Vietnam had a month to get POR qualified. I had to get all the shots, get my records updated, and qualify with all the different weapons I'd to be using. To make a long story short, I had two days to get all that done, where my contemporaries had a month. I had to go to the dispensary and had to get six shots. I hate needles anyway. I never will forget the two specialists that worked on me. I had my sleeves rolled up and they swabbed both of my arms. They stuck several syringes between their fingers, just kind of hit my arm with three on each side, and then hit the plungers. I said to myself, *I'm not going to faint*. Like I said, I was nervous about needles. Here I was, two days away from being a 2LT and I'm not going to faint in front of these specialists. And I didn't, but I was sick for the next few days as a result of getting all those shots as once.

Then I had to go qualify with the .45, the M-16, and so forth.

When I thought I was going to Fort Hood, I had planned to take 30 days leave, come back to Lawton, and get married. I'd then take my new wife with me to flight school at Fort Walters. Because I wasn't accepted for flight school and would be leaving for Vietnam, and that changed everything. We decided we'd move up our wedding plans, so my fiancée had to move all the plans up in record time. We were attending a local Baptist church in Lawton and it wasn't a problem with the pastor, so we moved up the wedding date and got the invitations sent out. I had two or three of my fellow officers, also 2LTs, in my wedding. My brother was already a 2LT and he was my best man, and two days later, I was best man at his wedding.

We couldn't lease an apartment because we weren't going to be in the area long enough. Fortunately, we had a friend in church who owned some small apartments in Lawton and he agreed to let us use one for three or four weeks. When I left, my wife went back to live with her folks.

I flew out of Oakland and happened to meet up with one of my OCS classmates, so we got to fly over together. The airplane was kind of a stripped down model. There were no niceties. There was some sort of condensation in the bulkhead above my seat and water was dripping on me. So, I took a pillow and stuffed it up there until it got soaked and had to replace it with another one.

It seemed like they had gone out and gotten the ugliest stewardesses they could find to put on that plane. When I came back from Vietnam, they all looked like queens, but on the way over, they all looked like the worst of the worst. Of course, on the way, back they could have been the ugliest women on earth, but if they had round eyes, they were pretty.

The plane was just as long as could be with three rows of seats on each side, all full of young soldiers. We stopped in Hawaii and Guam to refuel. In Guam, I saw my first B-52—they had a squadron of them stationed there and that's where they flew out of to bomb in Vietnam. I was really impressed with the size of those airplanes because the tail rudder was so huge that it looked to be 10 stories high. I'm sure it wasn't, but it sure looked like it.

We flew into Long Binh. As we were coming in, it was daylight. I looked around and could see a few troops take their briefcase and stick it underneath the seat, not the seat in front of them, but the seat they were sitting in. I asked what they were doing that for and they replied, "In case a round comes up through the bottom of the plane I want as much stuff as possible in the way of that bullet before it hits me." I thought to myself, *I'm sure if a round comes up through the bottom of this aircraft, that briefcase with a bunch of papers in it isn't going to stop too much.* But, I ended up putting my briefcase underneath me, too.

As I looked at the landscape, I couldn't imagine how many bombs had been dropped over the years to cause that much destruction. I saw one pothole after another. Those that had been there a while were filled up with rainwater while those that hadn't were still fresh bomb craters.

We landed in Long Binh, got out, and loaded onto buses. All the buses had heavy-duty grated wire on all the windows so someone couldn't throw anything like a hand grenade into the bus. That's probably when I first knew that this was the real deal—it was time to be serious and watch out for yourself and the next guy.

We got to the 190th Replacement Detachment and in-processed. While we were there, one of the things they announced was that everybody had to come back at a regular intervals to check the bulletin board to see where our assignments were going to be. Until that information was posted, we didn't know where we were going to go. It just depended on what was needed as to where they were going to send us. They told everybody that if our flight is scheduled after dark, we're going outside a 100-mile radius of Saigon (near Long Binh). If our assignments are within that 100-mile radius, we'd fly out sometime during the day.

I checked the bulletin board regularly over the next two or three days and my name didn't appear. Meanwhile, I had gone to the local PX and bought myself some stationery that had a map of North and South Vietnam on it. It had the major cities on it, such as Hanau, Da Nang, and Saigon, so I could kind of get an idea on where I was located on the map in relation to North and South Vietnam.

One night I went to the bulletin board and, lo and behold, saw my name, finally, and I was leaving at about seven o'clock at night. That told me I was going more than 100 miles away from Saigon/Long Binh. I gathered up all my stuff and met the bus, which took me to the airport and there they loaded us up on a C-130. That was my first time on a C-130. They had two rows of seats facing each other on each side of the plane. The seats weren't like regular aircraft seats. They were made of canvas or parachute scraps. I sat in my seat looking around at everybody else. You could tell who were the newbies because they had brand new boots, they had brand new fatigues, and everything was nice and green or black—maybe even still had a few wrinkles from being unwrapped. Meanwhile, the guys who had been in Vietnam for a while and were just catching a hop from Long Binh to somewhere else, their fatigues were faded and jungle-rotted, and the black had long since left their boots. I could tell they were the old hands, so I just kind of kept an eye on them and did whatever they did so I wouldn't act like a newbie.

As we're sitting there, all of a sudden we heard loud noises. It wasn't like in a commercial jet where, if you listen real close, you can hear some of the hydraulics and other noises. But in the C-130, I could *really* hear the hydraulics, and I could hear all the bells and whistles and gears grinding, and I'm saying to yourself, is this thing going to get off the ground? As we're taking off and we're hearing all this stuff, we're looking to some of the old-timers to see if they're getting excited. If they're not getting excited, we weren't going to get excited. Sure enough, the next thing I know some of the old-timers are asleep or half asleep, but I'm all eyes and ears watching everything. As we get further and further and gain some altitude, I feel a little more relaxed.

We flew for what seemed like forever before we finally started coming down. Now we were in Da Nang. We got off the plane, another bus met us, and we loaded up. We went to what I call a "tent city," a processing area with sort of a poor man's BOQ—just a bunch of tents. I checked in, got myself a pillow, some sheets, and a blanket. Then I found myself a cot that wasn't being used and that's where I slept.

I woke up the next morning and went into the community shower. That's where I had my first close-up experience with Vietnamese. They had locals helping in this tent city, performing cleaning chores. They also did the laundry in the showers and I didn't know that. I'm in there taking a shower with two or three other guys and all of a sudden, here come three mama-sans. They're two or three showerheads over doing their laundry. I thought to myself, *if it don't bother them, it don't bother me.* I'm lathering up, figuring what the heck. There was a warrant officer next to me and he was really embarrassed and had to leave. After he left, the mama-sans were giggling because they knew what had happened.

I went back to tent city where my bunk was and there sat a mama-san eating betel nuts, which I guess is kind of a poor man's snuff. The juice looked red, like blood, and it was coming out of the corner of her mouth. I thought at first that somebody had hit her and I said something to her. I then realized she wasn't hurt because she smiled just as pretty as you please. I could see her teeth were solid black. Later, I asked an old-timer about it and he told me they think black teeth is a sign of beauty.

I'd been told I was going to the 108th Field Artillery Group. I'm looking for the 108th and ask a sergeant, "Hey, sarge, where is the 108th Field Artillery Group?"

He tells me to go down the street three or four hooches, make a left, and you'll see a sign that says "In-Processing."

I walked into the In-Processing Center and saw a bunch of clerks sitting at typewriters. I asked about the 108th and the clerk directed me to another clerk at the back of the building. I introduced myself and told him I was there to in-process to the 108th FA Group. He invited me to have a seat and, after sitting, I asked him where the 108th was located here in Da Nang.

He said, "They're not located in Da Nang; this is just where the finance center is. They're located in Dong Ha."

"Where's that," I asked.

On his wall, he had a giant map of Vietnam, both South and North. I found Long Binh, where I came from. I saw Da Nang, where I was now. He pointed north of that to where Dong Ha is, right below the DMZ. I'm thinking, this ain't looking too good! I'm going to be closer to Hanoi than I am to Saigon.

That afternoon, I flew into Dong Ha. It was a dustbowl. The airfield was made out of corrugated PSP. When we came onto the airstrip, the C-130 didn't stop. As he was coasting down the runway, we were jumping off the tailgate and other guys were jumping on for the return trip. The C-130 went to the end of the runway, turned around, opened it wide up, and flew right out without ever coming to a full stop—he didn't want to present a sitting target!

I went over to the terminal, which was about a 10x12-foot structure, with plywood walls on the bottom, screen for the top half, and a plywood roof. Inside was a counter with a clerk behind it. There were some troops lying around the walls. They looked as though they'd been in country for years because their uniforms were like rags and their shoes had no black left on them—no color at all, because the sand and dirt had bleached them.

I told the clerk I was reporting into the 108th FA Group. He looked at me and said, "You can use that phone over there on the wall." I walked over to the phone, picked it up, and dialed zero for the operator. I told them who I was, what I wanted, and they connected me.

Some specialist answered and said, "Sir, I'll be over there in five or ten minutes to pick you up."

As I waited, the wind blew and the dust just flew through the place. I'm thinking, *jiminy, this ain't going to be nice at all.* About ten minutes later, a jeep pulled up. The specialist introduced himself, told me to put my stuff in the back of the jeep, and off we went to the 108th.

I showed up at the group HQ and about four or five of my classmates happened to be there. They'd gotten in a couple of days ahead of me. The clerks asked us what type of unit we'd like to go to. Mike Reid (who I'd met in Oakland) and I kind of stuck together. I told him, "If we marry up with a 105mm unit, we'd be moving all the time. But if we go with a bigger gun, they don't move as much as the 105s. Let's go with an eight-inch or a 175mm unit."

So that's what we asked for. The other guys didn't care what they got.

About 30 minutes later, this lieutenant came back and said, "Okay, LT So-and-so, you're going to such-and-such unit. Go with the sergeant and he'll get you processed into the unit."

And that's how it went until he finally got to Mike and me. He said, "Lieutenants, we don't have any openings in eight-inch or 175mm units. However, we do have a couple of openings in our target acquisition battery."

In field artillery, most of the training is on how to fire an artillery piece, whereas target acquisition is locating targets and calling in fire on those targets. There were different systems used to acquire those targets at Fort Sill. Target acquisition wasn't a big block of instruction back at Fort Sill, but we said we'd give it a try. We were thinking we'd be back behind the lines with a radar set, monitoring what's being fired at the friendlies. Supposedly, based on the radar information, you'd know where the round was fired from and you'd call in a fire mission on the mortar or artillery that had fired on friendly forces.

We had within our target acquisition battery what we called a sound platoon, a system where you'd put monitors out on the battlefield. Then, when an artillery piece or mortar fired, that sound would hit each of these sound systems, and the results from both systems were used to triangulate where the sound, and therefore the round, had come from.

We also had what we called a flash platoon, forward observers that would visually pick up where the muzzle flash came from and record the direction. If you had several folks doing this from different locations, then you could triangulate the origin just like you did with the sound system.

We really had a choice because they always needed somebody for 105 and 155 units, but we decided to give the target acquisition battery a try since we couldn't go with a large-caliber unit. When we got to the unit (F-Battery, 26th FA), we found out that it was originally sent to Vietnam TDY for six months. What happened is: after they got sent to Vietnam from Fort Bragg, North Carolina, after six months they let all the NCOs have an option to stay another six months to complete their tour, or they could go back to Fort Bragg. Most of the NCOs decided to go back to Fort Bragg, figuring this war wasn't going to last much longer. They didn't give the commissioned officers that option, telling them they had to spend a year there. When I arrived, it was about the seventh or eighth month after those officers had arrived in country, so a lot of them were getting ready to PCS in a few months. A few of the NCOs that had elected to stay fell into that same category. About two or three months later, some of those NCOs who had returned to Bragg after six months were now coming back to Vietnam for a *one-year* tour. Based on their records, only six months in-country, they hadn't gotten credit for a full tour. With the build-up in Vietnam, they needed troops and those guys got sent back to F-Battery, 26th FA, *for a year.* These guys were not happy campers!

I also found out that target acquisition was not done behind the lines—actually in *front* of the lines because that's where they put most of the systems used to detect targets. I guess that's why they called us *forward* observers!

About two or three weeks later, I became the radar platoon leader. My radar sets were located all along the DMZ, all the way from the coast to Camp J.J. Carroll, which was on a hilltop in the middle of nowhere. I had radar sets at Con Tien, Gia Lin, and Camp J.J. Carroll. They were a combination of MPQ-4 counter-mortar and MPQ-10 counter-artillery radars. When I got there, one of the Q-10 radar sets at Gia Lin had been hit and destroyed. A new one had come in-country, down in Long Binh. Our supply officer was out en route to Long Binh with some trucks to bring it back so we could set it up in place of the one we'd lost.

We were truly within 200 to 300 yards of the DMZ, so we were always taking fire on our bases. Just as you may have seen on TV, a Vietnamese would throw a mortar tube on his back and a couple others would put rounds on their backs, so they were mobile. They could move and get just about anywhere they wanted to go. The terrain was all jungle. You couldn't see far at all, except where the Air Force had come in and made a B-52 raid with napalm or daisy-cutters. There the terrain had been leveled and the vegetation destroyed. Otherwise, most of it was thick jungle.

Our firebases were situated high enough that we could look down into the DMZ. We had a good vantage point from where the firebases were located. The French had built most of these firebases originally. The one I stayed at the most was at Con Tien. It was a Marine firebase, commanded by a Marine O-6, and we were the only Army outfit on it.

When I first got there and they told me I would be the radar platoon leader, I thought, *fine, I'll learn what I need to learn*. Fortunately, I had good NCOs. Here I was, a brand new 2LT with less than a month or two beneath my belt. I was no fool. My daddy didn't raise me to be a loudmouth and not listen to what a seasoned soldier could to tell me. I knew I had good E-7s and E-8s that had been in the radar business for years, and that I should listen and learn.

I never had any problems getting along with any of the NCOs. I knew when I got over there that it wasn't going to be, "Yes, sir. No, sir. You salute me and I salute you." In a combat environment, we were there to watch each other's backs. I treated them like I expected to be treated, and it worked out great. I didn't have any problems with any of my soldiers.

About the time I left for Vietnam (1968), was when I started hearing stories about soldiers fragging their own officers and shooting people in the back. I didn't have that problem, because I got along well with the enlisted men. There were some officers over there that I could tell were headed in that direction. If I had heard that someone had fragged them, I wouldn't have been surprised.

We had a pretty good crew. Our base camp was in Dong Ha and all the different target acquisition systems were located all along the DMZ. I spent most of my time up at the DMZ. I'd come back to Dong Ha to maybe process some paperwork or do some administrative stuff, but I spent most of my time up at Con Tien.

For a while I was a pay officer, so I had to go to Finance, pick up the payroll, and then go out and pay the troops. If we had a helicopter, that made it easy because then I could just drop in and pay the guys and complete the job in a couple days. But when I didn't have a helicopter, I had to use a jeep. Of course, we had to travel the roads when we used the jeep, joining in with a convoy whenever they were leaving. Convoys were always leaving at certain times of the day and anyone who needed to travel just joined up.

There was another outpost out there called the Rock Pile, located between Camp J.J. Carroll and Khe Sahn. (Incidentally, I got to see Khe Sahn shortly after the first Tet offensive in 1968, and the damage was incredible.) I had a radar platoon at the Rock Pile. If you can just imagine flying out into the middle of nowhere and finding a mountain or a big hill sticking up in the middle of a forest, but because of all the bombing there's nothing growing on it.

There were bunkers on the side of the hill and foxholes, and some of my guys were out there in the middle of nowhere. You just couldn't imagine the living conditions those guys had to endure. When we landed in our helicopter, we had to land on a steep slope. I got out and didn't waste any time paying those guys. There were only about four or five of them, so I paid them real quick and got the hell out of there. I only had to be the pay officer for about two months since they rotated that job among all the officers as an extra duty.

We had some experimental equipment sent over from Los Alamos Scientific Laboratory in New Mexico. They brought this system over for us to test and a little civilian set up the system for us. That was kind of exciting. It was a neat system. It had a Battery Commander scope on a tripod. The BC scope looked like huge binoculars, over a foot long. The system also had a night observation device and a laser range finder. All those things were calibrated so that when you looked through the BC scope and put the crosshairs on a target, you could reach up and hit the laser rangefinder and it would give you the range to within five meters. The operator used bicycle grips to move the BC scope vertical crosshairs to determine target azimuth, then he'd move another lever that would move the horizontal crosshairs to determine target elevation. When he had both of those set, he could look on the console and see the digital readout of the target location. This information was so precise that you could call in a "fire for effect" on the very first round and expect a direct hit, instead of having to try to bracket the target with several shots.

I'll never forget my first trip to Con Tien, I drove up there not knowing what to expect. We had a radar set up there and a flash Observation Post. They had a bunker co-located. Another lieutenant named Larry Shaddix was the flash platoon leader and his folks were located across the compound near the OP, the highest point on the hill. We were the only Army unit up there; everyone else was Marines.

The first time I went into the OP, I saw this little old man looking through the BC scope. I could tell that he was wearing nice fatigues, had nicely spit-shined black boots, was wearing a black belt around his waist, and had what looked like a .38 strapped to his side.

I asked one of the soldiers, "Who's that little old fart over there?"

They replied, "That's General So-And-So."

He was an active duty officer who had flown in without anyone knowing that he was coming.

I'd been in-country for a while, so I had on a pair of old cutoff fatigue pants, a helmet, and a flak jacket, but no T-shirt or fatigue shirt. For shoes I had on a pair of what we called "Ho Chi Minh tiger paws." The Vietnamese could make something useable out of anything. They'd take old tires, cut them up, and make flip-flops out of them. That was one of the first things I did when I got in-country was to go down to the local Vietnamese shop and buy myself a pair of tiger paws.

So, there I was, dressed like I don't know what, asking who in the hell is looking through my BC scope. About that time, he turned around. He had one star on his helmet. I introduced myself and he asked me to show him the operation. I showed him how the BC system worked and he was real impressed with that.

I'll never forget a time before we had this new equipment, there was a Marine lieutenant in the OP, a forward observer for the Marines. He'd come into our area sometimes and use our equipment to adjust fire, and I didn't have any problem with that. This was the first time I'd met him, me being a new guy on the block. I came into the OP and there he was, looking through the BC scope, looking real hard at something.

I introduced myself and said, "Okay, where're the bad guys at?"

He points out into the DMZ and said, "There's some right there."

I moved over to the BC scope to take a look and the Marine tells me, "You don't need the BC scope. They're right over there. Just look off the end of my finger where I'm pointing."

Sure enough, probably 100 yards out is somebody with a shovel just digging like they're really serious. I'm saying, "You're kidding me! That's an enemy soldier?"

The Marine replies, "Hell yeah, that's a North Vietnamese building a tunnel. After he works up a good sweat, I'm going to call in a fire mission on him. You just watch."

Sure enough, the Marine waited about 30 minutes and then called back to the fire direction center in Dong Ha. They looked at the coordinates he'd provided, found an artillery battery within range of those coordinates, and told the battery to fire for effect. So the first thing I know, here come six rounds of high explosives. After all the smoke cleared, I looked out there and there's no activity.

I'm thinking, "Gee, this guy's pretty good." He'd apparently fired on this position so often that he could immediately fire for effect, that is, expect to hit the target with the first round. Normally, you have to fire a test round to see how close you can get. Then you fire another. Typically, one round will be short and the other long. Then you "fire for effect" on the third round by calculating the difference between the first two hits relative to the target.

He didn't fire on the digger as soon as he saw him. He wanted to let the guy work up a good sweat and expend a little effort. You've got to understand, those Marines were a little crazy anyway.

The firebase at Con Tien had been mined back in the days when the French occupied it. I was told never to step on any grass because it was probably mined. There used to be fences around the minefields with warning signs, but they had been destroyed a long time ago. Anytime I saw grass, I didn't walk on it, I walked in the mud or on the dirt instead. Many times I'd go outside and see a Marine just walking through the minefield and I'd yell at him, "Hey, do you know you're in a minefield?"

He'd usually just turn around and keep going. It just so happened that none of them ever got blown up. But sometimes when they were bored, they'd sit there and fire their M-16s into the minefield to see if they could set off a mine, and occasionally they would. I'm the tenant activity—they own the land—so I didn't raise too much of a stink.

During the July 4th or any other type of celebration, the Marines would all shoot, kind of like watching a celebration in Baghdad. They didn't have any fireworks, so they'd position their twin-40s, M-60 machineguns, or quad-50s and just start firing off into Never-Never Land. About every fifth round was a tracer, so you could see a stream of red going out into the middle of nowhere.

I enjoyed it because it was my first duty assignment. I really didn't have to report to anybody since our battery commander stayed back in Dong Ha. When I first got to Vietnam, I had a young battery commander, a captain, whose brothers and daddy were all West Pointers, but he wasn't. He'd gone to the Citadel, VMI, or one of those military academies to get his commission. He PCSed not long after I got there.

Then I got a guy by the name of Captain Joe Stanley. Joe was an E-8 before he got his direct commission. He was an old troop. I want to say that at one time, he had been a commissioned officer back during the Korean War, but because of the downsizing in the Army following the war he reverted back to his enlisted rank. When Vietnam came along, the Army re-commissioned Joe as a captain. He was just as even-keeled as could be—you couldn't upset CPT Stanley no matter what you did.

Later, I went back to Fort Sill as a 1LT and then got promoted to captain. I worked as one of the branch chiefs in the Target Acquisition Department. Joe Stanley came back following his tour in Vietnam, reverted back to E-8, and worked for me. In Vietnam, I worked for him as a 2LT and back at Fort Sill, he worked for me! About as soon as he reverted to NCO status they promoted him to E-9.

He'd been a great guy to work for, and we hit it off great when the roles were reversed. You know the old saying about not burning your bridges because you might have to cross them again? In this case, that proved to be true. He worked probably another two or three years before retiring right there in Lawton, OK. Great guy. Great guy!

I didn't know if we should have been in Vietnam or not. I was just a soldier following orders. My orders said go to Vietnam, so that's what I did. While I was there, I did wonder why we couldn't do certain things. For instance, we couldn't fire into the DMZ because the diplomats were sitting around the Paris Peace Table trying to negotiate an agreement. Well, I was sitting on the DMZ and there wasn't supposed to be anybody in the DMZ, not Americans nor Vietnamese, but there were.

Where we were at, there was a river that went down the middle of the DMZ, and a bridge crossed the river linking North and South Vietnam. Well, that bridge had been knocked out a long time ago and wasn't useable. On the other side, the north side of the DMZ, was kind of a blockhouse. One time I reported that I saw a flag being raised above that blockhouse. The next thing I know I get a call from some colonel saying that what I was reporting would be going straight to the Paris Peace Talks.

I said, "Sir, I'm not reporting anything that I didn't see. I saw a North Vietnamese flag being raised within the DMZ."

He challenged me, saying he didn't think I really saw that. It just so happened that soon after that, I looked out and not only saw one flag flying over the blockhouse, I saw about a thousand flags waving all along the DMZ! I reported that, and within an hour I had two helicopter-loads of folks show up. They were all dressed in nice fatigues and came running up the hill wanting to know who this lieutenant was reporting seeing flags. By that time, I'd put on my shirt. I still had my Ho Chi Minh tiger paws, helmet, and flak jacket, but for this special occasion I put on a shirt, too.

I told them what I'd seen and once again, they were skeptical.

"Where'd you see this?" they wanted to know.

I took them to my observation post and one of them started looking through his binoculars. I said, "You don't have to use binoculars, sir. You can see it right out there."

It was one of those kind of flags you see out in front of Kroger's, about 30 feet by 40 feet. It was a huge flag, and you could see it with the naked eye. They realized that someone had to put it up there, and it obviously wasn't any of the good guys since it was a North Vietnamese flag.

I had other occasions where they challenged what I had reported. We weren't supposed to be flying above the DMZ, but sometimes I could see aircraft lights up there. I didn't know if they were ours or theirs, but

I reported that I'd seen a helicopter. They said it couldn't be, that we don't have any flights in that area. There's not supposed to be any birds up there.

I said, "Well sir, there's something up there because I can see the lights. It's not a UFO because I can see the lights going up, down, and sideways. If it's not one of ours, then it's got to be one of theirs."

They tried to come back later on and tell me that it was probably a jet, that I'd probably seen the exhaust of a jet in the distance. I thought, *If that's what you think, okay, but I'm here to tell you that when I can see the lights going up, down, and sideways and when it hovers in one spot, that ain't a jet! To me that's a helicopter.*

One time I called in a fire mission on "elephants in the open." The VC used elephants and water buffalo for packing ammunition. I had a Marine major, whose company were perimeter guards, come up to me and say he wanted me to call in a fire mission.

I said, "Okay sir, what do you want me to call it on?"

He replied, "There're some elephants who hit a tripwire over there and I want you to fire on them."

I said, "What?"

He said, "Elephants."

I said, "Okay," and called in for an illumination round.

The fire mission came out and lit up the area, but I couldn't see any elephants. I asked the major where he thought they were. He got upset with me because I wouldn't go ahead and call in a fire for effect mission on this area—he was afraid the elephants were going to disappear. I told him I can't hit what I can't see.

He was very upset and I finally said, "Okay, I'll tell you what I'm going to do, sir. I'm going to call in a fire mission in the general area of where you say the elephants disappeared, but I'm only going to call in one round of fire for effect."

I'd fired in that area long enough that I had pinpointed on my map exactly where the rounds should go. That particular night, there must not have been much else going on. I called in the mission to Fire Direction Center in Dong Ha, elephants in the open. The FDC, in turn, transmitted the fire mission to a battery within range of the target. But as I mentioned, it must have been a slow night because a lot of other batteries that were within range of the target decided to fire, too. I sat there expecting about six or eight projectiles coming in when, all of a sudden, all hell broke loose. The whole side of the mountain just came alive.

The O-6 firebase commander was shook up by all the commotion. It woke him up and he called wanting to know what the hell was going on, and I told him.

He said, "Lieutenant Howell, I want you over here within the next five minutes!"

I knew I was in trouble. I got over there and walked into the colonel's office, once again in my usual uniform: Ho Chi Minh tiger paws, flak jacket, and helmet.

He says, "What in the hell just happened."

I told him, "I only called in one round, but obviously there must have been a lot of folks listening in who decided they wanted a piece of the action. I only expected six or eight projectiles, not 20 or 30."

He asked me who told me to call in the mission.

I said, "Sir, I didn't even want to shoot the fire mission, but Major So-And-So said he saw elephants in the open and he wasn't going to leave until I called in a fire for effect mission."

The colonel immediately got on the phone and said, "Major So-And-So, I want your ass over here. Lieutenant Howell, you're dismissed."

I got back in my jeep and drove back over to my bunker. No sooner had I gotten back to my bunker than my battery commander, Joe Stanley, had gotten word back through the grapevine that Lieutenant Howell had a fire mission on elephants in the open. He called me up by landline and said, "Bill, have you been drinking?"

I said, "No sir. Why?"

He says, "The FDC just called and told me you had called in a fire mission on elephants in the open. I'm just checking."

I told him the story. He said, okay.

That started the little incident where we got fragged once. Our bunker shower consisted of a suspended 55-gallon drum with a showerhead on the bottom. We filled the 55-gallon drum by hauling 5-gallon cans of water. You'd stand under it and pull the chain to release water through the showerhead. One day, after this elephant debacle, someone threw a fragmentation grenade into the 55-gallon drum. None of my folks were around but the shower was ruined.

A little later on, someone threw a CS grenade into our bunker. It wasn't a fragmentation grenade, but, when a grenade comes into your bunker, you don't take time to look and see what kind of grenade it is. You scramble out of the bunker and that's what we did. We couldn't use the bunker for a while after that because of all the fumes.

When that all happened, I reported it to the colonel. I said, "Sir, my folks didn't do this. It had to be your folks, and I think it was Major So-And-So as a result of the events a week or so ago."

The next thing I know, the colonel had a bunch of Marines down there rebuilding my shower. I didn't have any problems from then on; I think Major So-And-So must have gone someplace else. That was the only time I had any problems.

My radar chief warrant officer knew the technical workings of our radar sets. When a set went down, he was responsible for fixing it. We had NCOs that were technicians, too, but the warrant was supposed to be the smart guy. My radar sets, as I mentioned before, were located all along the DMZ. He tried to fix most of them via telephone by telling my NCOs what to do. He wasn't too keen on going out there himself, especially if he thought he'd be subject to being shot at.

We had ration cards over there that authorized us to get five quarts of liquor a month. A lot of us didn't use our ration cards, so this warrant officer would ask us for our ration cards so he could buy booze for himself. One of the drawbacks of being in Vietnam is that, if a soldier was susceptible to becoming an alcoholic, he could do it very easily. The liquor was so cheap and we didn't have much else to occupy our free time. If a soldier didn't have something to do—write letters, read books—then he could become an alcoholic. I saw a lot of good people who did just that, and this warrant officer was one of them. He could take a canteen cup, fill it to the lip with vodka, and drink it like it was water.

Our hooches were kind of like the air terminal I mentioned seeing when I first arrived in Vietnam. They were built of plywood, but about halfway up, they were made of screen. The chief had built himself some bookshelves in his hooch but he didn't have a damn book in there. He had it lined with fifths of booze!

Once, I had a radar set go down at Con Tien and my sergeant couldn't fix it. I told the chief, the one who didn't like to go to the field, "You and I are going to go up there this morning and fix that radar set."

The NCO had already told him the parts that were needed. Unfortunately, the major convoy had already left for the day, so we were the only two jeeps on the road. Me being the convoy leader, I was in the front jeep with my driver and the chief was in the back jeep with his driver. We had radios and called in at checkpoints as we went up the road to advise the base camp of our progress. We're doing 45 or 50 mph, which is pretty fast, when all of a sudden the chief's jeep passed me!

I told my driver, "You catch up with that son-of-a-gun or I'll be driving this jeep!"

My driver caught up with them and I motioned for the chief's driver to pull over to the side of the road. I got out and asked that driver, "What the hell do you think you're doing?"

He said, "The chief told me to move it, you were driving too slow."

I chewed out both the chief and the driver. "As long as I'm the convoy commander, you follow me. I don't follow you."

The chief was scared and didn't want to be on that road any longer than he had to. We had radar problems two or three times a week, but this was the first time the chief had ever been out of the base camp. The elephant grass along the sides was as high as a deuce-and-a-half or a five-ton truck. It wasn't anything for someone to come right up to the edge of the road and we couldn't tell that they were there. Some months later, they came out with Rome plows and plowed back the underbrush about 100 yards from the road.

When we got up to Con Tien, the chief had that radar fixed in record time and was ready to head home, so we came back to the base camp—he didn't want to stay up there that night. He was fine as long as he was back in our base camp.

On the way back, there was a dead Vietnamese lying alongside the road. We didn't know if it was a good guy or a bad guy. The chief had his driver stop and take a picture of him with his gun out, pointed at this dead Vietnamese. He was good about writing letters back home to his wife, and he was giving her a war story about how this was a Vietnamese he'd killed.

This guy was the technical expert on my radars, but other than that, I didn't count on him for anything else. As I said, he stayed at our Dong Ha base camp and I stayed mostly at Con Tien. We didn't see much of each other so I really don't know if all the booze affected his performance.

Our tours in Nam only overlapped for about three or four months. He had a brother that worked in personnel back in DA. After he had 10 months and one day in-country (minimum length of a combat tour), he mysteriously got orders to come back home because his mother was sick or dying. He had the absolute minimum time and he was out of there.

There was an in-country R&R in Vung Tau, down close to Saigon. I never got down there, but Vung Tau was one of those places where you could go and let off a little steam. I'd been in country six or seven months when my battery commander asked me if I wanted to go to Vung Tau on R&R. I'd gotten married about three weeks before leaving for Vietnam, so I was still a newly-wed. I had planned on meeting my wife in Hawaii, like most married couples, but I didn't want to do it at the half-way point knowing I had to go back to Vietnam for another six months. We decided we'd try to do it around the ninth or tenth month. That way I could come back, finish my tour, and would be heading home within a couple of months. That was the game plan.

One of my fellow officers, 2LT Smith (not his real name), had been to Vung Tau and had come back with an STD. He had to go through all the penicillin shots and other medications, but he swore he'd had a great time.

I said, "I guess you did if you can survive the penicillin and everything."

He was a single guy so I guess it could have been worse.

We had another officer's billet come up for three days R&R in Vung Tau and it was my turn to go.

I said, "In about three months I'm going to Hawaii to meet my wife. There ain't no way in hell I'm going to take a chance and go down there and mess up my Hawaii trip. I don't want to go."

Smith piped up and said, "I'll go!"

I said, "Are you sure?"

He said, "Yes, this time I'm going to stay with just one woman. Last time I had several. She's A-Number-One."

He showed me a picture of the lady and she looked to be a cross between Vietnamese and French. She was absolutely beautiful.

I said, "More power to you."

Lo and behold, a few days after Smith got back from Vung Tau, drip-drip-drip, and he had to go see the medic again. That told me I'd made the right choice.

He said, "Bill, I just can't understand it. She's so pretty."

I said, "Smitty, stop and think now. Do you really believe every Tom, Dick, and Harry is going to go down there and sleep with the ugly girls? No, they're going to sleep with the good looking ones, just like you did."

I got on a plane a few months later and went to Hawaii, arriving about a day ahead of my wife. I had rented a room at the Outrigger on Waikiki Beach. At that time, I think there was only one Outrigger in Hawaii; today, there're probably about 15 different hotels with Outrigger in their names.

I hadn't seen my wife in nine months when I went to the airport the next day to pick her up. I came up on a gal who had her back to me and I knew she was my wife. I had a lei of flowers in my hand and decided I'd sneak up on her, throw those flowers around her neck, spin her around, and plant a big wet kiss on her mouth. About the time I got ready to throw those flowers around her neck, the lady turned around and it wasn't my wife! I got embarrassed and she was scared to death—she didn't know who the hell I was. I apologized and told her I was sorry.

I walked a few feet and, lo and behold, there was my wife who, fortunately, hadn't noticed my earlier faux pas. We went back to the hotel, ordered room service for a couple days, and just stayed camped out. Then we rented a car and drove around the island. In those days, early 1969, the island wasn't too crowded. There were quite a few beaches where we just parked the car, walked along the beach for miles, and never saw a soul. We had a good time. I left again for Vietnam and she left the next day. When I got back in-country, I had about three months left to the end of my tour.

Where I was at, I didn't see a lot of death. We had a MASH unit located at the base camp. Sometimes, when we had some of our folks who had gotten hurt from incoming shrapnel or whatever, we had to go to the hospital and assist them. We could see a lot of medevac helicopters coming in with mostly Marines because that area was full of Marines. I can remember seeing a trashcan outside the hospital with arms and legs and other body parts hanging out of it. That kind of brought me to realize that this was the real thing, and that people were getting hurt and killed.

I had a couple of guys, one injured and one killed, at that radar site in Con Tien but it was from "friendly" fire. We had a couple of F-4 Phantoms that were in the area and those jets have indicators on them to advise the pilot when they've been targeted by a SAM missile. What happened, is my guys were out doing some maintenance on an MPQ-10 radar set and they had turned it on to test it. They had it pointed horizontally, but somehow the beam hit some concertina wire and ricocheted up into the sky. When that happened, a jet passed through the beam and thought it was a beam from a SAM missile. The automatic reaction of the pilot was to fire a rocket to backtrack the beam to wherever that transmission was coming from. That rocket hit about halfway between the radar set and the concertina wire that had caused the beam reflection. The rocket hit the ground, wounding one of my guys. He had a piece of shrapnel go through his hand and the pick handle he was holding. The other guy was killed—he got hit in the head and wasn't wearing a helmet. I had to take his body and belongings down to Da Nang to be flown out of the country.

I'll never forget that this guy didn't have any life insurance for servicemen. He was single, didn't have a wife or kids, but still he had a mom and dad back home. Back then SGLI was a buck or two for $20,000 worth of insurance. He didn't have any, and that's one of those things that should be mandatory for any troop, even if he doesn't have somebody to leave it to. He could just leave it to his estate to pay off his bills, burial expenses, whatever if something happens to him.

When I was at Dong Ha, we had an ammunition supply point where there were several bunkers of ammo. One time Charlie got lucky and lobbed a round into one of those bunkers. It was like the Fourth of July because the entire ammo dump blew up.

I had guys who didn't think there was any danger because we were no longer taking in-coming fire. They were standing on top of our bunker watching the ammo dump blow up, until all of a sudden we could hear an eight-inch round coming pin-wheeling through the air making a whop-whop-whop sound. It landed in the middle of our battery area, and when it did it hit several different things and wiped them out. When my troops saw that, they all dove inside our bunker.

As the ammo dump was blowing up, projectiles were being thrown into the air and it was just like a big chunk of lead coming. Two or three different ammo dumps got blown up while I was there. All an incoming round needed to do was get close enough to start a chain reaction.

We never knew who the opposing units were. We were told there wasn't supposed to be anybody in the DMZ, but of course there was. Often we'd look out through our BC scope and see all kinds of enemy activity.

I once got to adjust the fire from the battleship New Jersey. A Marine Lieutenant came on station and wanted to adjust fire for the New Jersey, which was sitting offshore 10 or 15 miles away. The New Jersey had 16-inch guns that fired 600-pound projectiles. With that kind of firepower, all an FO really had to do was identify a grid square and the round would wipe out just about everything in that square. It was really something. You could hear those son-of-a-guns coming. It sounded just like a train and, when it hit, it was just like a B-52 raid. It really did light up the sky.

I asked the lieutenant, "Do you think I could do that once?"

He said, "Sure."

I'd been sitting there listening and watching as the lieutenant called in the fire mission. There were some concrete bunkers up in the hills in the DMZ that we'd been trying to destroy. I'd called in fire missions a couple times myself, but not with anything like what the New Jersey could deliver. He let the folks at the other end of the radio know that an Army FO was going to be calling in a fire mission. I had the coordinates down pat and called in the fire mission on those bunkers. When they fired, they cut loose with either three or four projectiles and they just disintegrated the hill.

The B-52s were stationed on Guam and conducted what were called arc-light raids in Vietnam. We had several of them while I was there, and that was an impressive thing. If you've never seen one, it makes you glad that they're on your side! You could see a B-52 leave a vapor trail from 50,000 feet, or however high they were. Then, all of a sudden you'd see him turn around and head back in the opposite direction. You'd wonder, isn't he going to drop anything? Actually, he had already dropped huge 10 thousand-pound bombs, but he was so high you couldn't see the bombs. Then, you'd look out and see the shock waves when those daisy-cutters hit. At nighttime, you could see a huge ball of flame. During the daytime, you'd see the shockwave itself and the ball of flame wasn't quite as impressive. You just couldn't imagine anything living through something like that, and nothing did!

Whenever there was any activity in the DMZ and we thought the enemy was getting too close to the firebase, we'd call in F-4s. They'd come over and they'd rock their wings back and forth in response to us waving at them. Then they'd drop their ordnance, be it napalm or bombs. I was always thankful those guys were on our side and not with the enemy. I don't know how I could have stood being on the receiving end of something like that.

There were helicopters all over the place. Most of the ones I rode in were either UH-1 Hueys or OH-6A observation helicopters.

One of the gunships we had was a DC-3, called Puff the Magic Dragon. They had mini-guns along the side that sprayed out something like 3000 rounds of .30 caliber ammunition per minute. One of my first experiences with Puff was when I first arrived in Long Binh, waiting to come up north to my permanent assignment. There was some enemy activity in the Saigon area. I watched Puff from a distance and could hear a loud humming noise and saw three or four red streams from the ship to the ground, like several hoses spraying liquid fire.

I was talking to one of the old-timers and he said, "What you're seeing is every fifth round, the tracers. The other four are regular bullets, so you can imagine the amount of firepower that thing is putting out."

I also got to see Puff a few more times up north around the DMZ. They'd come on-station and literally just tear up the jungle. Once again, I'm glad they were on our side and part of our team.

So how did Charlie live through all that? Those guys were tunnel rats—they lived underground! It's hard to hit them when you can't see them, but there's no telling how many got buried alive. Whenever there was a B-52 raid or an F-4 raid, the next day our Marines would go out to do a body count of the enemy as a means of assessing the damage. Plenty of times the Marines would come back and say, they had found plenty of body parts but no bodies. The VC tried to reclaim as many of their dead as possible to give you the impression that you really hadn't done that much damage.

When I was in Vietnam, I personally didn't see any troops smoking marijuana. I didn't see them shooting up dope. I didn't see any empty syringes lying around. Where I was at, we weren't able to mingle with the local community. Whereas, in Da Nang or Saigon or some place like that, they were among us and we were among them. There weren't any Vietnamese on my firebase. You had what the troops called the "gook shop" outside the gate where you'd go to get your laundry done or get your haircut and stuff like that, but they didn't allow any of them on the firebase. The same way when we were out on the DMZ, we didn't have any locals out there. Going to and from our firebases, we'd drive through villages, but that was about it.

We had a good old boy, an enlisted man from Ozark, Arkansas, and we nicknamed him "Ozark." In Vietnam, the outhouses consisted of a piece of plywood with a hole cut in it. You sat on the hole and did your business. Under the plywood was half a 55-gallon drum with diesel fuel in it. About every other day, Ozark would go around to each latrine, pull out the barrel, stir it up, and then set it on fire. That's how we got rid of the waste. There weren't too many guys who were interested in that particular job, but Ozark liked doing it. When the battery commander asked him if he'd be interested in doing something else, Ozark said no. In fact, he extended his tour to do that. My battery commander wondered, where else are you going to find someone who'd volunteer to burn shit?

If you're at all familiar with diesel fuel and what happens when it burns, you can picture Ozark being covered with black soot and imagine the aroma on him from the other products that he burned. Ozark would go into the mess hall and would always have his own table. Nobody else wanted to sit next to him!

Ozark was just an old Arkansas hillbilly and he once told me, "There's a true art to burning shit. It's the way you stir it, sir."

There wasn't a human being in our unit that wanted to do what he did, but he loved doing it. Everyone stayed out of his way and he stayed out of theirs. He was something.

I was in Vietnam before the Army had the fat boy program. Our mess sergeant, nicknamed Big Daddy, ran our mess hall so we called it Big Daddy's Delicatessen. Big Daddy was about six-foot-six or -seven and weighed probably 350 pounds. A large man! He used to sleep in the senior NCO quarters, which was really just another hut but it housed E-7s, E-8s, and E-9s.

Those senior NCOs would tell us that, when we started taking incoming, nobody moved until Big Daddy had gone through the door.

Usually, whenever we got incoming, everybody jumped up and ran for the bunker. The first time that happened, Big Daddy ran over two or three troops and hurt them so bad that they just decided to take their chances with the rounds and let Big Daddy get to the bunker first. He was a typical mess hall sergeant.

I'll never forget the first time I sat down in the mess hall. I was eating bread, looked at it, and said to one of the lieutenants who'd been there a while, "I don't know if I'm going to like this rye bread."

He says, "Rye bread? That isn't rye. Those are just bugs in the flour."

I looked a little closer and, sure enough, they were little mealy bugs that had been cooked right into the bread. I figured, if these people can eat it I can, too!

We had a black cook named SPC Carter who had a stuttering problem. I used to tease him. I'd go out to Con Tien and stay a month or so where they had no cooked meals, just things like dehydrated pork chops. You'd take a pork chop out of the can and it looked like a piece of chalk. You had to let it sit in water or beer or something to soak up some type of moisture before you could cook it.

Whenever I came back to the base camp mess hall, I'd tell Carter how much I was looking forward to his home-cooked food. Then, I'd tell him, "You know, some of the guys up at Con Tien sure would like to have you come up there and fix them a home-cooked meal."

Carter would say, "N-n-n-no, suh! I b-b-b-burn baked beans!" He'd get real nervous—he didn't want to leave that base camp.

Vietnam is notorious for its rats and centipedes; they have some of the biggest centipedes in the world. One day as I sat in my bunker at Con Tien, I heard a scratching noise and couldn't figure out what it was. I was sitting at a little table writing a letter back home when I leaned back from the table and looked down between my legs. Right between my feet was one of those centipedes, about a foot long. It was crawling right between my feet! When they sting, they leave a hell of a welt.

I waited until he crawled all the way through, and then I got up and grabbed a can of Army-issue DDT. Today you'd probably get thrown in jail for having chemical/biological hazardous waste, but back then that's what we used for bug spray. I went over to that centipede and sprayed him and that centipede rose up almost like a dad-gummed cobra! I said, *to hell with this*! I grabbed a machete and cut that thing up in about three pieces, and those three pieces all ran off in different directions. That was something I didn't want to fool with.

Vietnam was a hot, muggy place, but during the monsoon season it got cold. In fact, I once wrote home and asked my wife to send me some long-handles. It rained and it rained and it rained. Up at Con Tien, we didn't have any outhouses, we had what were called Papa Tangos, or piss tubes. All that is is a powder canister sunk into the ground with a tube sticking up and a funnel on the end.

We also had an in-ground bunker, and in there was a 55-gallon drum with plywood across the top and a hole cut in it. When you went in there, you took your toilet paper with you and did your business. But during the monsoon season, that bunker would fill up with water, so anyone who went there had to wear boots (I didn't wear my tiger paws during monsoon season) because I'd be sitting there in calf-high mud.

When I went in there at nighttime, I made sure to take toilet paper, a flashlight, AND a .45. At nighttime, you never knew what might be in that bunker with you. The bunker was probably only about three feet by four feet deep, just big enough where you could crawl in there, bend over, sit down, and do your business.

I hated to go there at night, but when you gotta go, you gotta go! I'd sit there with that flashlight on and I'd be searching the inside of that bunker, knowing I'd see some beady eyes. Those eyes were the rats. I remember wasting as much as a clip or two, shooting rats while I went to the bathroom.

We had some of those big wooden rattraps and we baited them with peanut butter from the C-Ration cans. It got to be where you had to nail that rattrap down or the rats would carry them off when they got caught. Sometimes you'd catch three or four rats at a time. The biggest one I ever saw probably weighed three or four pounds and had a tail that was about a foot long. It was about two feet long, overall, and almost looked like an opossum.

I finally got tired of this bunker outhouse and told my men, "I don't care what you have to do, but I want you to build us an outhouse on *top* of the ground."

We got some materials and we built an outhouse on the opposite side of our bunker from the DMZ. That worked out fine. All you had to do before you sat down was to make sure that there weren't any centipedes near the top of the hole. One of my guys didn't do that and he got stung on the scrotum—he was in pain for about a week.

The OP I had consisted of several layers of sandbags, and we also used the same PSP that they used on the aircraft runways. We intermingled those two items and made a pretty effective roof over our bunker. One day, I called in a fire mission when we started taking rounds. Someone was firing at us with a mortar.

He did exactly what I'd have done: fire once long, once short, split the difference, and keep doing that until the objective has been achieved, that is, a direct hit. I could hear thump, thump, thump. The ones that you can't hear are the ones that are close. The ones you hear are either going over or they're falling short. This guy was landing short but kept walking them closer and closer. I tried to locate him while he tried to hit me.

He finally fired one over my OP and, when he did that, I told the two guys in the bunker with me, "You guys need to get down and grab hold of something because he's got us bracketed and this next one is going to be close."

Sure enough, the next round came and it hit right on top of the OP. When it did, one of the guys was standing and got thrown into the wall. He got bruised up a little but otherwise no one was hurt. It blew sand and PSP all over the place, making it look like more damage than had really been done. Evidently, the mortar operator must have thought he'd done enough damage or maybe he thought he'd wiped us all out. Maybe he was discouraged when he saw how little damage he'd done, or maybe he thought he'd better beat feet before we found him. In any event, we didn't take any more incoming rounds after that. That was probably my closest call in Vietnam.

My replacement came in a few weeks before my tour was over, I turned things over to him, and that left me with not too much to do. I said to myself, *I'm not going to do anything, I'm going to stay right here, and I'm not going to go anywhere.*

Then I got to thinking, I've been kind of footloose and fancy free, not worrying too much about my situation, and I hate to think I'm going to change now in my last week here.

There were two systems we used in Vietnam for convoy security. One was what they called a quad-50, four fifty-caliber machineguns on a pedestal mounted on a 2½ ton or five-ton truck. All four guns fired at the same time, and it was about like Puff the Magic Dragon but not quite as awesome and destructive. There were metal plates mounted vertically along the bed of the truck to protect the gun operators. Those quad-50s would be placed at the front and rear of the convoy, and maybe in the middle if the convoy was extra long.

For convoy security, we also used a twin-40 or duster, a track vehicle with two 40mm canon mounted side-by-side. These guns fired slugs that were over an inch-and-a-half in diameter. One gun fired and then the other gun fired—they kept that up automatically as long as the operator pulled the trigger.

They also used this vehicle to sweep the roads every morning to make sure it was safe before the convoy used it. Most of the roads, you could tell if they'd been tampered with. The surfaces were hard enough that you could tell if there'd been any type of damage or digging done to the road. When the crew saw one of these disturbed places, someone would get out and run a minesweeper over it to see if there was anything buried beneath the surface. If there was, they removed it—*very carefully*. So, they cleared the road by just driving over it and looking at it, unless they saw something that dictated closer attention.

We used the road during the day and Charlie used it at night, and sometimes Charlie left us a little present.

One of the lieutenants had extended for six months to get his full year in. He was working in a twin-40 outfit, sweeping the roads every morning to clear it for the convoys. He asked me if I wanted to go along, so I decided I would. Come to find out, I was on the outside of the twin-40 while his folks were taking minesweepers and sweeping back and forth on the road to see if there'd been any mines planted there overnight. I figured I would be inside the armored vehicle. I decided that coming along hadn't been too smart an idea, especially since this was my last week in-country.

But, the next day I went out with one of my survey sergeants and a couple of his troops. Artillerymen lay out survey points to use as a reference. Nowadays they use GPS, but back then they had to have survey points. I didn't think it would be too hazardous so I agreed to go along.

We got out on the road and we're in the middle of nowhere, about half a mile into some elephant grass. I got kind of concerned because I'd never been in that area.

All of a sudden, he stopped, jumped out, and said, "We're going over here and see if we can find the survey point we put there about a month ago."

So, he and the two troops go out into the elephant grass. The next thing I know, I'm there all by myself, I don't hear them, the grass is waving in the wind, and I'm looking around saying to myself, "What a spot to be in! You don't have to put yourself through this. All somebody would have to do is stick a rifle through the grass, shoot me, and they're gone."

Now I got worried. I jumped up in the jeep, stood on the seat, and tried to look over the grass to see if I could spot my cohorts. I couldn't see them. The jeep had a tripod with an M-60 mounted on it. I locked and loaded the machinegun—damned if I'd let Charlie's take me without a fight!

About that time, the sergeant called out my name. He probably realized that I was getting nervous and didn't want to get shot. So, they come out of the grass and see me standing behind that machinegun, ready to draw down on them.

They start laughing and I said, "It might be funny to you but it's not funny to me."

They said, "Are you ready to go home?"

I said, "You bet!"

When I got back to base camp this time, I did not leave it again until I was on my flight home.

We (the guys who'd finished their tour in Nam) flew into McChord Air Force Base, just south of Tacoma, on the way back to the states. From there, we were supposed to catch a plane at the Seattle Airport. I didn't know where McChord was in relation to Seattle, and I was in such a big hurry to get back home that when I got off the plane I went right outside. I didn't want to wait for the bus that was going to take everyone else to the Seattle Airport, so I hailed a taxi like I knew what the hell I was doing.

I told the driver where I wanted to go and not to spare the horses. He took off and it seemed like we were driving for an hour or more. I thought, *man, I don't know what this taxi bill is going to be.*

Finally, off in the distance I saw a plane take off so I figured we must be getting close. Sure enough, we finally pull up at the terminal. That was back in 1969 and I think the taxi bill was $25 or $30, which was a little expensive but I didn't care what it cost. I thought I was going to beat everybody else and get home sooner, but once I was at the airport, I had to wait seven hours for my flight! The bus finally showed up with everybody else and they didn't have to pay a cent to get there.

If I were a young trooper in the Army today, I wouldn't hesitate to do what I did in Vietnam. Somebody has to defend our country and I wouldn't have any problem doing that. In today's environment, we wouldn't let what happened in Vietnam happen again. I think we learned our lesson. You can see that in how we fought Desert Storm/ Desert Shield: we hit them with everything we had. However, we did stop short of doing what we should have done, and that's to go in and get Saddam Hussein.

I'd like to see us bring all our folks back home and let everybody else fight whatever fight they're going to fight. Then, whoever the winner is, if they want to co-exist with us, that's fine. If they don't, then we'll take on the winner!

Other than what I'd seen on TV, I had no idea how much we'd been involved in Vietnam before I went there. After the fact, I learned that some of our clandestine folks had been over there since the early 60s.

A few years before I went over there, General LeMay ran for vice president on the Goldwater ticket and one of his comments impressed me. He said he'd bomb from the DMZ all the way to Hanoi. He'd get it over with. That impressed me because most of the politicians were kind of waffling back and forth on whether they wanted to support the war or not. Originally, I thought General Westmoreland was a soldier, but I think he became a politician that just happened to wear a uniform. He certainly wasn't a Norman Schwarzkopf.

Some vets had trouble adjusting to life after Vietnam with things like Post Traumatic Stress Syndrome. Luckily, I had no such problems, not even recurring dreams or nightmares. However, for a year or two after I came back, anytime there was a loud noise while I was sleeping, I'd sit straight up in bed and try to determine if it was an incoming or outgoing round.

You can look at today's environment and see what we have the capability of doing, and we had a lot of that capability back then, too. Our weaponry might not have been quite as sophisticated, but we had the firepower to win that thing.

It was a different war and a much different environment. We were fighting in a jungle atmosphere, versus fighting out in the desert where you could see your opponent two or three miles in front of you. In Vietnam, you sometimes couldn't see him two or three feet in front of you. If the politicians had gotten out of the way and let the military run the war and do what they were trained to do, I think we'd have had a different outcome. I think a lot of the time we just went through the motions.

When Bill Howell left the service during the post-Vietnam downsizing in 1973, he returned to Cameron University in Lawton and completed his degree. He then landed a civil service job working at Fort Carson, Colorado, and then Fort McPherson, near Atlanta, GA. Upon leaving active duty, he joined the Army Reserve, eventually got promoted to LTC, and earned enough credit to qualify for a military retirement. He's now retired from civil service, too, and lives in the Atlanta area.

CHAPTER 2
ARMY SPECIALIST FOUR GEORGE ENGEBRETSON

Infantry

We made a hasty retreat and came back out of this peninsula thing to where there were some big anthills. I remember I was behind a tree and the incoming fire was very heavy. I was moving and the damn bullets were hitting beside me. There were four of five gooks behind us. So our hasty retreat kind of got stymied. The guys behind us ran into more gooks. We were in the bunkers by now, so everybody just got down and spread out. We were catching it from all four sides there for a while.

George Engebretson grew up in a very small town. His dad, George Sr., was a wounded WW-II veteran and a legendary baseball coach in northwestern Iowa. George Jr. graduated from high school in 1966, went to nearby Buena Vista College for a year and a half, became disenchanted with school, and dropped out in December 1967. He lost his student deferment and got drafted in June 1968, attending boot camp and Advance Infantry Training at Fort Lewis, Washington. George served in Vietnam 1968-69.

After I quit school, a high school classmate named John Binder and I decided we'd go out and conquer the world. We were going to Florida, but decided we'd like to go to Colorado Springs first because John's brother Bill was stationed there in the Army. So, we stayed in Colorado Springs, near Fort Carson, for a couple of months. Bill didn't go to Nam until after I got back. I saw Bill again at Fort Carson when I got back from Nam, just before he went to flight school. When he finished flight school, he went to Nam and got killed when his chopper was downed by ground fire during a reconnaissance flight.

When I got drafted and sent to basic, I figured, hey, I've got some college. There's no way they're going to put me in the infantry. *Wrong!*

Ninety percent of my boot camp class, including me, moved across post for Advanced Individual Training. After four months of training and two weeks of leave, I went across the pond, leaving from Oakland Army Terminal. That was the middle of October 1968. I flew to Alaska and Japan before arriving in Bien Hoa Airbase, near Long Binh.

When I was a kid of 12 or 13, my friends and I thought we'd be Army Rangers or Airborne. We were really into that stuff. We had all kinds of military gear. By the time we were 15 or 16, our interests shifted to cars and girls. I was still in high school (1965, 66) and the war was going hot and heavy. We saw it on the news and in the papers but really didn't have any opinions about it. We grew up in the Kennedy era. My dad was a veteran of WW-II and had been wounded, so we just thought it was our duty to defend our country. We grew up with Vic Morrow and "Combat" on TV, so I didn't have any qualms about doing it. I figured I'd go to Vietnam and fly helicopters. Close! I flew *in* them. They'd drop us off and then pick us up one to three weeks later.

When I flew out to California en route to Vietnam, there happened to be a guy on the plane that I'd gone through basic and AIT with, a fellow Hawkeye from southwestern Iowa. I ran into three or four other guys in Long Binh from my units in basic and AIT. When the levies came down, two of those guys went right with me to the same company. I was a PFC when I arrived in Nam, in October '68 and, bang, I made Spec Four almost immediately.

My first thoughts when I arrived in-country were that the place stunk. As soon as they opened the door of the plane, I felt oppressive heat. There's an odor to that country that's just must and decay all mixed together. It just hit me when I stepped off the plane. I smelled rotting vegetation and human waste.

We arrived at three or four in the morning. It wasn't much of an airport terminal. There were guys there who had just come out of the field and were going home. They were in ratty fatigues. They looked at us with strange eyes, just like in the movie *Platoon*. "Fresh meat," they said to us. They knew which of us were infantry because of the insignia on our uniforms. There were a few chairs around but most people were sitting or lying on the concrete. I thought, *ooh, this is going to be an interesting place.*

Then it was onto a bus with windows that had heavy screens over them to keep grenades out. We went through the city to the Long Binh in-processing center.

We were in formation and they read off a list of names, assigning us to our units, saying these guys are going to this division and these guys are going to that division, etc.

I wanted to be in the 1st Cavalry Division. I had been trained by a couple of drill sergeants who had been in the Cav and it sounded to me like those guys had their shit together. So, I was happy when I got assigned to the Cav, too.

Meanwhile, while waiting to be assigned, at morning formation, they said they needed people to work details. The first thing they did was asked for volunteers for a Chaplain detail and about 20 guys raised their hands. Then they assigned some of us who were left for sandbag detail and some for water detail, etc. Later in the day we saw the guys who'd volunteered for Chaplain detail: they were burning shit! After that first time in the formation everybody except the new arrivals knew better than to volunteer for Chaplain detail! I guess we spent two days there doing detail work and waiting for our exact unit assignments. They had an Enlisted Men's club there with a rock band and a stripper, and that's how we spent part of our down time.

In a matter of hours after we got our levy, we got on a plane and flew about a third of the way up the country, north to where the Cav was based at Ahn Khe. When we flew in, we circled this mountain that had the top cut off of it, there was a communications base up there, and on the side of the mountain was a huge 1st Cav patch. Seeing the size of that patch gave me a feeling of security about being assigned to the Cav. I said, "Yes, this is good!"

We went there and had about a week of in-country training. We sighted in our rifles and got acclimated to the country. There was a mountain inside the perimeter of the 1st Cavalry base area, surrounded by wire and bunkers. They'd taken Rome plows and pushed back the underbrush and everything a hellacious distance. But here's this mountain in the middle, called Hong Kong Mountain, and it's full of caves. Guess who was living in those caves? There were gooks, North Vietnamese, inside our perimeter living in this mountain!

The North Vietnamese, as opposed to Vietcong, were full-time soldiers. The NVA had nice uniforms like ours, new AK-47s, that type of stuff. They were the regular soldiers, hardcore, 24 hours a day. But the Viet Cong were the guerilla fighters, that is they were farmers or peasants in the daytime and at night they'd go dig their weapons out of a stash somewhere, turn into freedom fighters, and go out after you.

At Ahn Khe, we had regular billets, which were frame buildings with tin roofs. Inside, there were bunks with real mattresses on them. We were told that, if we heard incoming while we were sleeping, we should just grab our mattresses and lay them on top of ourselves, and then get under the bunk. Sure enough, the first night we were there shit started coming in, rockets and mortars, maybe 10 or 12 rounds, just harassment fire. Welcome to Vietnam!

A few nights later, I'd been put on KP and had to work quite late into the night. One of our tasks was to clean out the grease pit and what a horrible job that was. It was just a trench that ran through the kitchen and the cooks dumped all the cooking grease into it, which of course accumulated. While we were cleaning the pit, we heard rockets and shit started happening on that mountain inside our perimeter. A Puff the Magic Dragon fired up its mini-gun. It was just like a constant bolt of lightning as it fired 3000 rounds a minute into the mountain.

The next day, we went out to the rifle range to sight in our weapons on a range outside the perimeter a short distance. There were some more large hills or mountains not too far in the distance and the Air Force was working out on them. We weren't in any danger, but we could definitely see things getting blown to hell out there.

While we were there, a company of infantry came in out of the field. They were shuffling in and I'm thinking, hmm, this is what I'm going to look like in a few days. It was quite a sight to behold, the first time especially, to see real warriors coming right out of the field. It was very eerie.

When we left Ahn Khe, those two fellows I'd gone through basic and AIT with and me, we all got assigned to the same company, A Co, 1/5, based at Camp Evans. For the trip to Evans they put us in the back of a deuce-and-a-half. We had our rifles and they gave us each one magazine, which held 20 rounds. We had no escorts or anything, although there may have been a machinegun mounted on the cab of the truck. Down the road we went, through some villages, past some water buffalos, by some rice paddies, to a big firebase with artillery batteries inside the perimeter. I don't recall if there were one or two battalions of us there.

They took us to the Alfa Company area. The company was out in the field at the time and on their way in. The executive officer and first sergeant were there. We hung out there for an hour or so before the rest of the company came back to camp. They came in, single-file carrying everything they had to live with on their backs. Plus, they had picks, shovels, five-gallon water jugs, and an assortment of utensils. They looked like a walking junkyard. You don't think of a soldier carrying stuff like that, but you needed those picks and shovels and other things.

The company commander came over introduced himself to us, then assigned us to our platoons. He put me in the first platoon and the other two guys in the second platoon. Then the first sergeant announced that the whole Cav was going to move south to Tay Nihn. He put me into a squad just for a few days so I'd have somebody to hang with—they had to assign me *somewhere*. These guys were old heads—they'd all been there six or eight months. I was the new guy. They said, "Come on and hang out, man, and learn what it's all about."

They were having a few beers and they had a little whiskey and shit. I'm just watching and listening. It was a great time for them, so they're smoking and joking.

Pretty soon, they started doing splits with bayonets. They stood facing each other, threw their bayonet into the ground, and the other guy had to put his foot where the bayonet stuck. Then he did the same thing and the other guy had to put his foot where that bayonet stuck. They kept going until one of them couldn't reach far enough and fell over. It was just something to pass the time.

I'm watching these guys and one of them decides he's going to throw his bayonet right next to the other guy's foot. Bad plan, worse execution. The next thing I know, here's this guy standing there with a bayonet sticking out of his foot. He pulled it out, took his boot off, and pours whiskey over the wound.

"I can't go to the medic," he says. "I'll get in trouble for stabbing myself."

He came out of it okay; he didn't get infection or anything, but no purple heart either.

This same guy made it almost all the way through his tour, to within 12 days left, and then got killed. He was out on an ambush—should *not* have been out—should *not* have been in the field with that short a period of time left! He was a hell of a nice guy, too, named Jim Agnew. Everybody loved him. Another guy from my unit, John Gayman from Davenport, and I went to visit Jim's parents in Missouri about 13 years ago. The Agnews really appreciated our visit. It was one of the most rewarding things I ever did.

I got hooked up with my company at Camp Evans and we just hung out there for a couple of days. That's where I started sleeping on the ground. That's just the way it was. You rolled up in your poncho liner, laid down on the ground, and that was it. It didn't take long before you were used to sleeping that way. It wasn't that hard. Of course, it was pretty warm even though it was mid-October.

We hopped on C-130s and flew to Tay Ninh, which is about 70 miles northwest of Saigon, not far from the Cambodian border. There was a large firebase outside the city. Our portion of the Cav was there, or it could have been the division rear—I can't remember exactly. Also, the 25th Infantry Division was based there, and there were Philippine and Australian Army units there, too. It was a big compound.

We just hung out there for the day, waiting to go to the field. I'm the new guy and we're going out to the field tomorrow. We'd been issued gear, about 20 magazines of M-16 ammo, a couple of fragmentation grenades, a smoke grenade or two, trip flares, Claymore mines, all that good stuff. We got loaded down with probably 60-80 pounds of gear.

This guy who'd been there a couple three months is talking to me and he's taking care of me. He's telling me this and he's telling me that. I'm thinking maybe I should have some more hand grenades, and he agrees with me. "Why don't you go see our first sergeant," he suggests, "He'll give you a couple more."

So, I go booking over and find the first sergeant. I tell him I'd like a couple more frags. In my mind, I thought, *we were going out to the field and sure as hell tomorrow we're going to be in a big battle and I'm going to run out of frags and will want more.* The first sergeant got me some more frags but he looked at me kind of strange, like he didn't know if I really needed that many.

I come back to our area to where all my gear was lying. I look at my poncho liner. Being a new guy, I'd been issued a brand new one but this one is about six months old and it's all full of holes and shredded. Well, the guy I'd been talking to is gone with my nice new poncho liner and I've got this raggedy old thing. I went after him and told him he'd ripped me off.

"Oh no," he said, "I wouldn't do a thing like that."

It takes all kinds. I didn't have any respect for that particular individual after that. It's just a fact of life that, if you get that many people together, you're going to have a few shysters in the crowd. The last time I saw that guy was shortly before I got wounded the second time. We were at this rubber plantation and he got heat stroke. He was all tied up in knots and spinning around in circles and shaking. They had to medevac him out and I thought it served him right!

The next morning, we flew out to this place called Katum, which was very close to the Cambodian border. It was an ARVN compound, with a village nearby and an airstrip. We landed there and got off the Huey, thinking all kinds of hell was going to break loose. It didn't happen. The Huey came in and landed, we got off, and pretty soon the whole company is there, a hundred or so of us.

They took us out and we formed a perimeter around one side of the ARVN compound. We just started digging holes and building bunkers. This is going to be our firebase, where our artillery would be located. The ARVNs had some artillery there, too. Katum is located in what we called the "parrot's beak" because of the way the Cambodian border curves right there. We were talking to some of the Vietnamese asking, "Where are we?"

They showed us on the map that we had Cambodia on three sides.

We stayed in Katum for a day or two building bunkers for the firebase. There were remnants of a dead North Vietnamese lying in the brush right next to our position. In that climate, they didn't last long. He was just a bag of bones and some clothes lying there. I remember that well.

I think it was either our first or second night there—everybody took their turn pulling guard duty—I'm under my poncho liner trying to sleep. I just laid down on one half of the poncho liner and pulled the other half up over myself, head and all, to escape the bugs. I'm lying there trying to get some sleep when I heard these fellows talking. I think it was my squad leader, a guy named Trevino from Dallas. He was a cool dude. This Pedro Trevino was a pretty good-sized Mexican guy, just a nice guy.

Anyway, I hear Pedro saying, "Hey George, don't move. There's a rat sitting on your head. I'm going to smash him with my steel pot."

Sure enough, there was a rat there but Pedro didn't whack him. He was just kidding.

We stayed there for several days, and then our platoon had to go out and patrol outside the perimeter. This was my first patrol, so off we go. You couldn't believe the amount of shit we carried! We had a LAWS rocket, probably three frags, a couple smoke grenades, a Claymore mine, three trip flares, a gallon or gallon-and-a-half of water, 20-25 magazines of M-16 ammo, and everybody carried one 30-pound can of M-60 ammo (the ammo bearers carried two cans). Man, that pack was one heavy son-of-a-bitch! That's why I wore a towel on my neck because otherwise the straps would just cut into my flesh. If someone happened to trip, he was going down. If he lost his balance carrying all that weight, that was it.

Once we got to Katum, they reassigned me to the machinegun squad. That's the way our outfit did it: when you first came into the company, you became an ammo bearer for a machinegun. We had two machineguns in our platoon. Each gun team had a machine gunner and two ammo bearers. The ammo bearers each carried two cans of 7.62mm ammo, 400 rounds per can.

So, we take off and we're hopping along through the bush. We probably hadn't been out an hour and the guy walking point ran into some enemy troops. He just cuts loose with his M-16 and everybody hits the ground. But we were in tall grass and I couldn't see anything. I thought, *What the hell am I doing here?* We stayed put, called in artillery, they put about 18 rounds into wherever those gooks were last seen, and then on we went. I don't know if we hit anything—at least we never did find anything. The point man was a real short-timer, so he might have just been nervous. He left the company within a few days of that incident.

In another day or two, we went out to the field for real. Here came the helicopters—there were six Hueys to a lift—and they landed on the airstrip. Half the guys from a squad got on each side and away we went, a squad per bird. We took off and circled a little bit until the other birds got off the ground.

I didn't know how far it was to the landing zone we were going into, but we circled again when we got there. We were near Cambodia and could look across the border and see tin sheds, billets just like we had back in our rear area. But, guess what? They were not ours. They were theirs!

We landed not too far from there in a clearing. I was sitting in the door. I always liked to do that, although I don't know how I got to sit there on my first trip. Just before we landed, the door gunner tells me, "Don't get off until we get on the ground because, if you go jumping off, you'll upset the balance of the helicopter."

I said, "Cool, I won't."

We get down to the clearing and there was elephant grass all over. As the bird came down, I'm standing on the skid and the grass is up to my knees. I think, shit, we're practically down so I'm stepping off. I stepped off all right, and it was about another four feet to the ground. I landed on my ass with all that gear on but, luckily, only hurt my pride.

I jumped up and the company took off single-file at a high rate of speed. In fact, we were damn near running. I'm carrying all this stuff, we're moving through the bushes, and I'm wondering, do we move this fast all the time? We followed a trail for a thousand meters or so, then stopped to take a break so everybody could catch their breath. Just about the time we stopped, you could hear this chump-chump-chump sound. The enemy had seen us land and they were putting mortars into the LZ, but we had gotten far enough away. *That's* why we were moving at a high rate of speed. I was a new guy, but the old heads, they knew the score. Nothing else exciting occurred that day.

Every day after that, we got up at dawn and got all our shit together. Then we'd get coordinates for the objective of the day, shoot an azimuth, and off we'd go through the bush.

I carried the ammunition probably for a month. Then, as new people came into the company, they became ammo bearers and I moved up to a rifle squad. Humping ammo was just hard work, but it gave me a chance to figure out what the hell was going on. The bad part was, if you did get into the shit, the machine gun was very crucial. The machineguns weren't in the front of the formation; there were 5-10 guys ahead of us. We tried to stay spread out, at least five yards apart. If the point man runs into some shit, the first thing he yells is, "Guns forward." So, the machinegun squad has to run up to where the action is and the ammo bearer has to keep the machinegun fed. The machine guns draw plenty of enemy fire and, therefore, so do the bearers.

One difference between being an ammo bearer and being in a rifle squad was that I *got* to walk point in the rifle squad, be the first man through the bush. It was a rotating thing. One day, the first platoon would be in the lead. The next day, the second platoon had the honor, and so on. Within each platoon, they'd rotate which squad was out front and, within the squad, which soldier was out front. That way you didn't have to walk point too often, but we were so understaffed that we only had two rifle squads and a machinegun squad most of the time, so every other day my squad was point for our platoon. Frequently, I was the point man for the squad.

As we moved through the jungle, we were always getting caught. There were these wait-a-minute vines with little thorns that would just grab us and rip our clothes or catch us on the eyelids.

I was in a rifle squad for two or three days before I got the honor of walking point. The first time I ever walked point, I started out in second place behind this guy and we were in some pretty heavy brush. It was a rain forest, a tropical jungle. This guy walking point wasn't a real big guy. He was from the east coast somewhere, kind of a city kid. But, he's up there and making his way through. He had his M-16 in one hand and his machete in the other. The guy behind the point, or the second guy back, that's me in this case, would have a compass to keep us on course.

The point man had a complete breakdown about halfway through the day. He just couldn't hack it I guess. Maybe he just wasn't a real strong person. Let me put it that way: Physically, he was okay, but he just whacked out. Instead of fighting it and making him try to continue, our leaders moved him back in the formation. He ended up getting sent back to the World for a death in the family, or maybe he had gotten the word just before this incident and that could have been part of the reason why he cracked up. He was gone for about two or three weeks, and then he came back out. I don't think he every walked point again.

Anyway, my squad leader said, "George, you're going to have to do it sooner or later, so you're the point."

I finished out the day walking point. It's pretty close to hell. The next time you chop through some heavy underbrush, you never know what you're going to see on the other side. I got through that. Being a tall kid from Iowa who did a lot of hunting and fishing and athletics and stuff, I moved pretty fast. So it got to be like, oh, we need a point man? George, hop in there.

The way it worked out was, I could get through the stuff fast and keep a fairly straight path.

If our objective was eight clicks today or 15 clicks or whatever, we had all day to get there. So, if we left at 7:30 in the morning, we were expected to arrive at around five in the afternoon. Then we'd set up our main support base. If I was fast and could get us there by two o'clock, we wouldn't bother telling the rear that we were already there. We'd take our time getting our bunkers dug—every night we dug foxholes big enough for three or four guys. We carried sand bags with us, which we then filled and used for overhead cover. It worked out well if we could get there early and get all that stuff done. Then, around four or five o'clock, about the time we should be getting there, we'd radio in and report our arrival, tell the rear we'll be setting up stuff, so go ahead and send the log birds out.

Most every night we were able to get re-supplied with water, and frequently things like hamburgers, mail, and ammunition. That was one thing about having helicopter support is that they could get out to us almost every night. That was decent, real good support, and I really appreciated it.

Walking point, I had developed a good friendship with another guy—well, we were all tight—I mean it's unbelievable how tight you get with six or seven guys. There was a fellow from Texas, Charlie Lansdale, and we just kind of became a team. If I was walking point, he was walking second. If he was walking point, I was walking second. We could cut right through that stuff.

Most of the time, we didn't run into anything. We got mortared that first time at the LZ, but for quite a period of time after that, we'd just go out and hump every day. We were always waiting for the shit to hit, but nothing was happening. It was mostly, go out and search and destroy, but we weren't finding anything. The enemy must have been rebuilding, probably staying over in Cambodia. Cambodia was a safe haven for the North Vietnamese at that time.

The area that we were in was where the Ho Chi Min Trail came down through Cambodia and dumped right over the border. We found all kinds of bunker complexes and training areas. We found classrooms made out of bamboo, like a square building, or at least it had latticework on top so they could sit in the shade. They had little benches for seating and their training materials were still there. We went into one place and the pots were still cooking. They knew we were coming, but I don't think they wanted to screw with us because they knew we had the support. They were also probably saving up for the springtime. They had the big Tet offensive in '68 and another in '69.

This may not be the greatest story ever told, but on December 31, 1968, we came out of the bush to Firebase Eleanor. Believe it or not, I can't recall whether we humped in out of the rain forest or were charlie-alfa-ed, slang for combat assault, but we got there in the morning hours. We spent two or three hours on the edge of the airstrip waiting to fly into Quan Loi for a three-day stand-down. I guess the Cav had set up an area there for line infantry companies to come in from the field, and really kick back, pretty secure. Well sure, for Christ's sake, instead of having a trip wire, claymore, and a few feet of fire zone between the enemy and us there was one hell of a perimeter, with somebody else on guard duty. Let's go!

It seems to me we weren't even told where we were heading at first. Perhaps the brass didn't want us to get too unruly early in the day. I do have several pictures taken on the edge of the airstrip at Eleanor while we were waiting for transportation to Quan Loi. It's amazing how much stuff 80-100 grunts can carry. As I look at those pictures now it's almost like a walking junkyard: shovels, pickaxes, five-gallon water jugs, machineguns, M-16's, ammunition up the wazoo, frags, smoke grenades, machetes, and steel pots strewn everywhere along the edge of the perimeter of Eleanor.

They didn't let us on the firebase that day, just hunker down along side the airstrip and wait. First sign that I remember of us getting ready to fly out was a low-flying Caribou circling the airstrip, and then buzzing us. He came in really low and fast at a 90-degree angle to the strip, then swooping up, making a turn and landed so quickly. They could land those things in such a short distance it was hard to believe, and taking off was no different. It seems to me that our platoon first sergeant put us on a C-130 for the trip. The crew at A Company's rear on Eleanor had made plans for us. Many of us were carrying cases of beer onto the plane. The usual was Carlings Black Label, however, I had Millers. By this time the New Years Eve idea began to kick in.

During the flight to Quan Loi, the crew chief of the C-130 put down the cargo door at the rear of the plane. He walked out on the door and looked over the edge, crazy in my eyes but what the hell. Someone gave him a smoke grenade, he popped that sucker, and flipped it out. It was interesting to watch it falling to the bush below, trailing red smoke all the way down.

Upon arrival at Quan Loi we were zipped to the stand-down area. Wow! Big-ass tents with wooden floors, shower's made from jet fuel tanks with almost hot water (warmed by the sun), and a whole pallet of beer, 144 cases to be exact. Hmm, more than one case per sky-trooper. Well, I guess we were going to be there for three days.

The first thing that happened when we hit the company area was a meeting. We were instructed to turn in all ammunition, grenades etc., which was probably a smart idea. However, you are not going to get a grunt's weapons away from him, not all of them at least. Then came the steak dinner, showers, and free time, picture taking time, letters and tape recordings for home, and just plain kicking back.

Oh yeah, and there was that pallet of beer!

The men of A Company spread out all over Quan Loi that afternoon and evening. The place was built right on a rubber plantation with lots of straight lines of trees to follow in order to get somewhere. At least we could walk in straight lines—sort of.

I don't really remember what all I did that afternoon and evening. I think I stayed fairly close to the company area, had a few beers, etc. As midnight was drawing upon us, a bunch of guys came by and enticed me to take a walk with them. They had been out partying pretty hard somewhere on the base, talked of how some MP's had been hassling them for one reason or another, that is until someone threw a frag at them and the MPs left. I would think they would have known better than to mess with line infantry just out of the field.

So we walked a ways, over to a line of big metal containers—CONUS containers we called them—fill 'em up, put 'em on a ship, and send 'em anywhere. They make pretty good jail cells, also. Why these guys decided to hang out by the containers, I had no idea, other than the fact that someone there had a big old pipe and it was getting passed around. Being a hick from Iowa I didn't realize what the heck was going on until someone handed that thing to me. Hmm. Our LT was there but didn't much care what we did.

We all stumbled back to the Company area just before midnight, and got ready to crash and burn for the night. Keith W. had *not* turned in all of his ammo (surprise, surprise) and at the stroke of midnight he let his M-16 go on rock 'n roll, straight up into the darkness, 20 rounds, and every single one of them a tracer. What a sight it was! God, we laughed

Shortly thereafter we were in the tents just smoking and joking, whatever. We were kind of noisy I guess, because some 1st or 2nd lieutenant from a neighboring billet came into our tent and told us to "shut the hell up, his men were clerks and had to work the next day, and we were keeping them awake." I guess when he felt the barrel of the loaded .45 pressing on his forehead he decided to go back to his own tent and call it a night.

Don't mess with a bunch of grunts just out of the field.

Strange as it may seem, our three-day stand-down was over the next morning. They loaded us up, flew us right back to Eleanor, and then right back to the field. Someone was getting hit pretty bad and we were the Quick Reaction Force going out to help them. By the time we got to their position, the firefight was over. But the look in those guys' eyes told the story. No words needed to be said.

After New Year's, things started heating up. Until then, we'd get reports such as, *S3 has determined that there is a large enemy force and a good possibility they'll hit you tonight.*

Each night in the bush we had trip flares and Claymore mines positioned around the perimeter. The claymores were set up so their fields of fire overlapped. There'd only be a few guys awake at any one time during the night, pulling guard duty, one to each position. Once in a while, one of the trip flares would go off and the guard would blow his Claymores. The next morning, we'd go out and look to see if there were any casualties. There never were, so it must have been a branch falling that tripped the flares. Or, it could have been a gook trying to sneak through. Maybe they hauled off the bodies

There were also ambushes that went out every night. For my platoon, about every other night we'd go out and set up an ambush. We'd just take a squad of men, like our seven and a machinegun team, maybe ten of us altogether. We'd take a radio, no operator, and we'd go out about 1000m. We'd find a trail or some other likely enemy route, and we'd set up our ambush. We'd find a place that had good cover for ourselves and set up a tripwire across the trail for the flare. We set up Claymore mines so that, if something did hit the trip flare, we could blow the mines and then cut loose with our rifles.

That was interesting because we didn't have bunkers. All we took was our fighting gear and our bedrolls, maybe some C-Rations and tropical bars. The tropical bars were pure Nestlé's chocolate; it was good chocolate with some sort of additive to keep them from melting. That's why they called them *tropical* bars.

One time, our company was set up on the edge of a wood line next to a large open field. I suppose the grass there was knee-high and there was a trail running right through it. It happened that our firing position was right in front, and we could see right out across that field. On the other side of the field was a clump of trees, and that's where our ambush crew was setting up. I didn't know that—I never knew where any of the ambushes were set up, unless I was part of it.

The next morning, just as the sun came up, all of a sudden, BOOM, an ambush blew a Claymore. Then there were AK-47s going off, and M-16s going off, and M-60s going off. Bullets are flying all over hell. I jumped up, standing behind our bunker. From the edge of the clearing, I could see these three gooks running along a trail in the field. I got my M-16 and drew a bead, but my platoon sergeant had run over to me real quick and he pushed my 16 up, saying, "Don't shoot! Don't shoot! You'll hit our ambush."

So, I got the pleasure of watching the gooks run right in front of me, they were probably no more than 30 or 40 yards away. I could have dusted them. They were wearing nice green uniforms, ponchos, and one guy had a steel pot. They were *not* our guys—they were *not* friendlies—they were definitely NVA. The platoon sergeant was a good guy; he just didn't want me firing into our own ambush sitting across the field beyond the trail. Boy, that was so frustrating!

I jumped up and ran out to the edge of the clearing to where I knew our trip wires were because I had set them. I figured, maybe I can get them as they're moving on down through that clearing. But, evidently, they didn't go too much past us before they went up into the bush. I could have zapped them so easily. They would have been toast. I had no qualms or hesitation. It was such a clean shot and I was ready to take it before the sarge grabbed my 16.

A couple days later, my squad went out and set up an ambush in that same spot. There wasn't much going on that night, so Lansdale and I got a wild hair to go do a little roving ambush of our own. We told the squad leader what we were doing. It was kind of a full moon that night when the two of us took off. We went out there tromping around in the brush for 15 minutes or half an hour, and then thought, *what the hell are we doing out here?* We went back. We just got gutsy, showed a little bravado, figured we'd been lucky so far.

Shortly after this we started getting into some shit. There was a thing we called "The Bridge Incident." The way we operated, we'd go out for 21 days into the brush and then back to the firebase for a week. There were four companies, A through D, and we rotated, each spending a week back at the firebase and then three out in the boonies.

We got up one morning at our night position in the woods. I think it was just our platoon, not the whole company, and away we went with just our fighting gear. We humped along until we got to this area that had just had the shit shot out of it by cobras. You could tell because the bamboo and all the surrounding trees had bullet holes about every six inches. Those mini-guns were something else! It was pretty obvious when one had been shooting up an area.

We were humping along single-file and I heard some rustling in the nearby brush, but I couldn't see anything. There were bunkers in the area and they were freshly dug. There was also a river that made a curve and we were in sort of a peninsula formed by the banks of the river. At the point of the peninsula, there was a bamboo bridge across the river. We stopped and took a break for 15 minutes or half an hour to have some C-Rations. It was probably 10 o'clock in the morning. I remember sitting on the bank close to the edge of the river reading a *Sex to Sexty* magazine when all of a sudden an M-60 opened up.

The platoon sergeant yells, "What the hell's going on?"

The guy that was on the M-60 yelled back, "If I see a gook, can I shoot him?"

"Yeah," the sergeant replied.

This gook had stuck his head out of a bunker on the other side of the river and the machine-gunner had basically blown it right off.

Then one of the officers, either a lieutenant or a captain, came down and stepped out on that bridge. BOOM! All hell broke loose on the other side. The gooks were on three sides of us along the opposite bank of the river. The officer wasn't hit, but the guy with the machinegun took a bullet through the groin area. He lived through it.

We made a hasty retreat and came back out of this peninsula thing to where there were some big anthills. I remember I was behind a tree and the incoming fire was very heavy. I was about the only one left out there, so I hurried back. I was moving and the damn bullets are hitting beside me. I got back behind an anthill [not your normal anthill, these things were six-foot-tall cones that were hard as bricks] and then pulled back into the bunker complex I mentioned earlier. Wouldn't you know it? There were four of five gooks behind us. So our hasty retreat kind of got stymied. The guys behind us ran into more gooks. We were in the bunkers by now, so everybody just got down and spread out. We were catching it from all four sides there for a while.

I was helping this guy, Jim Davis, and we jumped in one of these nice deep bunkers with no roof. We're sitting down there when the platoon sergeant came over. He was ballsy. He was like 19 years old and he's already an E-7. His desire in life was to become *the* Sergeant Major of the entire U.S. Army. He's walking toward us with shit flying all over. He looked down at us and says, "That's a good spot for you guys. Just hang in there while I see where everybody is and figure out what we're going to do."

POW! A damn bullet nicked his earlobe. He wiped it with his finger, looked at the blood, and then went on about his business as though nothing had happened.

I couldn't believe it. He was a gung-ho guy.

We called in the jets, F-4 Phantoms I think, which was nice. They were coming in close enough that we could see the pilot's eyes. It's really an exhilarating feeling when they come in and drop their bombs. It shakes the ground like a son-of-a-buck. Of course, all that shrapnel doesn't stop. It goes up in the air and rains down on friend and foe alike. I had a piece of shrapnel hit right between my legs. I thought, *ooh, a nice big chunk like that could have taken my unit right off!* Luckily, nobody in my unit got hurt too badly from this type of shrapnel; maybe a burn was about the worst of it.

After the air support left, I got out of there and crawled toward the riverbank to see if I could spot some gooks. I was out there a ways but couldn't see anything. They were shooting from across the river but they were dug in, so I crawled back to our hole. After a couple of hours, there a medic came to get the wounded out of the bunkers. We're standing there watching this with our heads sticking out of that hole in the ground. No sooner had we sat back down in the hole, DING-DING-DING, right in that pile of dirt behind where our heads had been. If we'd still been standing there, we'd have been history.

We opened up on the gooks behind us, with a rifle squad and a machinegun laying down suppressing fire. Then the guys with the M-79 grenade launchers, fired three or four rounds into the bunkers, and eliminated the enemy.

All this must have taken three or four hours. All this time the jets were working out on the other side of the river. We had at least three wounded but nobody killed. We had a lieutenant who got shot in the leg and a platoon sergeant, a black guy, had been hit in the gut. He just took a jungle compress, put that sucker on there, and continued fighting. He was with his men. He was taking care of them. I remember him running back and forth and shouting out commands. It was exhilarating to see him in action, very inspiring.

We went out to check on the enemy and I remember one guy was just hammered because we'd put so many rounds into him. Among the enemy casualties, we found one GI that had been there the night before, although we certainly didn't know it at the time. He'd come there with another company the day before and had run into the same shit, the same situation we'd just been in. There were some of his guys that were wounded up on the front, and this guy that we'd found, a medic, had gone up there and pulled the wounded back. I don't know how many there were—two, three, four—he made these trips up there to pull these guys back. He went back again, thinking there was another guy up there but there wasn't. I guess that's when the enemy fire got so strong that his company had to pull back, leaving him alone on the front. Now, whether he got killed that day, I don't know, but I think he got killed during the action we were in. In fact, I'm sure that's what happened.

By now, it was five o'clock in the afternoon and time to get the hell out of there, back to the place we'd camped the night before. We didn't have all our gear and it wasn't a nice place to be in the daytime, let alone at night. So, went back through the bush and our squad got the duty of carrying the body of the medic back. He was with the 1st Cav, but I don't know what unit.

There's nothing like a dead body to carry. It's just dead weight. Lansdale and I had him in a poncho between us. When we stopped on the trail, the dead guy's arm flopped out of the poncho and I noticed that he was wearing a wedding ring.

Whoever was walking point was having a hell of a time. We weren't getting anywhere. So, here comes the word, "Engebretson and Lansdale, go take the point and get us back to last night's position."

So we went up there and away we went. We were there quick. A good point man is somebody who can get through the bush in a hurry. He has to be alert, be able to handle a machete, and be damn lucky. As mentioned, the first time I was asked to relieve the point man was when he kind of cracked up. This time I'm not sure what the point man's problem was. Maybe he was less experienced because we just weren't making any time.

They were going to have log birds come in and we wanted to take the body down to the LZ. We got him started home so we wanted to get him the rest of the way. We took the guy down there and, when we arrive, we checked him out again and his Goddamn wedding ring was gone! I suspect that the arm flopped out again when the other guys were carrying the body. We figured someone might have taken it. That was disgusting. We were pissed. What a real bummer! But, maybe somebody took the ring and put in the guy's pocket—at least I hope that's what happened.

The B-52s wiped out the area of "the bridge incident" after we'd pulled out. Then the Army sent the 173rd in there, instead of us, to see what was left. That was kind of irritating. I don't remember for sure, but I think the 173rd did run into a few enemy remnants in the area. But, from what I heard, guys who managed to survive a B-52 strike weren't much of a threat. I know the concussion was enough to bounce us up off the ground and we were quite a ways away.

The sky in Vietnam was a beautiful dark blue at night, one of the most beautiful skies I've ever seen, with stars all over hell. It was really neat. When the B-52s were working at night, we'd be sleeping on the ground and look up in the air. You'd see these lights moving across the sky. They'd get way over there on the other side of the sky and, all of a sudden, clear over here the ground would just shake. There'd be a big arc light and we'd bounce all over the place. The whole sky would just turn white.

We saw some daylight B-52 strikes. They weren't nuclear strikes but they did create similar mushroom clouds. Whenever we went into those areas afterward, there'd be huge holes 10 or 12 feet deep. Pretty amazing.

One of the reasons I wanted to go to the Cav was that they had helicopters. We were usually on duty as a QRF. Say, another battalion got into a big battle, firefight, or something, we were the unit designated to go and assist. We might be on a mission in the boonies somewhere when we'd get a call telling us to stop, clear yourself a landing zone, and we're going to come pick you up so you can go help this other unit. That happened fairly frequently. In fact, you were awarded an Air Medal after 25 missions—I got two of them!

What normally happened is that by the time we got there it was all over. A firefight is only going to last about half an hour or so—the enemy is going to hit and run. But we'd hop on a chopper and fly into a red LZ. We'd think we were going to get into the action, but usually nothing would be happening. However, there was one time that we went into a big clearing. There were a few rounds fired off at us as we were coming in and our door gunners were cutting loose. Usually, if we were going into an area, the cobra gun ships would go ahead of us and prep the area, just blast the hell out of it, try to encourage people to leave.

Anyway, we hopped off the helicopter and we're making a beeline for a tree line. I got off the left side of the bird and the damn pilot pulled out his .45 and is popping off rounds just as I ran under his window. Jesus, my ears rang for a few minutes! In fact, my ears have been ringing ever since—tinnitus, I guess. There was so much noise anyway.

In February of '69, we went to a place on top of a mountain called LZ Dolly, a beautiful place. There was a Michelin rubber plantation down in the valley where there had been some pretty sizable battles back in '65 or '66. Since that time, there had been no U.S. troops on that rubber plantation. I guess they decided it was time for us to go back in there and we were one of the first units to go.

So, one morning we took off from the top of the mountain and flew down into the rubber plantation. The rubber trees were planted like a checkerboard with a tree at the corner of each square so you could look down the rows in any direction. We went in there and I got to walk point that first day. It was easy walking—just get in between the trees and go down the row. There were all these shadowy figures out there. I could see a long way, which was unusual, maybe a hundred yards or so. I could see that there was stuff there, but couldn't really make out what it was.

Nothing happened right away and we made it through that day. But, that afternoon, one of our sister companies ran into some shit. Just when we were starting to dig in, we got the call to go down and assist. As we're getting close to them, we had the gooks between our sister company and ourselves. That was fine, except I'm walking the point and our sister company had called in Cobra gun ships, and they always come in from behind and raze everything in front. Something didn't compute very well for me because I was walking *into* cobra gunfire. Fortunately, they broke it off before we got too close. I really hesitated. I was getting there but it was like, I'm getting behind this tree and then I'm getting behind that tree.

We went back to our base for the night and were finishing setting up. There were enemy out there. You could just get a glimpse of them, never enough to cut loose on them. The next morning we got up and our platoon went out on a patrol. I think we were planning to come back to the same place that night. We were going through the trees at an angle when we came to a trail and spotted three or four gooks. Everybody got behind a tree and waited in ambush. The gooks were carrying AKs and one had a rocket-propelled grenade launcher. We were probably 50 meters or less from them when one of our machine gunners cuts loose. Wow! We all cut loose—I fired off seven magazines myself. We're killing the shit out of them—feathers all over the place.

When this one gook went down, apparently his B-40 rocket was pointed in my direction. It went off and hit up in a tree in front of me. I must have been in the act of reloading my M-16 when, BOOM, it felt like somebody hit me in the chest with a hammer. I looked down and the blood is squirting out of my chest. It went on like that for a while but then it stopped. I'm thinking, Jesus, I hope that wasn't a bullet. Fortunately, it was just a little piece of shrapnel. It stuck right in my sternum, a surreal sight, a stream of blood shooting out of my chest arcing toward the ground.

I looked over at the guy next to me and said, "Look at this shit!"

A medic came over and put a jungle compress on me. He and I were the only ones left there. Everybody else went to check out the bodies, and the medic, he was in a big hurry to go over and check the bodies, too. I'm thinking, do you suppose there are any more gooks coming around behind us? Luckily there wasn't.

They put me on a medevac bird and sent me back to the rear. When I got there, they laid me on the table, and the medic goes digging around in my chest with a tweezers or forceps, and pulls out this little bitty piece of shrapnel. I say, "Shit, is that all it is?"

He says, "Yeah, but what if it had hit you in the eye or something like that?"

I had to take a dose of penicillin every day for a few days, to prevent infection.

I ended up back in Tay Ninh and that was when 1969 really started to heat up. My first night there, there wasn't much for bunkers around and we were getting rockets and mortars, maybe 30 or 40 of them.

Eventually, I "got" to go back out and join the company. I went to LZ Dolly and that rubber plantation which had not had any U.S. troops in there for a long period of time. Consequently, the gooks were really well entrenched and had really good bunkers, concrete even. They were using trucks and the story that I had on it was, supposedly, we [the U.S.] were going to have pay $300 for every tree that we destroyed. Sounds like a bunch of shit but I don't know if it was true or not.

We had a lot of enemy contact all the time because it was a big enemy staging area. They'd been using if for so long they weren't going to give it up. When I got to Dolly, I couldn't get out to the field for a couple of days because they were filling the birds up with supplies, ammunition and stuff, so they didn't have room for me. But I eventually made it. I got wounded on the 23rd of February and went back out to the field on the 3rd of March.

The night before I got out there, our company's overnight position got attacked. The enemy had tried to come in with sappers. What they did was to move in some mortars and the guys would try to run in behind the mortar fire with their satchel charges. One of our machine gunners looked up out of his bunker and saw these guys coming in. He cut them down and saved a bunch of lives by doing that.

One of those Vietnamese had taken two M-60 slugs in the forehead. He had bandaged himself up and tried to crawl away before he died. It's amazing what the human body can take. It's different in a car accident where people go into shock so fast. But, in a war, a person can take a hell of a lot more than you realize. Everybody was amazed that this guy had bandaged himself up and tried to crawl away.

We got up the next morning and the whole company moved out. I didn't know where we were going. A buddy of mine was on the point and we got into five firefights that day. Every time we turned around, we ran into gooks. We'd move a few hundred meters and all hell would break loose. We didn't take any casualties but I don't know if we scored any body count or not.

We got through that day, my first back in the field. That night we set up our night position. About 11 o'clock, we got mortared. They knew exactly where we were. There was a crossroad nearby and they had set up a mortar right at the crossroad. They rained it right in on us. There were mortar rounds blowing up in the trees all around. At that time, we had our mortar platoon along, which was very rare. Those guys came out of their holes and fired right back at them.

We were in the bottom of our hole. First one in, yeah, that was me, and all the other guys were on top. It's kind of chaotic when you and four or five other guys are all in the same hole with your M-16s. We got mortared pretty heavily that night.

We got up the next morning and took off at an angle through the trees. We spotted a few gooks. In fact, we blew away three of them. We were congregating around the bodies, checking them out, when there were three more gooks spotted not far away. The platoon sergeant told our squad and a gun squad to go out after them there. We went out in kind of a frontal assault. We got to a point in the rubber plantation where the vegetation had filled in with bushes. Where I was, the bushes were too thick to get through, so I curved around behind this other fellow. He went through the bush, too, and, as soon as he got to the other side, there were four or five gooks right there. They saw him and cut loose. He jumped for the ground and I'm walking right behind him. Everything they were shooting at him was coming right at me! I jumped to the ground and, luckily, there was a hole there, probably about three feet deep. I got right down in it. I figured I was in pretty good shape since the bullets were flying above me. They were really cutting loose on us. We were getting some suppressing fire back at them. I started looking around in that hole and, shit, I was in the bottom of an old latrine! It was all dried out, but it was just an old dumper. I figured, when things calm down a bit I'm going to get the hell out of here.

When I got the chance, I got up out of the hole and started crawling parallel to this brush line where the gooks were. As I'm crawling along, they cut loose with a B-40 rocket. It hit a tree right behind me and a piece of shrapnel hit me in the neck. I'm lying there face down, when that son-of-a-bitch hit me. I thought, *oh shit, it chopped off my head*!

Curiously, no more than a night or two before we'd talked about how a person will still be thinking about 12 seconds after his head's been chopped off before the blood supply and oxygen run out. I'm wondering if that's what's happening to me!

Luckily, I had a towel that I always wore to keep the straps from the pack from cutting into my neck. That piece of shrapnel went through about seven layers of towel before it went into the back of my neck. I'm lying there thinking, oh shit. I yelled to one of my buddies and said, "Hey Rex, I got hit again."

He said, "Oh yeah?"

And I said, "Yeah, it's a little worse than the first time."

He said, "Just hang loose and we'll try to get over to you in a while."

Eventually, Carl Bahnlein came over and jumped down beside me. He looked at me and says, "Oh my God!

I said, "Carl, don't you know you aren't supposed to tell a wounded man he's hurt bad?"

But, I have to give him credit. He went out under fire to come to my aid. He wasn't even the medic, just a guy in my squad. He was a good shit. He ended up with a sucking chest wound later on. They call him "Sucking Chest Wound Carl" now, but at least he's still alive.

We called in the artillery. I was probably lying out there for an hour or two before we got everything all squared away. It was a real nightmare because there were trees all over. We got the gooks all suppressed and got our shit straight, and then a medic came over and put a bandage on me. I remember he had to cut the towel off me.

We were going to walk back to the company area, but I got up to walk and it was lights out. I stood up for a couple seconds and everything went white. I think it was the shock, heat, and trauma. I stood up and down I went. They picked me up off the ground and carried me.

When we got back to the company area, they called in a medevac. However, in this location there was no place to land so what they did was to drop a jungle penetrator. They strapped me in while the chopper hovered, and then they pulled me up. Once I was aboard, considering the amount of shit going on in the area, the chopper did not hesitate to leave. In fact, they took off as soon as the penetrator got above the treetops. They reeled me in even as they were pouring on the coals.

That was interesting! Better than Six Flags!

When we got to Tay Ninh, they took me off the bird, put me on a stretcher, and then in the back of an ambulance, a small truck really. The medevac team took me from the airstrip to the hospital. The doctors there were MASH types, up-and-coming young guys. They looked at me and decided they'd better send me over to X-ray.

So, it's back in the truck. I don't know how far it was but it seemed like it was clear across the base. It was a ways. I was bouncing all the way over there. They took the X-rays, gave me the pictures, and sent me bouncing back across the base to the hospital.

The doctors took one look at my X-rays and said, "Oh shit, don't move around too much! That piece of shrapnel is between the vertebrae and kind of close to your spine. Try to stay still or you could have big problems."

Oh yeah, thanks a lot, I'm thinking. I've just bounced across base and back in the back of a truck, and *now* you tell me not to move around too much!

They said, "We're going to have to operate."

I asked them if they'd save the shrapnel for me as kind of a souvenir.

"Yeah, we'll do that," they said.

I had an almost new pair of boots. When I got wounded the first time, I got a new pair of boots while I was back in the rear. An infantryman's boots are very near and dear to him. When they were going to prep me up for the surgery, they started cutting my boots off.

I said, "Hey, don't do that! Just untie them. There's some grunt out there who needs a good pair of boots. Give them to him."

I don't know if they unlaced the boots then or continued cutting. That's just one of the little things I remember.

They did the surgery on me and when I woke up, I thought, *cool, I survived that.*

The doctors came in and I said, "Where's that shrapnel you took out of me?"

They said, "Oh man, we had a hell of a time getting it out. When we did get it out, POW, we threw that son-of-a-bitch as far as we could!"

They were frustrated and I didn't get my little souvenir.

I stayed there for a couple days in an inflatable hospital ward. The gooks were still rocketing and mortaring. That concerned me because I couldn't get out of the bed very fast. I just stayed right in the damn hospital when the attacks came, didn't even try to get out.

There was a North Vietnamese soldier across the aisle from me and I had empathy for him. Those guys were just like us. They were warriors just doing what they were told. They had their beliefs and we had ours, so I had respect for him. He was shot up pretty badly, so I wasn't too worried about him slipping out of bed at night and slitting my throat. I could tell he wasn't going to do anything to anybody for a while.

Also, there was a black guy a couple beds away. He was a real dark-skinned man. I never talked to him or anything, but here I was, a lily-white farm boy from Iowa. We'd both been wounded in action; we both had tubes running into our arms and legs, so I guess we're all pretty much the same color on the inside. Our blood is all the same.

After two or three days, they flew me down to Cu Chi and that was where they sewed me up. Until then, they had left the wound open to let it drain and try to keep the infection out. I think they may have irrigated it with saline solution. Cu Chi had just taken a big hit a few days earlier. They had had gooks inside the perimeter. Of course, they didn't know in those days that there was a massive enemy tunnel complex right underneath the post.

The next day, the doctor was looking at my record and noticed that this was my second wound in about 10 days. He said, "I'm going to send you home."

I said, "Thank you very much!"

I hung around Cu Chi for a few more days and then made the trip home. I went to Saigon, onto a plane to Japan, to Clark AFB in the Philippines, and then to Travis AFB in San Francisco. From there, it was Fitzsimons Army Hospital in Denver to convalesce.

I was in Vietnam only six months and really developed a camaraderie with the guys in my unit. I can only imagine what it would have been like if I'd finished my one-year tour, but when you get wounded twice in the period of time I did you're out of there. When they said I was going home, I said, "OKAY!"

I wasn't in Vietnam long enough for an R&R. I could have gone on one, but I wanted to go to Australia and the guys who'd been there longer had priority. I could have gone to the Philippines instead but I passed on that one. I was there on the way over and wanted to go someplace different.

Morale in my unit was pretty good. We had a very good company commander, at least the one that was there the majority of the time I was there. His name was CPT Joe Davidson. My platoon leader, a first lieutenant, was David Neff. They were good guys who looked out for us.

There were no big drug problems in my unit. There were a few guys from California, guys who had been hippies in civilian life. They found some pot along the trail one day just before Christmas. Toward the end of the day, they shredded the pot and laid it out on a paper to dry. It didn't take long in that heat. And then they fired it up. Heavy duty! Far out! I was there early enough that drug use wasn't rampant, like it probably was later in the war. I was there right during the peak of the build-up and people weren't really dejected yet. We were there to kick ass, at least that's what we thought. We didn't know what was going on for sure. Nixon had just gotten elected and we're thinking, oh God, he's going to have us home by Christmas.

After Fitzsimons, I went to Fort Carson, near Colorado Springs, where they put me in a tank outfit. I didn't know a damn thing about tanks. When I reported to the unit, the first sergeant says, "The company is out in the field so what can you do?"

I said, "Do you see these hands? They can type. I'm infantry, but I can type."

He put me right in the orderly room. I was a SP4, having gone to Nam as a PFC. I got promoted after being in Nam about a month. I was in an E5 slot, a fire team leader. I was in first platoon, first squad, fire team B. That worked out to 1-1-B, quite a coincidence since 11B is the Military Occupational Specialty code for infantry. I thought that was an interesting coincidence.

Six months later, I got a hardship discharge—my dad had to go in for surgery on his legs. So my whole military career was only a little over 18 months. A soldier had to be on active duty for 18 months in order to qualify for veteran's benefits. My company commander at Fort Carson had just returned from Vietnam. He was a tanker and he'd been blown away about the same time as me. Most of us that were back from the Nam were pretty tight. When I started processing my hardship discharge, I think he dragged it out just long enough so that I'd qualify for benefits. He was good.

Every Christmas, my dad had a big, free sandwich spread at the bar he operated. I arrived on a Friday night, home from the army, and the next day he had his big spread. I didn't spend much of my own money that day—I may not have spent a dime! Everybody around home was so supportive. They treated me really good. Guys like my dad who'd been in WW-II treated me good and I really appreciated that. They'd ask questions and I'd tell them what they wanted to know. I figured, why not?

There are some fellows around, though, who are real basket cases and can't talk about their experiences. But, in my case, I consider it good therapy to get it off my chest. I did have some pretty wild dreams, but not so much lately. When I do have them, it's always the same one: I see a bunch of gooks coming and my damn ammo won't fire. That's a pisser!

I was very adamant about cleaning and lubing my weapon every night. I could fire a magazine through it so fast it'd make your head spin. When I got wounded, I couldn't take my weapon with me on the medevac, so someone else got it, an officer who'd been carrying a shotgun. He blew the damn thing up after I left.

I thought the M-16 was great. I had no trouble with it. If you take care of it, it'll take care of you. We kept ours clean all the time. Your weapon is your friend.

It wasn't unusual to see a Bouncing Betty along the trail. I saw them sticking up out of the ground. You had to watch your step all the time. I didn't run into any booby traps or have to crawl into any enemy caves. We did run into some bunker complexes, but what we did was just put a guy on each end and they dropped frags simultaneously. Then we got the hell out of there. If the cave were full of ammunition, there'd be a lot of fireworks.

When I came back to Travis AFB, I was on a medevac plane and didn't have to go through a civilian terminal, so I missed out on any protestors. I stayed in the military medical system until I was through at Fitzsimons. When I left the service, I flew from Denver to Omaha, but in the Midwest, I had no problems even though I wore my dress greens.

Years after I left the Army, another fellow from my company, John Gayman from Davenport, Iowa, made an effort to look up some of his old buddies. He remembered that I was from the Storm Lake area, so he just got Directory Assistance and asked for Engebretson. That put him in touch with my brother Al. He called me up and we talked, and then we got together in Iowa City and viewed our pictures and stuff. We both knew this guy whose name was Jim Agnew. He was just such a nice person—everybody loved him. Gayman and I talked about this guy and decided if we could figure out where he lived, we'd go look up his parents. He was from New Franklin, Missouri. Agnew called them up and said we'd like to come and visit you. They said, yeah, come on down.

The day after Memorial Day, 1989 or '90, I took off from home and John took off from Davenport. It was like an eight-hour drive to New Franklin. My brother Doyle went with me. We got there about three in the afternoon, had a nice visit with them, stuck around for three or four hours, and then headed home. The Agnews were very appreciative.

After leaving the service in 1969, George resumed his education and received an A.A. in Business from Iowa Central Community College and a B.B. in psychology from Mankato State College. He was in sales briefly before going to work for the Illinois Central Railroad. In 1982 he joined the U.S. Postal Service, became the postmaster in a small town not far from where he grew up, and recently retired.

CHAPTER 3
ARMY CAPTAIN JED DUTY
Battalion Surgeon

One night we were sleeping when suddenly there was small arms fire and all hell broke loose. The sergeant and I both hit the floor in the aid tent and bullets were flying over our heads, at least we could hear them echoing, hitting trees, and all that sort of thing. We thought we were okay until we looked up and saw this big oxygen tank right between us. We realized that, if a bullet hit the tank, it would be all over for us.

*J*ed Duty was born and raised on the grounds of the Toledo State Hospital, *a mental institution where his father was the superintendent. He attended Libby High School, a public school in Toledo, graduating second in a class of 350 in 1957. He went to the University of Toledo and earned his undergraduate degree in three years by going to school year round. He then entered medical school at Ohio State University, graduating there in 1964. Throughout high school and college, Jed worked at a gas station to earn money.* Jed's served in Vietnam 1965-66.

I did my internship at *the* Toledo Hospital, not the mental facility. I use my childhood environment to explain the way I am today [Jed laughs]. So, basically I came back home. That was July 1964 through July 1965. In the spring of '65, I became aware that I probably was not going on to my residency because I began getting communications from the Army. "Welcome," one of the later letters said [Jed laughs]. I found out that my orders were to report to Fort Sam Houston in San Antonio, TX, for the five-week Physician's Indoctrination Course. That was my boot camp. Also, that spring I received orders that, following indoctrination at Fort Sam, I'd proceed on to Fort Benning, GA, and join up with the 11th Air Assault Division. While I was at Fort Sam Houston, the 11th Air Assault became the 1st Air Cavalry Division, a newly designed helicopter-mobile force. They left for Vietnam before I finished my basic training at Fort Sam Houston, so I got reassigned. My new orders sent me to the 1st Infantry Division at Fort Riley, Kansas.

Boot camp wasn't just medical stuff. There was an introduction into what the Army Medical Corps was all about, and how the logistics and bureaucracy of Army medicine worked. We were also taught how to function in the field as a GI, which meant we had to learn how to use weapons, break them down, and clean them. We also had to go through the most traumatic part, and we knew what that was as soon as we got there because everybody told us about it: the Infiltration Course.

It's basically a course that is mud, dirt, and barbed wire, and we had to execute this course with .50 caliber machineguns shooting over the top of us. We had to crawl through that thing. Of course there were all sorts of ghost stories about how some guy got up too high and got shot in the head, or some guy's foot got up in the air and he got shot in the foot. Those things probably weren't true, but they sure did scare the hell out of us. So we sucked a lot of dirt—we imitated a worm to the nth degree. We did the course once in the daytime and that wasn't nearly as bad as at night. At night, they used tracers and we could see them flying over our head as we navigated the course. That was probably the most exciting moment of the five-week course.

Naturally, I was down there from the 1st of July until the middle of August. In San Antonio, that's got to be the best (read: hottest) time of the year, and in a car that had no air-conditioning! I learned that, even though it was the middle of summer, it was a good idea to have a pair of gloves in the car. Otherwise, when you get into a car that's been locked up all day, and you put the key in the ignition, which is metal, you'd burn your fingers.

I got drafted as a first lieutenant, and when I finished the five-week boot camp I made captain. The whole reason for this isn't that they were just trying to give me something. It's basically for pay purposes. Even a captain is making peanuts compared to what he'd make on the outside in private practice. In order to keep doctors, and attract even more doctors to come into the service in the first place, the Army needed to offer extra compensation. Otherwise, Army life would be decidedly unattractive to an MD.

I was married at the time, so my bride went with me to Fort Riley. We didn't have our specific assignment until we got there. This whole time I'm thinking I'll be assigned to some hospital unit. I knew I'd probably be going to Vietnam because the 1st Infantry Division was gearing up to go overseas. I figured being assigned to a hospital unit was for the good, pretty much out of harm's way.

When we first arrived at Fort Riley, we moved into a condo on the campus of Fort Riley, kind of a quad thing. We were there for about a week, had the furniture all unpacked and everything. Then they moved us up on Custer Hill, the 1st Infantry Division's area, so we got to pack and unpack everything again. They had all these split-level quarters up there with carports instead of garages. We were in one of them for about three weeks, in the officer's area.

It was a great life if I didn't have to go overseas and get shot at. Many career guys liked Army life because there was plenty of golf time, and lots of freebies and officer's clubs and stuff like that. And the work wasn't heavy. They weren't out there killing themselves, being on call all the time like they would have been in private practice.

I got my assignment and was shocked to learn that I would be a battalion surgeon and not assigned to a hospital unit as expected. I didn't even know what a battalion surgeon was, but soon learned it meant I was the only MD in a battalion. That was the bad news. The good news was I was assigned to the 1st Combat Engineer Battalion. One of my Fort Sam buddies was assigned to an artillery battalion in the 1st Infantry, and several others were assigned to infantry battalions. Those were the worst assignments because those units were always in combat; the doctors assigned there were always patching up bullet wounds and worse, real meatball surgery.

The guy I roomed with in med school was unmarried when he went over there. He spent his year with the Montagnards. There were maybe a few U.S. Special Forces guys up there, but he was a medic up there, taking care of Montagnards in a Montagnard Special Forces camp. He had a crap assignment.

At the engineer battalion, I was the rawest of rookies while all the other guys there had been in the service for quite some time. My sergeant basically ran the show for me since I had not a clue as to what was going on militarily. He handled all the soldier stuff while I just played doctor.

My battalion commander, a lieutenant colonel, wanted me to learn all the engineers' functions before we left Fort Riley. I had to get up at four a.m. and run with the other officers, do pushups, and all those things. At the time, I was only 26 years old and in great shape. I've never been in perfect shape, but I was much better physically than most of those officers. Some of those guys were way overweight and just in really bad physical condition, so I was able to keep up with them easily.

The commander also had me out in the field with the engineers, setting charges, and learning how to detonate them. I don't know if he thought I was going to be a terrorist in later life or what [Jed laughs]. I always get the feeling I know a little bit about what terrorists must go through when they're blowing stuff up because I was out there lighting fuses, and then running and diving behind a little mound of dirt or whatever.

The battalion regulars probably didn't appreciate what a medic was. I think they thought I was a loaner from the hospital because the battalion surgeon's position had never been filled as long as they had been at Fort Riley, until I got there. A lot of divisions are kind of skeleton crews at home station. There were doctors at Irwin Army Hospital on Fort Riley and the physicians up there probably took turns going out to the troop areas to do whatever needed doing.

We rode a train from Fort Riley to Kansas City, not all the troops, just the officers. The enlisted folks got to ride a train, too, all the way to San Francisco. When we got to Kansas City, I took my first airplane flight. I was as nervous as hell because I never did want to fly in the first place. We flew to California and there about 3000 of us boarded a merchant marine ship. It took us about 20 days to get from there to Vietnam. As I watched the Golden Gate Bridge fade into the distance, I started getting sick. I knew this was not going to be a good trip.

There were three of us sharing a room—nice quarters—officers quarters. There was an artillery captain, an infantry captain, and myself. I was in an upper bunk and I stayed in that damned bunk for a week. At mealtime, the other guys would bring me an apple and some saltine crackers from the mess. I would stay there, mostly flat on my back. When I did roll onto my side, it'd take a minute to regain my equilibrium. Once in a while, of course, I'd have to get up to take a pee. Every time I got out of bed and ran into the head—we had our own private head, thank goodness—I had to puke before I could take a leak because just the motion was enough to upset my equilibrium and make me absolutely sick.

I took Dramamine but it didn't help. We all kidded with one another and said how this is all just in your head. To avoid seasickness you just look at the horizon and everything is fine. Well, my head didn't know that; it wasn't responding as it was supposed to do.

Believe it or not, there was an advantage to being seasick because I didn't gain any weight on the trip. Most of the other guys who didn't get sick were pigging out, eating good meals on the ship. They'd get out on the fantail and do a little exercise, but it was nothing like what we were used to at Fort Riley.

When we got close to Hawaii, we ran into a horrendous storm. That was during the first week when I was still sick. I remember one night, we had this little porthole window in our cabin, and the guy who slept under the window had it open because it was pretty warm in there. In the middle of the night, a damn wave came right over the side of the ship and just poured water in through that porthole. The guy under it flew out of bed, and he and the bed were totally soaked. Even as sick as I was, I just broke out laughing.

Because of the storm, our ship changed course and headed south to get out of it. When we got past Hawaii, I recovered, went out on the deck, and started moving around. I was able to perform a little sick call duty, but my appetite still wasn't that good. The trip from that point on was like being on a South Seas cruise—very pleasant.

I remember there were these flying fish. You could look over the side of the ship and see these little silver things just skipping through the waves. I don't think they really flew. They were going so fast they just kind of jumped between waves. They could jump significant distances, 20 or 30 feet, and they weren't that big, maybe the size of a three-pound bass or something like that.

We stopped in the Philippines and by then, I was doing pretty well. We laid over at Subic Bay Naval Base. There was also an airbase near there, but the name eludes me. The funny thing was that all the officers were invited to go the O-Club, but we didn't have any dress uniforms. If you had your dress blues along and you could get them out of your footlocker, then you could wear those and get into the O-Club. The

Subic Bay O-Club required formal dress for some reason. Everybody was disappointed because most of us didn't have our stuff with us.

We were supposed to take our dress blues with us to Vietnam, but most of us left them at home. They said we could get in real big trouble if we ever had to go to an event where we needed dress blues. I said, "Bull, I'm not going anywhere over there, I'm going to be out in the boonies, so screw that."

We went to the PX and they had some flowery, frilly white shirts that qualified as formal dress. You could wear those shirts with *anything* and it was considered a dress uniform. I had my khaki pants and my field boots on with one of those things. The shirt wasn't even the right size because, by the time I got in the PX, most of the shirts were gone and all I could get was an extra large. At that time, I weighed 160 pounds so this thing was draped on me like a tent. But I got into the O-Club; the white shirt satisfied the dress requirements regardless of how horrible everything else looked.

There were drinks, dancing, and carrying on half the night. The folks in the O-Club made a big deal over us because we were going to Vietnam. They treated us royally. One of the guys knew somebody who was stationed at Subic and we got invited over to the place where this guy lived. He had houseboys! I mean the place where this middle-grade officer was staying looked like a palace, a little different from where we were going.

We left Subic after three days and it took us another three days to get from the Philippines to Vietnam. I can't remember the name of the place we landed—Long Binh seems like a possibility—in southern Vietnam. We rode landing craft from the ship to shore, probably like the troops storming Normandy in World War II only there weren't any enemy on the beach shooting at us. The landing craft came into the shore, dropped the front, and we disembarked. But those things were not very user friendly. They had big ribs across the deck to allow vehicles to get traction. We were wearing boots and you had to be careful because it was very easy to trip. I remember one of the lieutenants, a company commander, fell getting off the landing craft and opened up his knee. He wasn't looking where he was going and, bingo! All of our medical stuff was packed up, but one of my medics came up with some sutures and things, and I sewed up the lieutenant's knee on the beach.

After we landed, we had to set up our tents and stuff because there was no formal place for us to go, no permanent buildings or anything. Later on, as the war progressed, they probably built buildings and things like that, places for people to stay. But we had this temporary area and we ended up leaving after a few days—I can't remember how long it was.

Then we went out and set up to our base camp near Di An, about 25 miles north of Saigon. Di An was just out in the middle of nowhere. The Republic of Korea, the ROKs, had a division that was fairly close by. I think they came in a little after we did. The engineers were responsible for building everything for the 1st Infantry, from base camps and buildings to roads and bridges. The engineers were responsible for the whole division setup. So basically, we lived in pretty crappy conditions for quite a long time.

I was in the battalion headquarters, collocated with the 1st Infantry Division HQ. The engineers were divided into companies with one company assigned to each brigade of the 1st Infantry Division. The four infantry brigades were not all contiguous because of the logistics of the war. They were in the same general vicinity, but you just couldn't go from one to another by land because the enemy might nail you. So, I couldn't just hop in my jeep with my driver and go visit one of the engineer companies. We had to hitch a ride in a helicopter to go safely from one area to the other.

I remember that for the first six or eight weeks all we had to eat was Spam and salmon. One day, we'd have two meals of Spam and in between, we'd get salmon patties. The next day it was salmon patties morning and night, and Spam at noon. That was our three-meal-a-day menu, except Sunday morning when the cooks fixed us powdered eggs. What a treat! Yuk!

For the first six weeks we were there, diarrhea was rampant. I remember a second lieutenant running across the compound to get to the crapper but he never made it. He was a mess! We needed lots anti-diuretics. The dietician should have been shot.

We had all had our shots before we went over there: gamma globulin for hepatitis, immunizations for cholera, and all that sort of stuff. We were taking anti-malarial pills every Monday and the medics were responsible for passing them out.

We got our base camp established and I lived with the rest of the troops in this big tent for quite a while. Then, because we really weren't going out on a whole lot of missions, they built me another little thing with a framework and some screen. I could use the tent as my aid station and my living quarters, separate from the rest of the troops. But most of the time, I stayed with them. I had a cot in the tent and I just stayed with the E-3s, E-4s, E-5s, and my lead NCO who was an E-6. We had netting for mosquitoes over our cots, which we slept under all the time.

We had kind of a central location for the battalion crappers, and the medical personnel were responsible for maintaining them. We took 55-gallon drums, cut them in half, and slid them under the seats in the latrine. We were also responsible for burning them out, the easiest way of eliminating the accumulated waste. We'd pull them out from beneath the seats, dump in some kerosene or whatever, and just burn them out once a day. The battalion commander had his little bailiwick pretty close to that area, and the boys would always have a good, hearty laugh whenever the wind was blowing in his particular direction during burning. I don't think he was in his tent much during that particular time of day. The fire in the drums would burn for about three hours. We'd do the burn around nine in the morning after the troops were fairly well through with their ablutions and there was a lull in the use of the facility. Maybe by noon it'd be all done.

I went out in the field and had some close calls, but not as frequently as the guys in the infantry units. We weren't a front line unit, but we still had our perimeters to guard. The engineers were as equipped as anybody else to fight a skirmish. They had all the same weapons and had similar training. They just had other duties to perform as their primary mission. During the day, the infantry would guard the perimeter while the engineers were working.

The first few months we were there, we concentrated on getting the base camps built up. Most of the construction was within a guarded perimeter and there wasn't much risk, although you had to be a little careful. You didn't want to be out there walking around where people could see you in the daytime. Even at night, you pretty well stayed in your own area. As soon as we got there, we dug holes and placed sandbags around them, and then put timbers over the top of these little bunkers so we could go hide in the event of a mortar attack or whatever. We practically never used these bunkers. In fact, I don't recall ever running down into one during the time I was in the base camp area.

From late November or early December until the middle of March, we didn't have one drop of rain. Nothing! Winter over there was the dry season and it was dry as could be. I couldn't believe it. I thought in the jungle we'd get rain practically every day, and we did but only during the spring, summer, and fall. Practically every afternoon there'd be a thunderstorm or downpour. The roads we made were crowned with drainage ditches along the side, made with laterite, a kind of red clay. There were pits of that stuff over there and the engineers mined it to make roads. It was good stuff, but during the winter, the dust on those roads would go over the lower half of your boot.

But during the rainy season, you could hardly walk on them because the roads were crowned. You couldn't get across the road without slipping or falling because it was just a quagmire. The combination of slope and sliminess made it very treacherous. The trucks could navigate it okay because they had pretty good treads. I did not see a paved road in Vietnam except for the few that were probably left from when the French were there. Any roads we built were all earth roads and they were well designed.

The airstrips the engineers built were flat and covered with some of this clay, and on top of that, they put PSP. That's short for porous steel planking, and it's got one-inch holes in it. It comes in big sections and it kind of hooks together. That's what the fixed wing aircraft landed on. The aircraft over there were mainly helicopters, but we also needed bigger planes to bring in supplies. We didn't have many big helicopters, mostly utility helicopters called UH-1s or Hueys. There was a pilot and copilot up front, machine gunner at each side door, and room for maybe five or six passengers in the middle. They also used the Hueys as medevacs to transport wounded.

At some point during the late fall or early winter, we went out on a mission to build roads between the base camps of the different brigades so we wouldn't always have to rely on helicopters to travel back and forth. Or the roads could have been for infantry units to move their equipment—I don't recall for sure. They probably never told me what they were for. What does a medic need to know anyway? I never needed to know anything. I just knew we were going out on these missions and this was going to be my first one.

We got out there and after a few days, we were bivouacked in a clump of trees. Like I say, we had weapons so we didn't just rely on the infantry out there to protect us. They protected us during the daytime when the engineers were building stuff, but they secured their own areas at night and we had to secure ours.

The engineers split up the all-night duty to guard the perimeter. One of the guys on the perimeter that night had an M79 grenade launcher that jammed. He was on his way back into camp after being relieved and tried to disarm the thing but couldn't get the grenade out, so he decided to just pull the trigger. Sometimes these guys didn't use all the synapses they were born with! The launcher fired, launching the grenade which exploded up in the trees surrounding our camp, raining shrapnel down right over our tent, the aid station.

I was up in the front of the tent with my sergeant. We had this little dugout, not fortified or anything, a little foxhole that the four or five of us in the front of the tent could fit into. There was another near the back of the tent for the guys at that end. When the grenade exploded, my sergeant and I dove out the front of the tent and landed in this hole. At that moment, a gung-ho captain happened to be walking past our tent. The next thing we knew, that captain was in the hole with us. He was due to be promoted and rotate back to the states. Like I said, this captain was gung-ho but he knew he wasn't tougher than a grenade.

We heard some moans and groans from the guys at the back of the tent, so we went back there. Nobody was seriously hurt but shrapnel had hit three of my medics. We fixed them up and then they had to go into the hospital for a couple of days. I don't know if they got purple hearts for being wounded by friendly fire.

There was another friendly fire episode while I was in Vietnam where an artillery round, a short round to be specific, killed about eight guys in our HQ base camp.

On the same trip, probably the biggest venture that we had, we set up camp in another treed area and stayed there for several days. Normally, we just kept moving as the road construction progressed but, evidently, we were doing a lot of construction in this particular area. One night we were sleeping when suddenly there was small arms fire and all hell broke loose. The sergeant and I both hit the floor in the aid tent and bullets were flying over our heads, at least we could hear them echoing, hitting trees, and all that sort of thing. We thought we were okay until we looked up and saw this big oxygen tank right between us. The tank was a cylinder about four feet tall and nearly a foot in diameter. We realized that, if a bullet hit the tank, it would be all over for us. That thing would surely explode and blow shrapnel right through us. We got the hell out there in a hurry and jumped down in our little bunker outside the tent.

We had just started to feel a little bit relieved when we heard someone cry for a medic. One of the guys in the bunker with us went out to see what the problem was. While the firefight was still going on, someone yelled that they needed me, so I had to climb out of my little refuge and head over there. The problem was a 19 year-old kid who had a big three-inch diameter, penetrating chest wound, right in the middle of his chest. He'd been hit by a round or a piece of shrapnel. I didn't turn him over to see if it was through-and-through because he was gone. Whatever hit him blew right through his sternum.

What we theorized happened was that, after everybody had been awakened by the firefight and had taken off to get into their protected areas, this kid just went back to sleep or maybe never woke up in the first place. In any event, he never knew what hit him. I think somebody would have noticed if he'd been hit before they left. When they noticed he wasn't in the protected area, that's when they went back and found him. That was the first casualty on one of our field trips.

I do recall seeing one other casualty. Unfortunately, I didn't really get to treat many living beings because most of the time they'd helicopter those people right over me to one of the hospital units. We were out in the field, but we were there mostly for physician advice on first aid and that sort of thing, and to help keep up the health of the troops from day to day. We'd treat their infections, tend to injuries received during construction mishaps, and that sort of thing. But, if somebody got hit by enemy fire, chances are I wasn't going to be close enough to get to them before a helicopter came in there and took them out. I wasn't involved with helicopters, except during a couple of fights. I started IVs and things on the wounded, but then I got off and those patients were flown away.

At the end of one particular firefight, there were 100-200 Vietcong killed by our troops. Some appeared as though they were barely into puberty or even younger, but they all had weapons and knew how to use them. There were dead bodies all over the place. We decided to haul them to a nearby B-52 bomb crater and bury them in a mass grave for sanitary as well as esthetic reasons. Unfortunately, the only vehicle available was our mess truck. So, the troops loaded bodies and parts of bodies into the mess truck and hauled them all to the burial site. That was a little bit unappetizing for most of us. Needless to say, we washed down the truck very well when we finished the burial detail, but still nobody had a major appetite for a couple of days. Whether that had to do with nerves after the first big battle or if it had to do with who had been residing in our mess truck, I was never sure. I do know that we ate a lot of C-Rations the next few days, lots of pre-packaged food.

Speaking of C-Rations, one time they experimented on us with freeze-dried rations that we reconstituted with water. I forget what the name of those rations was—I mean the *official* name, not what we called them [Jed laughs]. They had meats and other things in them, but everything tasted just like the cardboard that they'd been sitting in for probably years. Have you ever had a pizza that's been in a box for about three or four days? You're trying to clean out the refrigerator and you think it's a terrible thing to just throw this pizza away. So, you think you'll just eat it but the damn crust on the thing tastes just like the cardboard box. That's the way these experimental rations tasted.

They subjected us to about three weeks of this. Then we got little forms to fill out on what we liked and didn't like about this, that, and the other thing. We all felt like a bunch of guinea pigs. What a crappy way to treat guys who are in a combat zone laying their lives on the line. Why couldn't they do that to the guys over at the O-Club? Let those guys suffer a little! We had enough problems with our stomachs without having to go through that crap.

I recall an incident during another mission, although I don't remember exactly what it was we were doing. Claymore mines were a favorite weapon of the Vietcong. They would detonate those things to create as many casualties as they could. I remember this particular time our vehicle had already gone by where the VC had set up a Claymore. Maybe half a dozen vehicles behind us was a deuce-and-a-half with probably 10-15 troops in the back. That's when the VC detonated the mine. They just *nailed* this truck injuring most of the troops. My crew and I went back there and started IVs and whatever else they needed. Then the helicopters came in and took the wounded away.

That was the end of it for me. Basically, I was no more than an EMT over there, actually the head EMT or coordinator. That was my medical experience as far as taking care of patients the whole year I was in Vietnam. So, from a medical standpoint, it was a lost year of practice for me.

We had stuff going on every night so I never slept straight through a whole night the entire year I was in Vietnam. We'd have harassment and interdiction, or H&I, which was done randomly throughout the night. Our artillery pieces and mortars within our own compound would fire rounds outside the perimeter, basically to discourage any kind of assault on the compound during the night. We did H&I *every* night.

On one of our trips to the woods, we had a 155mm howitzer that was probably within 50 feet of the foxhole where I tried to sleep. When you think of foxholes, you probably think of holes where you could stand up and your head would be just above the surface of the ground. But most of our foxholes were more like little shallow trenches where at night you could sleep and the profile of your body would be below ground level so that any rounds and shrapnel would pass above you. The only time you'd get hurt was with indirect fire falling from above.

As I said, this 155 was being used for H&I during that night just 50 feet away from me. You can imagine the sound of that baby when it went off and how it affected my sleep. It fired a six-inch-diameter projectile and made a hell of a racket. Maybe they'd do two, three, or four, maybe up to a half a dozen rounds a night, all at random times. So, it was almost like being in a civilian hospital sleeping quarters next to the Labor and Delivery Room, as I was many times later on in my career, with a bunch of future mothers screaming all night long. Instead, I had this screaming artillery piece going off right beside me. I'd catch an hour here, two hours there, and that's the way I slept.

You got used to it and could actually go back to sleep fairly quickly. When you woke up, you listened to determine if it was outgoing or incoming fire. The way you could tell was you'd listen to the initial explosion when the weapon was fired and, if that was a lot louder than the blast at impact, then that's outgoing. That was good and it was safe to go back to sleep. If you heard a distant weapon firing and then a much louder explosion on impact, that meant it was incoming and was obviously of more concern. I recall that happening a few times when we were out on missions and we had artillery firing from other locations, not inside our compound. You could hear them firing and the impact explosion would be closer than the blast at firing. That was because the target was actually closer to us than the artillery piece. We didn't sleep much those nights.

I'm nuts about athletics and sports, and have always been that way. I haven't been endowed with great athletic ability but I've always been a more than willing participant. I played with the troops all the time. In fact, I commandeered a couple truckloads of laterite and we used it as a base for a basketball court. Then we requisitioned a goal, backboard, net, and a pole to put it all on. We did all this without the knowledge of the higher-ups. After it was finished and the battalion commander saw it, he was a bit perturbed. I said, "Look, I'm the doctor here and this is for mental health. My dad was a psychiatrist and I know what's good for mental health."

By golly, he bought it!

There weren't too many good basketball players there, but a lot of the guys liked to play football, so we played two-hand touch or what we called pass-and-tap. We got a good game going one day, basically the officers against the enlisted men. There wasn't that big an age difference. A lot of the officers were in their late 20s, while the enlisted men were mostly in their late teens and early 20s. Many of the enlisted men smoked where most of the officers didn't, so that kind of balanced things. Physically we were pretty much similar.

One of the lieutenants and I were both playing defensive back and someone threw a pass. We both went for the interception and banged our heads together. It sounded like a couple of coconuts. I ended up with a terrible black eye out of the whole thing, and it lasted for three or four weeks. I remember that night I had one of my medics come over periodically to do cranial checks on me. He woke me every couple of hours to check my pupils and make sure I was oriented as to time, place, and that sort of thing.

We also had a volleyball court that we set up smack in the middle of camp, probably a good quarter-mile from the perimeter. We played after dinner every evening when it was cool. I played with the lieutenants against the captains, although I *was* a captain. A medical officer is kind of a nonentity when it comes to military hierarchy. Nobody treated me like an officer and I didn't treat anybody else like I was better than they were.

We were playing volleyball one night when all of a sudden, there's a big bang and a round comes right through the volleyball court. We all hit the deck thinking it's a sniper round from the perimeter, which it was. There were also a bunch of tents right next to the court, sleeping quarters for the officers, multi-person tents. About 30 seconds later here comes this second lieutenant, staggering out of one of the tents, saying that he's been hit. I run over to him and he's got a wound in the middle of his back between his left shoulder blade and his spine.

We're thinking it might be a sucking chest wound, which means the bullet has actually entered into the pleural space, or lung area, and he could end up with a pneumothorax. That's where your lung collapses because there's no negative pressure to keep it inflated. We slapped something with Vaseline on it over the wound to seal it and then carried the guy probably a ¼ mile to the division medic's tent. They took an X-ray to see where the bullet was, but can't find it anywhere. The bullet just wasn't there, and there was no exit wound either! We're thinking, what the hell is going on here?

We took the bandage off and explored around a little bit. What it was, this bullet had just grazed his back. He was proofreading a letter to his fiancée and he said he had just bent over to make a correction. That's when he got hit. The round would have penetrated his chest, but because he'd just bent over the round just grazed his back. All he had was a small wound that didn't even go into the chest cavity at all. We bandaged him up and he walked back with us. He wasn't really hurt that badly—he'd only been nicked—and then we took care of him at our own place for the next week or 10 days.

We went into his tent and one of the metal poles supporting the tent had a piece chipped out of it. Lying near the bottom of the pole was the spent round. What had happened was that the round had grazed him, smacked into the tent pole, and then had just fallen to the ground. It didn't even penetrate the tent pole, so the round was pretty well spent. If it had hit him squarely, it probably would have hit a rib and stopped. But if had gone between the ribs, it might have penetrated a lung or at least into the chest cavity breaking the integrity of his pleural space. He was one lucky troop.

Whenever we were in the base camp and not out on a mission, the battalion commander sent me into the nearby villages to treat patients. It was a PR thing. I didn't do much good, though, because I had an interpreter assigned to me but he didn't know medicine. He just knew Vietnamese. He could tell me if the patient had a headache, or if the patient hurt here or there. But as far as trying to make diagnoses, I had to rely on physical exams with a stethoscope and my hands. A lot of times, I think these patients or citizens from these tiny villages would make up symptoms, get medicine from me, and then give that medicine to the Vietcong later on as a way of keeping on the good side of them so that they wouldn't blow them away.

Vietnamese civilians who lived in a war zone were forced into doing whatever they had to do in order to survive. When a Vietcong with a gun came around and said, "I want you to do this, that, and the other thing," what choice did they have? If they did it, they were aiding and abetting the enemy. But, it was basically whoever was there with a gun in his hand, they did whatever he wanted. In the daytime, they did what the Americans or South Vietnamese wanted them to do. At night, the VC had the run of the countryside and the villagers had to do what the VC wanted. They tried to stay on the good side of both of us.

We had at least 10 percent venereal disease morbidity rate within our battalion. One of the ways we tried to combat this was to treat some of the women that the guys would be associating with. We'd treat them with long-acting penicillin to try to cut down on the amount of venereal disease they could communicate. We really couldn't immunize or medicate the troops prophylactically. That wasn't allowed. You could treat them only *after* they contracted a venereal disease.

If you gave the troops any medication, you had to document it and someone was bound to ask why you did it. If you just said," It's because the troops are going out and having a good time," that wouldn't fly and for good reason. There was always a risk of an allergic reaction to penicillin and some of those reactions could be rather tragic. If someone was going to have a major allergic reaction, better to have it in one of the women. If they died, nobody is going to ask any questions. But if one of the soldiers died, that was a big problem. That's the hard, cruel reality of it. We were trying to curtail disease with the least amount of risk to the troops.

We never did get to the point of having ID cards for the women so the troops would know who was relatively safe. We knew who a lot of them were and gave them penicillin, but we still had a very high venereal disease rate. Penicillin would take care of some of the venereal diseases but it wouldn't take care of all of it, just the most common types. There were some penicillin-resistant strains of gonorrhea and we used tetracycline to treat it. There were other exotic forms of venereal disease that were much more rare and almost impossible to treat.

The guys would just go nuts over the women over there. It's just a matter of opportunity. We had GIs whose hormones were flowing, they were away from their homeland, and they'd seen nothing but other guys for six weeks. Those gals all started to look like Farah Fawcett to them.

Then there were all the social problems that came up later on, with one society clashing with another. It was tough. Plus the emotions sometimes wear off after awhile. In the military, there are a lot of wives of soldiers that are foreign-born. My sergeant was married to a German gal and our mess sergeant was married to an Oriental gal, very common situations among career soldiers. That's just the nature of it because the guys would meet these women, they're all single, and there's no one else around. Being in the Army doesn't always give you a lot of options when it comes to companionship. Sometimes the women the troops met around a military facility were looking for someone readily available to get married. That was their ticket to get to the United States and, sadly, maybe that's all they were interested in getting.

I only saw one or two American women the whole time I was over there. They were American Red Cross gals and they were called "Donut Dollies." That was the slang for them, but I didn't know whether it was because of their goodwill or maybe because they had round eyes. I didn't understand that part of the jargon. I was out in the boonies the whole time, so what would I know?

My major political concern regarding the Vietnam War was: I want to go home, and not in a box or a bag. I got an extra $35 a month for overseas duty, and $75 or $80 bucks a month combat pay. Everybody got the same, the privates, the officers, we all got the same. That was part of your compensation package. The big joke was, my God, I'd pay them ten times that amount not to be over here!

My politics when I was in country was, get me out of here! I didn't know that the war was un-winnable. I didn't know there was so much politics involved. I didn't even know that there was much of a protest against the war until we got back to the states. The only news we had over there was the *Stars & Stripes* military paper, and that was obviously propaganda. They weren't going to load it up with articles about people protesting the war. The whole year I was over there, I had no clue and I wasn't interested anyway. I was more interested in who's pointing a gun at me, and that sort of thing than the politics.

We doctors would talk about wanting to get out of the service. Even the career guys, men who'd been in ten years or more, were talking about getting out. All of a sudden, now there wasn't a lot of time on the golf course and an 8-4 job at the hospital with being on call maybe only three times a month. Now it was a matter of, when's my tour over? I knew that some people weren't happy that we were fighting the war. I was one of them while I was over there, but not for political reasons.

When I was a kid, I was into war stuff big time. I went to war movies, collected toy soldiers, and played soldiers all the time. I was just amazed at how much I didn't care for the military once I was in it. What was so much fun as a kid—you could get killed 20 times in one day and still get a good night's sleep that night—wasn't much fun when you were playing for real. As kids, we could play with our little tanks, guns, and soldiers, and then when the war was over they could all go back up on their shelves and look as good as new, like nothing had ever happened. I think the reality of it was, now I was over there and, number one, I had a job to do so don't do anything stupid. Don't volunteer for anything.

We had pretty good morale in our unit. I played a lot of pinochle with the enlisted men and bridge with the officers. When it came to playing cards, it seemed like the officers were more into bridge and the enlisted men were more into pinochle. You might say that kind of described the social strata of officers versus enlisted men. But it also described me because I could fit into either situation.

The main goal of the engineers was to build things for the division, but there were times when we could get a little extra stuff to improve our personal lives. We had a brick-making machine in our unit. We wanted to build an O-Club, so we did it using this machine to make adobe bricks. The engineers got the materials to make the bricks and we used the brick-maker to make them in our spare time. Officers of captain's rank or higher had a competition against the lieutenants; I was in with the captains. There were more lieutenants than captains, they were younger, they were harder workers, and all that—we had some pretty lethargic guys in our group.

Each group had to make 5000 bricks and whoever got through *last* had to do the masonry, using all 10,000 bricks to build the structure. One of the other guys and I were afraid that the lieutenants were getting ahead of us, so one night after everyone was in bed we sneaked out and made bricks all night. We stayed up the whole damn night making bricks! As a result, we got our allocation of bricks done before the lieutenants finished theirs and they were so pissed. They *got* to use all the bricks to build the O-Club.

I had the opportunity for R&R while in Vietnam but declined it because I didn't want to leave the base camp. It wasn't that I was gung-ho, and not taking R&R wouldn't have shortened the tour. I thought about going to Australia or Hawaii and that would have been nice, but there were other concerns. There was the economics of it; it would have cost a fair amount of money to go to one of those places. I could have met my wife there, seen her for four or five days, and then have had all that heartbreak of having to say goodbye again. Doing that once when I left for Vietnam had been tough enough. So, all things considered, I'm the kind of guy who just wanted to get a nasty job done rather than divide it up into doses. I just wanted to blitz on through the thing and get it over with.

I did take a few trips into Saigon, though. On my first trip, I remember going into a bar and there were all these good-looking women. They'd want to sit down and talk, and then they'd ask if I wanted to buy them a drink. I'd already bought myself a drink for a nominal fee. Then I bought the gal a drink and it's like about ten times as much. So, that was my introduction into the "you're paying for my company" type of thing. They're just drinking sugar water or whatever it was. I was clueless on that stuff, totally clueless.

We all learned that lesson. Haircuts went up ten times during the year I was there, from probably a nickel to about fifty cents. It just took a while for the Vietnamese to figure out what the GIs would pay, whatever the traffic would bear as they say, and then that's what they charged. Of course, guys would tip and that probably just inflated things even more.

Mosquito repellant wasn't readily available in Vietnam; it was all on backorder. But on the streets of Saigon, I'd see vendors like in New York City, selling this stuff in military-OD cans. Insect spray and stuff like that. The stuff had come in off the ships and it was, one for you and one for me. That's how the black market worked over there.

Here's a story to show you the craziness of the situation, the hormones involved, and the naiveté of some of our troops. When we were out in the boonies on one of our missions, one of the cooks had a gal that he'd met during the day. After he'd finished his duties for the day and it was bedtime, he snuck out of camp and went to meet this gal. Apparently, he'd set up something with her ahead of time. He snuck out beyond the perimeter and we found him there the next morning with a bullet between his eyes. That was his reward for going out there. It was just a ruse to get the guy out there. Unbelievable!

Later, there are all kinds of stories about drug use by our troops in Vietnam, but I was totally oblivious to it when I was there. I guess I heard a few stories about guys smoking marijuana, but that's all. I was totally oblivious to any narcotics or drug use of any kind. I'm sure others who were there when I was knew about it, but I didn't. I'm sure it happened later in the war, more than when I was there.

Being a physician in Vietnam, I probably would have been one of the last to know, even if I had tried to nose around. The troops sure didn't want the doctor to know that they were using drugs or whatever. My personal knowledge of drug abuse over there was that it never existed, didn't even happen. But I know it did from what I've learned since, I just had no first-hand information. I know it escalated over there as time went on, probably because it escalated in this country, too.

Growing up in the '50s, I'm sure there were some drugs in Toledo, but the people I hung around with in high school didn't even smoke, let alone use drugs. I never even had my first drink until I was coerced into it at a fraternity in college. I never had one sip of alcohol in my life until I was a fraternity pledge. I have never smoked, ever in my life, so you're not talking to somebody who's been into substance abuse at all.

Almost all the officers in our battalion got replaced before me. I may have been the last officer to go back to the states. Doctors were not easy to come by in the early days of the war because there was a physician shortage and the military was ramping up. They hadn't really caught up with their need to put a physician in every one of those little pigeonhole slots, the authorized physician spaces in the units. The Army was sucking up physicians right and left just to get them into those empty slots so the units could deploy to Vietnam.

That was the Army's priority; finding replacements wasn't. They already had me over there. If they had just punched my TS [tough shit] card and said, "Duty, old buddy, you get another six months over here," what the hell was I going to do about it, hitchhike to the ocean and swim home? So, I was one of the last guys to be replaced.

At the other end of the spectrum, the battalion commander was the first one to be replaced. His replacement came in and he wanted to do all sorts of stuff. He wanted to make his mark. I had been staying back from the previous couple of missions because there really wasn't much going on out there for me. But he says, oh no, I want Doc out there on every mission. As a result, I was still out in the field my last day in-theater. I had to be in Saigon that night to catch my flight back to the states. I had already shipped all my personal belongings and my footlocker ahead of me, but all my military gear I had to leave in the field.

Just before dusk, I caught the last helicopter to Saigon. I ended up waiting three days to catch a flight anyway, but who knew that? I was supposed to be in Saigon that evening or else my seat could have gone to somebody else, was all I knew. I was NOT going to let that happen, but I was out in the field living in one of those little trenches and almost did just that.

Everybody else was sitting in camp while their replacements went to the field, but I was out in the field my last day in Vietnam. When my replacement came in I basically said, "Hi and goodbye" to him, and I was out the door and gone. The last thing I wanted to do is spend my last year on this planet in a hell zone like that, and then get clipped just before I left. Better I just step off the landing craft and get drilled so I didn't have to suffer for a whole damn year.

I was very concerned and reluctant, but I went to the field my last day because that's what my battalion commander told me to do. Tragically and strangely enough, I learned that the following year this guy and his replacement were on an orientation tour in a helicopter, got shot down, and were both killed. He got it at the end of his tour.

Another guy had been over there only about three weeks. He was walking patrol with some other troops on a levee. On one side of the levee was a rice paddy and on the other side was an 18-foot-deep irrigation ditch. He fell into the ditch wearing full gear, went right to the bottom, and drowned. He had a wife and kids at home. I remember them bringing him into the aid station. He had weeds and stuff clutched in his hands. His eyes were still open and you could almost see the terror in his face. Imagine someone drowning. It's my worst nightmare. I'd rather have a coronary or a stroke, like we all would.

Because of the age at which I was drafted, I didn't have to participate in the Reserves when I got out of the service, although they certainly encouraged me to join. One of my friends that I interned with had the option of signing up for a tour in Germany, but then he'd have to stay in for three years instead of two. He had a wife and two kids at the time and was afraid a two-year tour ran too big a risk of going to Vietnam, so he took the three-year offer. He finished his three years, went into the reserves, and retired in 2000 as a brigadier general. He must have been a full colonel and then got bumped up to BG upon retirement. That's usually the way it works in the Reserves.

When I finished my year in Vietnam the Army reassigned me to Irwin Army Hospital back at Fort Riley, much to my displeasure. That was the last place on the map I wanted to go. Toward the end of my tour overseas, they had me fill out a dream sheet and put down my first three choices of duty assignments. They assured my I'd probably get one of them. Well, Irwin Army Hospital certainly was not on my list I guarantee you, but that's exactly where I ended up.

He spent the following year at Irwin Army Hospital before being discharged. He returned to school, specializing in anesthesiology, served his residency back at Toledo Hospital, and then went into private practice. He's now retired and living in South Carolina.

CHAPTER 4
ARMY SPECIALIST FOUR RICH SOUTHWORTH
Radio Operator

The enemy came running down, thinking they'd killed us all. When they came up out of the caves, we opened up on them. The enemy just couldn't believe that we were still alive, let alone putting up a fight. When we started firing, they did a quick reverse and ran back into the caves. They didn't want any part of us if we were going to shoot back. They couldn't understand what had gone wrong, why were we still alive and kicking.

*R*ich grew up on a farm in Michigan about 12 miles from Huron Bay *and about an hour and a half from Mackinaw in a little town called Twining where he attended Areneck Eastern High School. He graduated in 1964 and went to work for the Buick Motor Division in Flint. He was drafted in September 1965 and took Basic and Advanced Individual Training at Fort Knox, Kentucky. Toward the end of Basic, a soldier from Fort Benning, Georgia, addressed his class and convinced Rich to go to Airborne School. Following Airborne School, he went to Vietnam in April 1966 where he was assigned to the 101st Airborne Division. Rich Southworth served in Vietnam 1966-67 and 1969-70.*

We flew out of Norton Air Force Base, near Oakland, California. We were on a prop plane, soon experienced engine trouble, and landed in Hawaii for repairs. We were there about a day but had to stay in the airport. I guess they were afraid they'd never get us rounded up when it was time to leave if they turned us loose on the island.

From Hawaii, we flew directly to Vietnam, landing at Tan Sanut AFB, just outside Saigon. When they opened the door on that plane and the heat hit me, I just said, "My God!" The temperature must have been 115-120. There were no runways per se. All they had was porous steel planking. That was early in the campaign and there hadn't been much of a build-up yet—no permanent buildings—just dirt and tents. The second time I went over, there were Quonset huts and the airport had been built up. It was nice, compared to what I'd seen the first time.

It reminded me of my first jump at parachute training. I was very enthusiastic. I really wanted to get out that door, jump, and really get into the action. The second time, I knew where I was and what was going to happen, and I was a little hesitant.

On Tan Sanut there was an area called Camp Alfa and that's where you were critiqued, a process to ensure your records, next of kin, and everything else was in order, sort of an in-processing procedure. They showed us films on various things to include VD. Venereal disease was a big concern in the 101st because they wanted to keep their troops in good shape and fit to fight.

After about a week at Camp Alfa, I got assigned to the 501st Signal Battalion. Sergeant Major Yonkers must have taken a shine to me because he asked if I'd like to be his driver and I accepted. We were stationed in Phan Rang. Then he asked if I'd like to be an 05C instead of an 05B. A Bravo carried a radio where a Charlie also uses cryptographic equipment and required a top-secret clearance.

While waiting for my background check to be processed, my mother wrote that there were people who came to the house to talk to her, my dad, and my family. They also went over to the neighbors and other people who knew me. My background must have been okay because I got my top-secret clearance.

I operated a TT-4 teletype-machine with a KW-7 encryption device attached using an AN/GRC-19 radio for transmission. When we started moving around, we put all this equipment in the back of a jeep and joined convoys as the line units moved from place to place. We'd serve as a relay system to patch signals from one distant unit to another who were too far apart to communicate directly. With the KW-7, our transmissions were garbled so that only someone who also had a KW-7 could decipher it. If the enemy intercepted our transmissions, all he had was unintelligible garbage.

Once, we had to land atop a mountain to set up a radio relay station. A Chinook chopper brought in our jeep and other heavier equipment. Then they brought us in on Hueys and we had to jump out into this six-foot-tall elephant grass. Our company commander jumped right onto a pongee stake.

Convoy travel got hairy sometimes. We got attacked two or three times and one of the enemy's main targets was any big antenna, in order to knock out communications. Our convoys had V-100s—we called them Ducks because they looked like an amphibious craft, which they were. MPs were usually the operators, who were there to help protect the convoy. The V-100s had .50 caliber machineguns. The convoy also had the usual firepower, such as M-60 machineguns mounted on the trucks.

We went to Tuy Hoa, a big village with a river and a huge rice field. Our line companies were to guard the rice field in order to deprive the enemy of food. My detachment was attached to the 502nd Infantry Battalion, nicknamed the Panthers. They were pretty good.

From there, we went to Dak To. We went to the boonies one time and saw choppers come in with Vietcong prisoners onboard. The Republic of Korea Marines kicked the VC out of the choppers during interrogation to make the remainder talk. The ROK Marines were very tough—you *did not* mess with any of them. They were well trained.

The ROK Marines had two VC, which they'd been interrogating without success, so they blindfolded them and put them in the chopper. They took them up into the air about 500 feet and again started asking them questions. Naturally, the VC still wouldn't talk. The ROK Marines already had an idea which prisoner had information and was likely to talk. They took the blindfold off one VC and then kicked the other out of the chopper. The survivor immediately talked up a storm.

Incidents like that had nothing to do with us, though. We didn't do things like that, at least not that I ever saw or heard.

We put our jeeps and stuff on an LTD, an amphibious boat, and ferried across the water to Quan Tri, which was very close to the Ho Chi Minh establishment. We met a lot of Marines up there. Quan Tri was a fairly big city. Along with the Vietnamese, there were quite a few Cambodians there.

The 101st built what they called a Sixty-nine Club. The club was in a fenced in area with Air Police guarding it. In the morning, a medic would use a truck to pick up the girls downtown and bring them to the gate. But before they could go in the gate to the club, they were all checked to be sure they each had a tag. Girls could not come into the club unless they were wearing a tag that said they've been checked and had their shots. This was done because Phan Rang was full of venereal disease, things like gonorrhea, syphilis, and you name it. You'd get red-flagged if you caught something like that, meaning you couldn't go home until it was all cleared up. There were so many soldiers catching these diseases that the command decided they had to do something. The Sixty-Nine club was their solution and that stopped much of the problem.

They emphasized use of condoms if you were going to socialize, because you couldn't underestimate the diseases they had over there. Aside from the usual, they had some exotic stuff, too, like blue balls. If you had that, your testicles would swell up and often the disease could not be cured.

I had a problem myself where I kept getting infections. They gave me penicillin shots for it. I couldn't figure out what was going on because I hadn't been doing anything to catch VD. But I'd go to the medics, they'd check me out and find that my penis was dripping, so they knew I must have some sort of VD. They'd give me eight shots, four in each cheek!

The medics in the 101st had a system where they could hold four syringes in each hand and pop them into so quickly. Once you'd had that done to you, you wanted to be careful from then on.

Anyway, they kept doing that to me. One day, I went in and told the chief surgeon that I wasn't getting any more shots until he checked me out a little more closely. I told him I'd been in there a number of times, getting shots, and I haven't been *doing* anything. They kept giving me shots for VD but I couldn't have VD. He checked me and found out I was getting infections from not being circumcised.

I was 21 years old when they fixed that problem. That was not a fun thing, probably the worst two weeks of my life. In the morning, it was a real problem. They put about 15 stitches in me but they don't stretch *that* much. It really hurt but that solved my problem. I had gotten all those shots for nothing.

I came down with malaria and they packed me in ice for three days to keep my fever down. I have no idea how I caught it, except that it happened while I was out in the boonies. There were two types of malaria. We had been taking quinine pills daily and putting iodine in our water, all to prevent malaria. Rear echelon people didn't take their quinine pills and other things as religiously as the troops in the field. Maybe I didn't take mine like I should while in the rear area.

I'd also had shots for malaria but that didn't stop me from catching it. After three days in ice, they kept me in bed for a while and gave me a few shots, and then it was back to the boonies.

I had 12 shots at Fort Benning before leaving for Vietnam. They used the air gun to shoot the medicine through your skin without even touching you. You stand in line, start walking, and stop in front of the next medic. You don't want to flinch when it's your turn. It's just going to sting a little, one on each arm. I saw some guys flinch and the stream just ripped their arms wide open.

At Camp Alfa, they gave me a hemoglobin shot. People don't realize what that's like—some folks say it felt like a square needle. It wasn't square but it was a *big* needle, let me tell you. A hemoglobin shot was many shots combined. You name it and it was probably in that shot. When they hit you with that thing, I swear to God your leg ached. But it was probably good we had them.

From Quan Tri we went back to Phan Rang where I operated a MARS station relaying personal calls from troops to their homes or wherever they wanted to call in the States. We'd patch them through to somewhere like Bakersfield, California, where another operator would patch them into the phone lines to wherever they needed to go. That way the troops only had to pay for a call from Bakersfield to wherever they were calling. There were three of us operating the MARS station and we just operated in shifts. Between shifts, we were free to go anywhere and do anything.

I worked there for three or four months until I got orders to come home. It seemed like a quick year. I didn't have an opportunity to go on R&R during my first tour in Vietnam.

I left out of Cam Ronh Bay to go home. By that time, they were sending most folks home from there so they wouldn't cross paths with the incoming troops at Tan Sanut. That way, the newbies wouldn't get scared from all the stories the departing troops would tell them.

I landed in Oakland and ran into some ridiculous demonstrations. Folks were throwing stuff at us, cursing us, and you name it. I just could not understand it. You go to Vietnam, do your duty, and *this* is what you get?

Rich got out of the Army in August 1967 and went back to work at the Buick plant near Detroit. He got married but was divorced six months later. He developed a drinking habit, popped occasional pills, and smoked marijuana. He owned a muscle car, drove like a maniac, and was constantly in trouble with the police. Eventually, a judge told Rich he was on his way to prison—there was nothing else to be done.

As Rich sat in jail awaiting prison, an Army major caught up with him, apparently on a mission to get veterans to re-enlist. The major told Rich he was in serious trouble but that he could avoid it if he'd go back into the Army. That sounded good, but having been out over a year, Rich did not want to lose a pay grade. The major arranged for Rich to go back into the Army at the same grade he'd left (E-4) and also arranged to have his criminal record expunged.

He went back into the service in the summer of 1969 and was assigned briefly to Fort Knox, Kentucky, and then Fort McClellan, Alabama. He had applied for door-gunner training but instead got an assignment to the 1st Cavalry Division in Vietnam.

I drank quite a bit before my first hitch, but I drank even more in Vietnam and also started doing marijuana. Marijuana was big over there, just a natural thing. Most of the folks in my unit were using it when they weren't in the field. You could buy a pound of it for 500 piasters. You could get opium in a liquid tar form and soak the marijuana in it. That was some bad stuff let me tell you because you could get hooked on opium that way. My drug and drinking habits while in Vietnam probably contributed to my problems when I got back to the states the first time. It had made me a little more independent and authoritarian.

This time we went over on a commercial jet and stopped in Japan before landing again at Tan Sanut. As we made our approach, they gave us chewing gum because we were going to make a steep dive to the runway. They also told us to put a pillow between our legs and rest our head on it. I couldn't figure out what was going on until we landed. When they opened the door, it was obvious that there had just been a mortar attack. There were jets on fire and bomb craters all over the runway. It hadn't been anything like that during my first tour there. I couldn't believe it.

They rushed us off the plane to a Quonset hut where they told us to get a mattress and crawl under it. They didn't keep us at Camp Alfa too long, wanting to get us out of there and out of harm's way.

The 1st Cav Division's home base at that time was at Bien Hoa. We got on a Caribou, a plane with a drop-down tailgate, and that's how you got on or off. It's also the plane they usually used to drop paratroops.

At Bien Hoa we had to go out on maneuvers, run obstacle courses, and set up ambushes. The guys who had never been in-country before were very nervous about setting up an ambush. They were scared to death.

That Christmas, I recall that Bob Hope was at Bien Hoa, but I spent the holidays in the boonies in a foxhole and didn't get to see him. I was assigned as a radio operator to Charlie Company, 2nd Battalion of the 12th Infantry Brigade at Soung Be. Radio operators didn't have a very good life expectancy because the enemy always tried to kill them.

Back at camp, I had an E-7 come to me and say that Major Ward wanted to talk to me. I didn't know who Major Ward was, but he was with the battalion S2, the intelligence officer. I had no idea why he'd want to talk to me, just a SP-4.

Major Ward shook my hand and was very cordial. All the while, I'm wondering what the heck is going on. Then he asked if I'd be interested in going to another unit. He said they were putting together a group of five-man teams called Echo Company, a reconnaissance unit. We would set up conventional and automatic ambushes, and do a lot of reconnoitering.

It sounded good to me so I accepted. He said he was glad to have me, that he needed prior service people. That cleared up some of the mist: my prior service in Vietnam and the fact that I was a radio operator.

A week later at the most, I was out in the boonies in a foxhole on a big mountain called Nuey Bara not too far from Soung Be. That's where I spent New Year's. I remember that because everybody was blasting away with their weapons in celebration. My team was about halfway up Nuey Bara on a sort of ledge or plateau, sleeping on the rocks.

Our teams would go out for nine days and then come back in to rest for three, and then do it over. When we were back in, we had to stay right there in Soung Be. There was a post exchange, commissary, alcohol, soda, movies, and stuff like that, so it wasn't too bad. Soung Be was a forward support base for the 2nd of the 12th.

We got mortared almost every night. We figured it was coming from someplace on the mountain. We always had a platoon protecting the perimeter and another up there on the mountain with 81mm mortars.

Our teams never had to pull any of these security details because the only time we were back at Soung Be was when we were standing down for a few days. The folks who pulled security were from platoons that were probably gone for a month and then back for two weeks, but we weren't around long enough to pull security details.

Once on our way back out to Nuey Bara, we got a message from the inbound team that they had spotted two North Vietnamese soldiers. Our job was to flush them out and back down to where an ambush had been set up. We had an E-6 shake-and-bake named Yost who liked to go by the book. That's what happened with a lot of these shake-and-bakes; they wanted to go too much by the book because they just didn't have the practical experience. You couldn't do that in certain situations—you had to use common sense. He wanted to go by the Ranger Handbook. Sometimes you can get yourself into trouble that way.

We were supposed to go down the mountain and push the NVA into the ambush. We were walking down the mountain when Yost told us to stop and take off our backpacks. The first thing the point man said to him was that, if we take our packs off and the NVA see us, they're not going to run because they're going to know something's going on. They'll know that we know they're there.

Yost said, "No, this is what we're going to do. We're going to take our packs off and we're going to walk down."

One thing I learned is that you never underestimate your enemy. When you did, that's when you got yourself into trouble.

We eventually lost the argument and did as Yost ordered. We took everything off our packs except, being the radio operator, I had to carry the radio.

We had a point man and a slack man about 20 feet behind him. If something happened to the point man, the slack man took over. If the point man ran into enemy fire, the slack man did all he could to get the point man back to the rest of the group. We were going down the mountain and the trail curved to the left. When the point man and the slack man went around the curve, they came under enemy fire. The NVA were waiting for us and we ran right into them. They shot the point man and then shot the slack man. We didn't know how bad everything was, but Yost went crazy. He just couldn't handle it.

That was an example where a relatively inexperienced man, such as this shake-and-bake, might not do too well under fire. But someone who was prior service, had been in Vietnam before, and had experienced enemy fire might be cooler and levelheaded in that situation. I'm not saying all the shake-and-bakes were bad because some of them were good, but Yost just didn't fit the latter category. He just completely lost it and that's all there was to it.

Yost was panicking, "My God, what'll we do?"

I said to call in some artillery support, get something going. Gee whiz, we're pinned down here. You need to call somebody.

"I don't know, I don't know," he stammered.

We laid down a base of fire but by now, the enemy had taken off running. I knew they'd do that. They knew they'd been spotted—dropping our backpacks told them that. I knew they'd hit and run. I told Yost he needed to go up and look after the point man and the slack man. Find out what's going on.

"Yeah, yeah," he said, "that's right."

Yost and I went up there and learned that the slack man had gotten hit in the foot, but the point man had taken a round in the leg. When we rolled the point man over, blood just gushed out of his leg. Yost panicked and said, "Oh my God, this guy's going to die!"

Of course, that's the worst thing you can say to a man who's been shot. You just tell him he's okay and not to worry, and then you try to stop the bleeding. It's just common sense. But when the E-6 shot off his mouth the way he did, the point man went into shock.

I got mad and threw off my radio. I grabbed Yost and told him to sit down and shut up. "You're nuts," I told him. "You don't say something like that to a wounded man."

I stopped the bleeding by applying a tourniquet. He was in shock but we thought he'd probably be okay. Then I grabbed the radio and called in artillery and I called in a snakebird. A snakebird was our slang for an AH-1 attack helicopter, called a cobra. They sent a cobra to us and he spotted the enemy and killed them. But in the process, he caught a downdraft and crashed.

Now we had a snake down, but the pilot had already told us he'd killed the two NVA. We had to try to find the snake and see if the pilot was all right. At that instant, I took over the team because the E-6, Yost, was still in a panic.

Fortunately, we had a medic with us. Our team was originally composed of five people: a point man, a slack man, the NCOIC, the radioman (me), and the medic. The medic also served to guard the rear of the column, so he carried a weapon, too. Our guy, we called him "Doc," was really good.

Our team was now down to two people, just me and Doc. Yost was no good to us and the other two were shot. At that point, the other team came up from the bottom of the mountain. They had waited for the ambush but nothing had happened. When they met us, they told us to go back to base camp.

The other team found the snake and the pilot was okay, which meant we didn't lose anybody, at least no one was dead.

Going up the mountain was a hand-over-hand proposition. That's how steep Nuey Bara was, just like a cliff. To make it even more challenging, we had our backpacks, which weighed a ton.

When we got back to Soung Be, two of my guys went straight to the NCOIC, who went to Major Ward. Major Ward was the S2 but he was really the guy in charge of us. The NCOIC came to me and said he wanted me to take over the team. I reminded him that I was only an E-4. He said that didn't matter, this is Vietnam and he wanted me to take over the team. I had an E-5 who was coming onto the team and I was going to be over him? I didn't think that was going to go over too well. The NCOIC said he didn't care. He said it was my team, that's what the guys want, and that's what I want, too. I said okay.

Soon Major Ward promoted me to E-5 and told me to take over the team. That made it official. He took the E-6, Yost, and put him in charge of the Vietnamese people who came in to do cleanup, KP, and so forth. At least that's all I ever saw him do. That was January 1970.

The new E-5 gave me a hard time for one or two days, him being senior to me, longer time in grade, but then he figured out that I was pretty good and knew what I was doing. He really became a good asset to me after that—we really had a good team and never lost anyone.

My five-man team was the best. Everybody liked me and knew that I knew what I was doing, that I wasn't stupid. In fact, outsiders wanted to be on my team. Whenever I had a vacancy, there were always plenty of volunteers to fill it. I had an E-4 who came over to my team and he was a smart ass. I figured that out right away. I told him, "I don't know if I want you or not."

He says, "What do you mean?"

I said, "Because you're just a smart ass. You don't listen to anybody."

"Well," he said, "if you think you can beat my ass, you go right ahead and try it."

That's a no-no, for an NCO to get into a fight with a subordinate. But Vietnam was different. I had a system. I had two sets of boxing gloves and whenever someone mouthed off to me, I got in the ring with them. That way, it was legal. That's what I did with this E-4 and I beat his ass. He was bigger than me, maybe 40-50 pounds heavier. But I knew how to box and he didn't. I learned how to box in high school and even had a chance to go into Golden Gloves. I boxed his ears pretty good but when it was over, he came over and shook my hand. "You're a better man than I thought," he told me.

Before I "explained" it to him, he must have thought he could bully me. After that, he was the best soldier I ever had. Some times that's exactly what had to happen over there. Some of those guys came over there full of piss and vinegar, and just weren't going to take orders from anybody. But if you showed them who was boss, then they'd listen to you.

That was one thing about Vietnam: you had to stand your ground. If you were a leader, sometimes you had to use a little force against some of those guys because they just didn't understand. Many of them didn't want to be there in the first place. Sometimes you just had to put them in their place.

We didn't have any fragging incidents, where subordinates would toss a fragmentation grenade into an officer's hooch. We did have one case of a guy intentionally shooting himself in the foot.

The second time I was in Nam, the drug situation was the same as it was the first time. However, I was in a position that was a little different from the first tour. I knew I had to keep myself straight, especially when I was heading the five-man team. The first thing I told my people, "If I catch anybody whatsoever doing drugs while we're out, I'll kill you!"

That was my philosophy. I had a good team and there were no problems whatsoever. I had an E-4 named Dana. I didn't catch him doing drugs in the field, but he'd go off to go to the bathroom quite a bit. I couldn't understand it, but I really wasn't paying that much attention to him. He had liquid speed and he was drinking that stuff with coffee or water. Then I found out and I told him, "That's it, buddy, you're gone! You ain't with me anymore." He was a good E-4, too. He'd been in Vietnam before, and I wanted somebody who had prior service and knew what was going on. But he wanted to do drugs and I got rid of him.

Our team would go into an area and if we found a trail, first of all I'd check to see if it had been used recently and how much. If it looked active, we'd set up an automatic ambush and then pull back. An automatic ambush means that no one is there to set it off. There's a tripwire and when the enemy hits it, he sets off the ambush himself. You've got to know how to set it up. We used Claymore mines, grenades, C4, blasting caps, and detonation cord. Naturally, we had to mark the area so that friendlies didn't blunder into the ambush.

If we had our Claymores set up in a V, we could probably take out five or six people. We also wired up grenades hanging from the trees to blow at the same time. The grenades had a wider shrapnel pattern because they were up high and might injure seven or eight additional personnel. Another reason for the suspended grenades is that, after hitting the first few ambushes, the NVA wised up and started riding elephants. If they hit a tripwire and set off Claymores, the elephant got killed or wounded but the NVA were unharmed. To counteract that possibility, we added the grenades to get anyone who might be riding an elephant.

First Cavalry Division invented the automatic ambush. That was our job, to set up automatic ambushes and reconnoiter, but not to be seen.

With a five-man team, you don't have much firepower. No M-60s, just M-16s and an M-79 grenade launcher. Usually our medic carried the M-79 or sometimes the slack man carried it. The point man sometimes carried a shotgun if he wanted it but it weighed quite a bit, so he usually opted for the M-16. I carried a CAR-15, which is really just an M-16 with a wire butt stock. I also carried a .22 Ruger pistol. If we had to crawl into a cave or tunnel and we had to shoot, .45s made to much noise. People were ruining their hearing so we went to the .22 Ruger automatic.

We reconnoitered areas, as they wanted us to do. Because we didn't have much firepower, we had to walk quite a ways. They might drop us off half a day's march from our objective because we didn't want to be seen arriving. If the chopper had dropped us right at our objective, the VC would know that we only had five men and, as soon as the chopper left, we'd be history.

During with the long walks, we had to maintain silence for the same reason. We had to be very careful about the areas in which we were working. We only had five guys and any enemy we ran into would surely outnumber us. If we ran into the enemy, we had to do some escape and evasion, and do it quickly. It was a tedious job, but for some reason I enjoyed it. My adrenalin was flowing every time that I jumped out of the helicopter.

Because we were such a small group, we didn't set up any live ambushes. We'd set up automatic ambushes and then pull back. If one of our automatic ambushes went off, the next day we'd go back and check to see if how many casualties we'd inflicted. But usually the enemy would carry off the dead and wounded because they never wanted us to know if we did any damage. So most of the time you really didn't know how many had been killed or wounded. That was their way of keeping our morale from going up.

The Ho Chi Minh Trail came down through Phan Tien and Phuoc Vin. It extended all the way down to the Mekong Delta. We operated near Soung Be, also near the Mekong Delta, not even close to Cambodia. The Mekong Delta had a number of rubber plantations with dozens of trails through them.

When I was with the 101st Airborne during my first tour, we found an NVA hospital inside a mountain. It had running water, electricity, everything. It was fabulous. During my second tour, we found big caches of rice—big old caches of rice—hidden underground, enough to last them forever. We found tunnels that went for five miles. We were in their territory and they were very resourceful, so we had to be careful, especially since we had just a five-man team.

When we ran across a VC/NVA unit, we had a system we called SALUTE to report the enemy's characteristics. When you spotted an enemy unit, you always used the word SALUTE. That way you'd provide a complete report back to S2. They'd assess our report and decide what needed to be done or report the information up the chain of command.

One particular time, we were on a plateau or ridgeline on Nuey Bara and that's where we set up camp. We always slept foot-to-foot and took turns standing watch during the night, making an hourly radio contact with our battalion. When you were on watch, you could stand, sit, or lie down, but you had to make contact with the battalion every hour.

I usually took the last radio watch so I could look at the map and get organized. That way, when everyone else got up we'd be ready to go. I'd tell my point man the azimuth of the days march and how many meters we needed to go.

That was another duty of the slack man, to count off the meters. He figured a meter was one step and that told me how far we'd come or how far we still had to go. Everybody had a specific job to do during a march. If the point man didn't maintain a proper azimuth or if the slack man didn't keep track of the distance, we wouldn't know where we were.

That morning one of the men woke me up, saying there's something going on further down the mountain. When I asked him what he was talking about, he said he saw lights down there. Up on top, our guys occasionally fired illumination rounds. These flares came floating down on little parachutes. I asked if he was sure it wasn't one of those, or possibly the moon. He said he didn't know and thought I'd better have a look.

When the illumination went off, I looked down below and couldn't see anything. I waited until the illumination ended. All at once, I looked down there and saw something that looked like a fire, possible started by the illumination. I looked through my binoculars and, I'll be doggone, the lights we were seeing were flashlights!

I called the S2 who told me to wait until morning and then go investigate. I only had five men, but I said okay. He said there'd be another platoon that'll link up with you, and that made me feel better. *Good enough*, I said. We could have called in a 155mm round to take care of the flashlights and anybody near them, but we wanted to know what the enemy was up to. We had no idea what was going on. We'd already interrogated some prisoners and had intelligence that the enemy was going to hit Soung Be and Nuey Bara. That's what the two VC were doing earlier, trying to get the layout of Soung Be. They'd been mortaring Soung Be every night for a week.

As I said, our team would go out for nine days and then come back for three. Of my three stand-down days, I spent about two of them doing recon for our next mission area. They'd fly me out in a UH-2B, or Iroquois, an older chopper with a .50 caliber machinegun in each door. It was a forerunner of the UH-1 Huey utility helicopter.

They'd take me up and the pilot would tell me where we were on the map. I'd tell him where I wanted to go and he'd take me over the mission route. I made notes of terrain features and availability of water. This let me plan the types and amount of equipment we needed to carry. If we had to blow out an LZ, how much C4 would we need? How much ammo, Claymores, etc., would we need to bring?

The recon flights also let me plan how much water we needed to bring along. If there was no water in the area, each man would have to carry up to eight quarts. You didn't want to carry that extra weight unless it was absolutely necessary. If we didn't take our own water, we'd have to take extra iodine tablets. Anytime you used water anyplace in Vietnam, you had to put iodine tablets in it first to prevent dysentery.

To cut the weight of our backpacks, we carried LRPs, food that had been dehydrated. If there was no water in the area we were going to, we had to carry extra water in order to use the LRPs. You could eat the stuff dry if you had to, but most of the time, we'd use water to reconstitute it.

Back to the story about the flashlights: The next morning I packed everybody up and told them, "Let's go down through the ravine to the bottom."

That was stupid of me. That was not using my head because anytime you're on a mountain, you should stay on high ground. What I should have done is take my team across the plateau and followed the ridgeline down. It would have taken a lot longer but we'd have had the high ground, always a tactical advantage. I don't know why, but this time something told me to go straight down instead of following the ridgeline.

Just as we hit the bottom, something suddenly picked me up in the air and threw me about 10 feet. Aside from a big noise, that's all I remember. It was really something. I got knocked out for a while—I know that. The E-5 next to me wound up in the same place where I was. Just about the same thing happened to everybody. That's how much explosives the enemy had *on the ridgeline!* If we had walked the ridgeline, all five of us would have been killed. No question. There's just no way anyone could have survived. But, because we went straight down into the valley, most of the blast went over the top of us. The compression from all those explosives picked us right up in the air and threw us.

In Vietnam, they have what they call "triple-canopy bamboo." This stuff is so thick that no sunlight can get through it. It's so thick that, when it rains, water can't even get through. The explosives blew a huge hole in the triple-canopy.

When we recovered our senses, we checked to see if everyone else was okay. At about this time, my E-5 yells, "VC! VC!" The enemy came running down, thinking they'd killed us all. When they came up out of the caves, we opened up on them. If we hadn't come to as quickly as we did, the VC surely would have killed us all anyway. The enemy just couldn't believe that we were still alive, let alone putting up a fight. When we started firing, they did a quick reverse and ran back into the caves. They didn't want any part of us if we were going to shoot back. They couldn't understand what had gone wrong, why were we still alive and kicking.

When the firing ended, we were still dazed from the explosion. We had just been shooting on instinct. All at once, we heard something off to our right. It was the other platoon coming up to meet us. Were we ever glad to see them! They asked what had happened and I told them the VC had blown the ridgeline. I said that I'd done something I shouldn't have done—I'd taken my team straight down the mountain instead of following the ridgeline. The platoon leader said, "You're one lucky person, let me tell you! You guys would have been killed. There's no way you could have gotten out of that alive."

Our medic looked everyone over. Sure, we had scratches and bruises, but nobody was seriously hurt, except for my point man. He lost an eardrum but we didn't even know that until we got back from the mission. He got sent back home. Otherwise, everyone else was in good shape.

The other platoon went into the caves and found tons of rubber bands and other items. The rubber bands told us that they were stockpiling stuff for an attack on Soung Be. The VC sappers could crawl through six strands of concertina wire with no problem. Along with the concertina wire, we had trip flares set up to let us know when someone was trying to infiltrate. After the sappers got through the concertina wire, they'd put rubber bands around the trip flares so they wouldn't go off. After the sappers did their thing, then the main body of VC would come through and they wouldn't have to be concerned about setting off the flares. The flares were magnesium and, along with emitting tremendous light, would also burn a person severely if the magnesium got on him.

In Bien Hua, we watched a demonstration of what a sapper could do. This guy was like a snake. If you haven't seen one, you wouldn't believe what he could do. He crawled through the mud and water, and through four strands of concertina wire. He did it quickly and easily, and without setting off any of the flares we had rigged up. He not only crawled through all the wire, he also used rubber bands to disable the flares and turned all our Claymores in the opposite direction. If it had been a real attack instead of a demonstration, setting off the Claymores would have wiped out the good guys instead of the VC.

I watched this sapper do his thing and all I could think was, "You've got to be kidding me!" Fortunately, this was just a demonstration, but it really showed us what a sapper could do.

Our team got an award, possibly a Bronze Star, for surviving the ridge incident. My team got a lot of awards and I can't remember which ones came when. When we got back to camp, they had us go up to battalion where they stood us up and gave us the award. The battalion commander himself pinned the decorations on us.

As I mentioned, our base camp was getting mortared every night. When we came in from the ridge mission, they told us they wanted us to go out into a rubber plantation because they believed there were mortar rounds coming from there. The major told me he'd sent a platoon out there to search the area, to try to find out where the mortar rounds were coming from, but they couldn't find anything. Yet, we were being mortared every night and he *knew* it was coming from the plantation.

What am I going to do with a five-man team, I asked. He just told me to do it, so I did.

This is where common sense came in. I'm not saying I'm a genius or anything, but it's a knack or gift you either have or you don't have. My experience helped, too. Anyway, we went out there. I told my troops to be sure to stay spread out so, if one guy gets hit, they wouldn't get everybody. The point man stopped and we all came together.

I saw a pile of rocks nearby and asked him what that was. The point man said it was just a pile of rocks. I looked at it and said, "What do you mean, just rocks? Are there rocks in a rubber plantation?"

The point man and the E-5 just looked at me. I said, "Those rocks look out of place. How can you put one rock on top of another rock and think it's not something. That's got to be a sign, like the Indians used to have."

The point man said, "Wow! Maybe you're right."

"There's something wrong," I said. "Those rocks are put there for a reason. That's a checkpoint or something."

We went over to the rocks and looked at them. "I said, I'll tell you what. I'll bet these rocks are pointing that way. Let's go that way."

We did, and guess what? We ran right into the heart of the enemy mortar location. They had camouflaged over the trees, they had two spider holes and all kinds of artillery stuff. Now, why couldn't the platoon have found this stuff?

Once we found it and reported what we'd found, the major went running to the battalion commander, the battalion commander got into his chopper and came right out to where we were. He shook our hands and congratulated us. We got a Bronze Star for that. "I cannot believe this!" he said. "You guys found all this?"

When we got back to the base camp, the E-7 said, "I'm promoting you!" So, I made E-6 in June of 1970, only six months after making E-5.

About that time, I went to Formosa for two weeks of R&R. I really enjoyed it—it was nice.

When I came back, our three reconnaissance teams came together as a platoon because we were going into Cambodia. We called the area we were going into "The Fishhook" because that was the shape of the Cambodian border at that point. This was a top-secret mission because Cambodia was a neutral country and we weren't supposed to be there. We knew through intelligence that the VC came and went from Cambodia, so we decided we needed to go where the enemy was.

A platoon usually consists of about 40 people but we had 15. That's all we had. We had an M-60 gunner, M-16s, shotguns, and M-79 grenade launchers. We had a commander, a platoon sergeant, squad leaders, and a sniper. The sniper could kill somebody from 1000-1500 meters away.

They took us into Cambodia by chopper and dropped us off. We made the fishhook with me as point man. Because I'd been there longer than the others, I had volunteered to walk point. I guess, when you've done it so often, you can get a little too comfortable, not really thinking that well or staying that alert. I was walking and noticed that there were NVA walking in the opposite direction not 15 yards away. They were walking along a trail and we were moving through the jungle just off the trail. I couldn't believe it! The NVA might have been half daydreaming just like I was and probably thought I was NVA, too.

As I passed the NVA point man, I turned and looked at him and he looked at me. I hollered, "GOOKS! GOOKS!" Everything opened up—everybody started shooting. When it was over, we found a helmet that one of the NVA had, but that's all we found. We didn't know if we did any damage or just scared the hell out of them.

That was a real wake-up call for me. If I'd been any more relaxed, it could have been a disaster. After that, we started being a little more cautious.

We had a sergeant that had led one of the other teams. He was getting short and due to rotate out of Nam. He went back to the rear area and served as our supply rep. He brought out clothes, sundry packets, cigarettes, beer, and things like that to our forward support base. Our forward support base at Soung Be was called Camp Snuffy.

From Snuffy we went into Cambodia. Our supply rep said he wanted to go with us because he was getting tired of being a supply rep. He didn't have that long to go and he got lax. We were walking down this road, stepping over dead bodies, and the point man was talking to the M-60 operator when the NVA hit us.

You have a quick release on the left side of your rucksack. All you do when under attack is you reach across and grab the release. Naturally, your rucksack falls off your shoulders. At the same time, you swing your shoulders so the rucksack lands in front of you. You get down behind it and that serves as protection from incoming fire.

The platoon sergeant was lax and didn't hit his quick release. All he did was sit down. The rucksack was still on his back and held him up in a sitting position. The enemy just riddled him. It was terrible. We watched it and could see him jump every time the enemy fired. There was nothing we could do. We couldn't get to him. Because he became lax, he didn't think quickly and get his rucksack in front of him. I'd say he might still have gotten shot but probably wouldn't have been killed. As it was, they just riddled him.

Along with the platoon sergeant, our sniper also got killed. Our radioman had a $1,000,000 wound. The round went through his stomach. It wasn't a serious wound, but serious enough to get him sent home. Our medic got a Silver Star trying to save the sniper via mouth-to-mouth resuscitation. We couldn't get the medevac chopper in because of all the firing and the sniper didn't survive.

We found artillery, we found a truck, we found all kinds of rice, we found weapons still in Cosmoline. In fact, everyone in the platoon got a weapon out of that cache. I got a CSC, a Chinese rifle that takes a 7.62mm round.

Once we secured the cache, they sent in what they called a "blue team," a group that came out of Phuoc Vin if I'm not mistaken. They were demolition or explosive ordnance experts, and wore black cowboy hats and blue scarves. They blew the remainder of the cache in place. The cache was so huge we nicknamed it "Rock Island East."

The 1st Cav Division commander, Major General Maddox, found a truck and had it converted for his personal use, naming it The Rock Island East Express. All this was in *Look Magazine*, which carried a story about the biggest cache that was ever taken during the Vietnam War.

We were part of Delta Company, 1/12 Infantry. We were supposed to hook up with the 1/7th Infantry the next day. We went out walking and our commander put a shake-and-bake E-6 in charge because he wanted me leading a flank unit. I took 2-3 people and marched on the flank of the main column.

We were walking along and all at once, we look out and see a guy shoveling dirt just ahead of us. He was VC! We opened up on him. I don't know exactly what happened, but when the firing stopped and we went over there, we couldn't find anything. About then, we started getting incoming fire. Here we go again! An E-6 shake-and-bake Ranger had come with us. His name was Yost and he's the same guy I talked about earlier who had lost his head and had been replaced by me. Yost had an E-4 with him; I think his name was Benjamin or Bendix. The E-6 threw a grenade, which hit a tree and bounced back. It went off and blinded the E-4. I said to myself, *this guy is bad let me tell you! Everything he does is wrong. Can we put him on the other side?*

That was it for Yost—we never saw him again. Apparently, the commanders knew a liability when they saw one.

We finally linked up with the 1/7 who had also found a cache, a huge pile of rice. One of their guys had been shot in the stomach and they were trying to call in a medevac chopper for him. The medevac couldn't get in because of enemy fire. We tried to keep the troop alive. We found a cave and put him in it, hoping he could last until the chopper could get there. He was laughing and talking, so we figured everything would be okay.

We knew he'd been shot and that he was bleeding, but he was in good spirits. We were all playing cards until I got sleepy

About two or three in the morning, we heard somebody holler that the guy was dead. Internal bleeding finally got the best of him. The 1/7th had lost 10-12 people, including this guy.

We started walking at sunup, still in Cambodia. We began going up this mountain along a well-used trail. The point man for the 1/7th was walking up a hill with the rest of the company following him.

I was point man on a flanker team of 10-11 people, separated from the main column of troops. I had my M-60 gunner right behind me. All at once, I spotted an NVA who had his rifle pointed right down the trail, right at the point man of the 1/7th. The NVA spotted me about the same time I saw him. He turned and aimed his gun at me and, to this day, I swear he pulled the trigger. I *really* think he did. At the same time he pulled the trigger, I hollered, "NVA! NVA!" The only other thing I remember is hitting the ground. At that instant, my M-60 gunner opened up, just riddling the NVA. The guy had no chance whatsoever.

When everything was over with, we went up there and the point man from the 1/7th said, "Man, you saved my life!" I got a Bronze Star for heroism as a result of that incident and the Army sent a news release to my hometown paper, the *Arenec Independent*, to that effect.

I said, "I don't know about you but I know he shot at me. I heard that thing go click."

"Really?" he said. He picked up the NVA's gun, pulled the hammer back, pulled the trigger, and it went off.

I'm almost positive the NVA had his safety off—he would have *had* to if he was going to shoot the point man. Maybe he had a misfire or maybe he *didn't* squeeze the trigger. He was only 15-20 feet away, so he could hardly have missed. Whatever happened, I was just lucky.

After that encounter, we knew that we would hit more NVA as we went up the mountain. We pulled back, called in a napalm strike, and then we went up. I'm not sure what our objective was in going up the mountain. That knowledge resided with the commanders—I was just a grunt following orders—but it had to be something to do with clearing an enemy outpost. Like most of the other guys, I was pretty much in the dark about why we were doing things, unless I was in control and leading my five-man team. Otherwise, the commanders just told us where we were going that day, and that was it.

With all the things I've been through, you'd think I'd have gotten at least one Purple Heart. You have to get wounded to get one of those things, you know. But I was just lucky. For example, the time I led my team down the middle of the ravine instead of following the ridge the way I'd learned in combat training. It saved everybody, but that should have gotten me at least a Purple Heart, probably a ride home in a box. The same thing could have happened when the NVA fired on me as we were going up the mountain in Cambodia.

When I was in Vietnam, I was just doing my job. I felt it was my duty. Looking back now, I'd say we shouldn't have been there, at least not the way we went at it. We should have gone in and bombed Hanoi and gotten it over with. If we'd done it the right way, fight to win at all costs, then yes, we should have been there. But we did it the wrong way and that's all there is to it. It's as simple as that. I look back now and see how many people we lost and the way we did things, I would say that there's no way I'd ever want to do it again. It was stupid the way we did it. If we had to do it again using the same procedures, it would turn out the same way.

They're not a democracy in Saigon; they're all communists. So, what did we accomplish? It was politics. But if you weren't out front like I was, being shot at and having to step over dead bodies, you just didn't understand. The politicians just wanted to make themselves look good, I guess. It didn't bother me to have to kill the enemy because of what I saw on the trails, what I saw when we dropped in someplace or met up with another unit.

We did not have any of the psychiatric or psychological counseling available when we got back from Vietnam the way the troops returning from Desert Storm did. We were nothing but snakes in the grass to many people in the states. When you have someone throw things at you when you get off the plane, how would you feel? After I'd been over there and seen my fellow soldiers fall, it really made me angry.

Now I look back I believe that those demonstrations were in good faith. But what they didn't understand was that we were just following orders. They had a right to oppose the war but not the warriors. The whole thing was nothing but politics. I really believe that. They thought it was just a police action and that everything would be over quickly. That didn't happen and the politicians didn't adjust. That's why we lost so many people. If we had bombed Hanoi in the beginning, we probably wouldn't have had all the resistance we had in the States.

To send us over there in a guerilla warfare-type operation was a problem, too. We never had any training in guerilla tactics. The Special Forces had that kind of training, but not the rest of us. The regular troops out of Fort Bragg or the 101st Airborne Division or anyplace else, they had no guerilla warfare training.

Guerilla warfare was right down their alley for the Vietnamese. They would hit and run—that was their style to a T—that's the way they did it. When the NVA got involved, they started setting up ambushes and killing lots of GIs. I shot NVA but they just kept coming. They were doped up or something. If you didn't hit them square and put them on their back, they just wouldn't stop. It was terrible. Their adrenalin was so high and they were so full of drugs that they just kept coming.

If you took an M-16, shot somebody, and they just keep coming, that was scary. An M-16 slug tumbles when it hits someone—it doesn't just go straight through. If the slug hit a bone, it would just rip you and you'd go down. That's one reason I liked the M-16. I just didn't like it in the jungle because, if a slug hit a twig or something, it would throw off the shot. If you were shooting an M-14 and hit a twig, the 7.62mm round kept right on going where you aimed. That was good, but the M-14 was *heavy*, which is why they came out with the M-16 and its lighter 5.56mm ammunition.

Believe it or not, the AK-47 was a better weapon, but we couldn't use it because it had a distinct sound. If one of our other platoons heard it, they'd assume it was NVA or VC. That was the problem.

I always taped my M-16 magazines together in pairs, one upside down. When I emptied one magazine, I'd just eject, turn it around, re-insert, and start firing again.

Some people didn't like the M-16 because they said the bolt would hang up. But I never had a problem. I always kept it well lubed with LSA. After every use or trip to the field, I cleaned my weapon really well, and slathered on the LSA. Otherwise, in a firefight the buffer assembly will overheat and have a tendency to stick. If you kept the buffer assembly loaded up with LSA, you didn't have that problem. I never had a misfire in 24 months of action.

I used a CAR-15 the last four or five months I was over there. It's really the same rifle as the M-16 except it had a skeletonized wire butt stock, which made it even lighter.

Two weeks before I was to rotate, they put me in the rear echelon at Soung Be. I was in charge of the perimeter defense, and had my own hooch and my own maid. I just had to make sure that everything was kosher, that all the Vietnamese who came into our compound were supposed to be there, tagged and certified.

I knew I'd still be in the Army when I left Nam, so I really wasn't anxious to leave. I wasn't married at the time, so it's not like I had a family to go back to. In fact, they asked me to extend in exchange for a direct commission. I was thinking about doing it, really tempted. But then I heard on the radio that the US was getting ready to pull out anyway. If I had accepted a commission and then there was a draw down after the war, I'd lose the commission anyway. No way would the Army be able to keep all those officers who'd accepted battlefield commissions.

After assignments in Germany and Fort Bragg, Rich got out of the service in November 1980, and went back to Michigan. After remarrying, Rich and his wife moved to North Carolina where he works in a plastics plant. As a result of his service in Vietnam, Rich Southworth was awarded an Air medal, Combat Infantry Badge, and four Bronze Stars (one short of automatically qualifying for a Silver Star). He also received a Gallantry Ribbon, Meritorious Medal (Vietnamese), and 24 campaign ribbons (one for every month in combat).

George Engebretson (right) and friends at LZ Eleanor, early 1969

Bill Howell at Con Tien, 1969, on the DMZ during the monsoon season—
mud all over the place.

Bill Howell talking to some kids about their water
buffalo during a convoy delay.

Bill Howell (R) and MSG Cain outside their bunker entrance at Con Tien.

Bill Howell, Mike Reid, and Larry Shaddix (L-R) in front of one of the "Dusters" used to provide convoy security.

Ammo dump near Dong Ha, hit by mortars.

Bill Howell filling sandbags to protect his bunker.

Larry Touchstone (left) with two buddies cooling canned beverages on a
rare and valuable block of ice

Part of 2nd Platoon, C-1/5, in the village of Tic Thien, March '70

The crew of #1 gun in C-1/5 mortar platoon, left to right; Front Row:
Kyle Madole, Allen Collins, James Hillbloom; Standing: Richard
Blood, (unidentified), Larry Touchstone, Bob Murphy

CHAPTER 5
MARINE GUNNERY SERGEANT FRANK PANNULLO

Computer Programmer

On the way back, they decided to stop in Da Nang proper—at a whorehouse. Staff Sergeant Francis didn't go in. The other two guys went inside. While Francis was lying there, a grenade came flying over the top of the vehicle.

*F*rank Pannullo (pa-NOO-lo) grew up in the New York City area, graduating from Charles E. Gorton HS in 1954. He worked at various jobs before joining the Marines the following year. He hitched a ride with a friend who happened to be visiting a Marine recruiter, and Frank wound up enlisting, too!

*He began boot camp the day before he was to enter Brockport State College in upstate NY on a football/track scholarship. After boot camp at Parris Island, North Carolina, and advanced training at nearby Camp Lejeune, his first regular assignment was at Camp Lejeune as a disbursing clerk in the 2*nd *Combat Service Group. He soon tired of this and badgered his first sergeant into sending him to school, anything that would provide him with a marketable skill for when he left the service.*

That turned out to be data processing school, although he wouldn't leave the service for another 20 years. His duty stations included Washington, D.C; Quantico, VA; Okinawa; and Norfolk Naval Base, VA. In 1968, the Marines sent him to Pensacola Junior College to get his Associate's Degree. From there, he went back to Quantico to upgrade his computer skills and then to Marine Corps Finance Center, Kansas City, Missouri. In December 1970, Frank left for Vietnam. Frank served in Vietnam 1970-71.

I flew over there via Okinawa and they must have scoured a lot of the retirement homes to come up with the stewardesses for that flight!

Nevertheless, they were a nice bunch of people—I've got to say that. In those days, you could smoke on the plane and most everybody did.

We landed in Saigon and went through some initial processing. Even in December, it was hot and smelly over there, pretty much the odor that you'd get in any subtropical/tropical jungle, the smell of rotting vegetation.

From Saigon, they flew us to our specific assignments. I went to the 3rd Marine Division's Force Service Regiment, stationed north of Da Nang at a place called Red Beach. That's where the Marines made their much-ballyhooed beach landing. It was pretty much a low-key, non-combat type of organization. That's not to say that we didn't take some mortars or have to go into some areas that were "hot." We could sit in the staff NCO club at night, drinking ten-cent rum-and-cokes, and see tracers from helicopter gun ships involved in full-fledged firefights in the nearby hills. It was very interesting from that perspective.

My job title was Programming Chief for Special Projects. When I first got there, the Marine Corps was in the process of moving from one automated personnel system to another. Another gunnery sergeant, Jack Epperly, and I had to go out and verify the data. We had to go where the units were, be they infantry, artillery, or whatever. We'd go out by helicopter, we'd go out by jeep, and there were times we hitchhiked. You don't think that was spooky? We'd get to the units, ask for their records, and then sit down and verify the data.

Sometimes in our travels, we'd run across items that we would trade because this unit had something that we could use and we had something that they could use. For instance, we were at an Army base somewhere and they had a small club that had a ship's bell. We had huge 50-pound bags of onions and traded one of them to get that bell for our club. If you went into a Marine or navy club with your cover (hat) on, somebody would ring the bell and you had to buy the house a round of drinks. We *needed* a bell!

Right outside the building where we worked, was a huge open-ended medical warehouse. This buddy of mine, Jim Shields, and I always made it a point to walk through the warehouse at the end of each workday to pick up any items we might need, items such as extra pillows, bathrobes, sheets, whatever. We'd go down there and "appropriate" stuff and trade it with other units. I got a really nice field surgical kit and a first aid kit. Maybe I should have been a supply sergeant!

On our trips into the field, we were very fortunate not to run into Charlie. It was always like, "Boy, you should have been here yesterday" or "You should have been here last week." We must have had angels sitting on our shoulders. The worst thing that ever happened to us was, if you sat too close to the side of a jeep with your arm hanging out, the local kids would try to rip the watch off your wrist as you went by.

There was one close call, now that I think about it. Three guys from my unit went to the base at Da Nang to conduct some business at the data processing facility there. One was our admin clerk and the other two were data processors. They were riding in an all-purpose carrier, a 1½-ton truck with an open bed. On the way back, they decided to stop in Da Nang proper—at a whorehouse. Staff Sergeant Francis didn't go in. "I'm just going to sack out here on the seat and wait for you," he said.

The other two guys went inside. While Francis was lying there, a grenade came flying over the top of the vehicle. It wasn't really a grenade; it was a tennis ball filled with some sort of explosive, along with shrapnel or nails. He was being the good guy, staying out of trouble, but he's the one who got hurt. It detonated and Francis got all shrapnel-ed up. It was nothing too serious, but he spent some time in the hospital and got a purple heart out of it.

I went to Vietnam with a guy by the name of Sullivan. He was a master sergeant, and had come out of the Marine Corps Supply Activity in Philadelphia. A short, stocky guy, Sully was gullible and shaky. When he was at Kadena Air Force Base, Okinawa, on his way to Vietnam, he and a friend of his decided that since they were going into a combat zone that they'd get combat haircuts.

Sully's buddy said, "Let's get it really high and tight, you know, whitewalls close to the head."

Sully said, "Yeah, yeah, yeah! Let's go there looking like we really mean business!"

They go to the barbershop and there's only one chair open, so Sully's buddy lets him go first. Sully sits in the chair and says, "Okay, I want it shaved up the sides."

He comes out of the chair looking like a real gung-ho Marine. The other guy gets in the chair and tells the barber, "Just a light trim, please."

Sully wound up in the same unit with me. He was the NCOIC and worked for the colonel. Explosions going off at night got him a little spooky. We were in Vietnam about 10 days and it was pretty evident—everybody knew that he was spooky. We had plywood hooches up on stilts and the Seabees had poured a slab and installed very crude showers. We generally worked 12- to 14-hour days—we didn't have anything else to do anyway.

Sully was in the hooch one night, taking a shower all by himself. He was showering away when this other guy, Vic (sorry, can't recall his last name) went into the shower and spotted Sully. Vic hadn't made any noise coming in so Sully didn't know he was there. Vic picked up a metal GI can—garbage can—and slammed it onto the cement right behind Sully.

When Vic told that story about how Sully had jumped, I thought I'd die laughing. Sully must have been scared out of ten years living. Sully was *extra* shaky for another week after that. He plotted to get back at Vic.

What he finally came up with was, we had these outhouses with cutoff 55-gallon drums underneath. There was a trapdoor in the back through which the drums were removed so the contents could be burned. We also had huge rats that, for some reason, always hung around the outhouse. Sully decided that he was going to sneak up on Steed when he was on the john, reach through the trapdoor with some pliers, and pinch his testicles, make him think a rat had gotten him, but he could never get the job done.

One time, Vic filled up Sully's boot with shaving cream. Sully couldn't see the shaving cream until he put his foot in the boot and the stuff started coming out of the top. Another time, Steed nailed Sully's boots to the floor. This poor guy took a lot of abuse, but he was pretty good-natured about it.

One of the motivations for working 12- or 14-hour days was that the computers had to be air-conditioned; that was just a serendipitous byproduct for us working there. We had a lot of work to do, believe it or not. One of the jobs I had that my unit took over from the Army was their target acquisition program. This program would pinpoint enemy mortar launch sites Then they could feed the information into a computer and get coordinates our artillery could use to neutralize the mortars. The computer gave the most likely places the enemy was shooting from.

I hated program maintenance, so whenever possible I'd try to get into new projects where I could write new programs, even if it wasn't really in my field. This target acquisition system was one of those opportunities. My actual job title was Personnel Programmer. That was my MOS. Target acquisition was certainly not a personnel system, but I took whatever was available for work. Somebody had to do it.

I came and left Nam as a gunnery sergeant. I was an REMF [Rear Echelon Mother-(bad word)]. I say that jokingly because, even in Saigon, people were assassinated and attacked. I went to Saigon a couple times on business, and everybody who went there always had a list of things to buy for his buddies. On one trip, I brought back a dozen elephants, coffee table-size ornaments: two for me, two for my brother in California, and the rest went to other people who were on site. My brother still has his.

I went to Thailand twice on a one-day R&R. More formally, you had a choice of Australia, Hong Kong, Hawaii, or home. I had a one-week R&R coming after six months in country, and chose to go home. It was either that or meet my wife in Hawaii. I'd have liked to do the latter, but then I wouldn't have gotten to see my children and they wouldn't get to see me. I didn't think that would be fair.

The way it worked was, they would fly you to a military facility, and from there, you had to pay your own way. In my case, I had to pay my fare from Hawaii to Kansas City where I'd left my family.

The hardest thing about being overseas is leaving your loved ones to go home to your wife and family [Frank laughs].

My tour in Vietnam was after the riots at the 1968 Democratic convention in Chicago. I ran into some student war protesters when I was at college in Pensacola. It was a military town, so there were other issues, such as teachers pay. I didn't pay too much attention to the protesters because I had a job to do.

I thought we should be over there because of SEATO. We signed it and we had an obligation. Additionally, there was the Domino Theory and I bought into it because it made a lot of sense.

There were no drug problems in my unit (we just got high on computers) but lots of VD. As a matter of fact, our colonel, whose name shall be forever stricken, did his best to enlighten us about the dangers of VD. He brought in corpsmen to show movies about the effects of VD, and all the disgusting pictures. He even made arrangements to show sex films in the unit so that guys could get their sex vicariously.

Many of the buildings had a kiosk outside with a six-inch-wide pipe, called a piss tube, jammed into the ground. The stall or kiosk was probably about three feet square, walled in on three sides, and about chest-high. We had one outside the building where I worked, which was alongside a dirt road. Across the road was a village. All we had between the village and us was a chain-link fence. The opening of the kiosk was toward the chain-link fence so, while we're in the kiosk doing our business, we'd have our back to the village. Anybody could have poked a rifle through the fence and blown us away. They had the kiosk opening facing away from the work area for modesty reasons (apparently it didn't matter what the civilians saw) instead of the other way around.

You talk about a nervous piss! It was awfully tough to hit that tube while looking over both shoulders.

Troop morale for the most part was pretty good in our unit. However, there was a lot of dissension among the black Marines. It was okay to give the Black Power sign to your buddies and wear the hair bracelets and the shoelace crucifixes, all big fads of the time. That wasn't a big deal, but there were some other serious, serious problems.

One time, a group of black Marines barricaded themselves inside one of the hooches. They locked and loaded, fired up their weapons, and started to make all kinds of weird demands. The black Marines felt they weren't getting any respect. Now, you have to realize that, if you're in the military, it's a different mindset. That's not to excuse the sometimes-blatant discrimination that went on. It happened, but for the most part it wasn't even covert.

On the other hand, there was a lot of the same stuff going on stateside. Martin Luther King had certainly achieved an amount of prominence and that fired up the black Marines. Whether they were right or wrong, this gave them something to point to, something to think about, a cause. If you're told over and over and over that you're not good enough or that your race has been denigrated, abused, and taken advantage of for years before you were born, then pretty soon you might start believing it.

We had a couple of guys who were black racists, but one of the guys I worked with, Staff Sergeant Richard Hughes, a black Marine, really had a level head on his shoulders. If a white Marine had gone into that hooch, the black Marines probably would have whacked him. Richard went in there and defused that situation.

He and I eventually wound up in Albany, GA, on later assignments.

I think, for the most part, we were all treated in accordance with what we did. If you were a good programmer, you were treated well, regardless of your color. If you weren't getting the job done on time or if you were doing sloppy work, then you got your ass kicked. Color was irrelevant.

This was in the early 70s, about 16 years after Brown versus Board of Education, which was in 1954, when I was in high school.

I joined the Marine Corps Reserve with some other guys from my high school. We were in the 2nd Rifle Company, New Rochelle, NY, and went to Camp Lejeune for our summer camp. We had a couple of black guys in the unit with us. A group of us went into nearby Jacksonville, NC, a Marine Corps town. There we were, three white guys and two black guys. We went into a bar and sit down. A waitress comes over and we order, but she says, "Sorry, we can't serve colored people."

We really got indignant, but she said, "I'm sorry, but that's the law!"

We thought that was such a stupid law. We had never encountered anything like that. So, we got up and left. We weren't going to patronize this place! Of course, the two black guys knew and they said, "Look, the only place we're going to get served is in the black section, so that's where we'll go."

I went to a high school in New York that probably had less that 10 black graduates in a class of 250. It was an almost exclusively white school. However, there was another school that was very near a black neighborhood and had quite a few blacks attending. There was a trade school in that same area, and it also had a large black population, but in neither case was it a black majority.

I never had that much exposure to black folks when I was growing up, so I never developed an attitude or position on race relations. Most of the black students I went to school with were good students. One of them received a full scholarship to Yale, another received a scholarship to the Cincinnati Conservatory, another received a scholarship to some prestigious art institute, and one of them went to a school of design. They were all much better students than I was.

I hated the lack of support by our government who would not let us do the job that we could have done in Vietnam. We couldn't use carpet-bombing, we couldn't cross borders, and we couldn't go into areas that were "protected." The purpose of war is to kill people and break things, but they had all these stupid rules that prevented us from performing our mission.

Would I do it again? Only if I could get a clear shot at Jane [Fonda]!

Frank left Vietnam in September of 1971, was stationed briefly in Japan, and finished his career with a four-year assignment in Albany, Georgia. Albany was considered "The Country Club of the Marine Corps," but Frank's kids called it "Agony" instead of Albany. There were plenty of recreational opportunities for adults (hunting, fishing, golf), but not much for teenagers. Frank stayed in Albany and got his bachelor's degree in 1976 from Albany State, and then accepted a civilian job in automation working for the Marines. In 1981, Frank moved from Albany to take a similar position in Atlanta working for the Army. He retired completely in the late 1990s and passed away in 2007.

CHAPTER 6
NAVY LIEUTENANT COMMANDER WILLIS "BILL" UDE

Marine Chaplain

Every once in a while, we'd hear a whirring noise, a 250-pound bomb flying over us. The next morning when it got daylight, we could look around and see these 250-pound bombs lying all over the place. None of them ever went off! If they had, it would have been devastating, or if one had hit the building we were hiding behind, we'd probably have been wiped out.

*B*ill Ude *(pronounced: OO-dee) was born and raised in Deshler, a small town in south-central Nebraska. Upon graduation from the eighth grade and with his pastor's recommendation, his parents sent him to prep school at St. John's College in Winfield, Kansas, a Lutheran Church Missouri Synod institution. He graduated from high school there in 1944 and was given draft exemption provided he stayed in school year round. Graduating high school on a Friday, he began college the following Monday. He spent a year as vicar at his alma mater, the Prep School of St. John's, as a teacher and another at St. Paul's Lutheran School in Austin, TX.*

After graduating from seminary in 1952, he went to Navy Chaplain School at Newport, Rhode Island, a two-month course where he learned the Naval way of doing things. There were two groups of students there at that time, he relates, the skinheads and the retreads. The skinheads (a reference to their boot camp haircuts) were the newly commissioned folks like Bill, and the retreads were officers being recalled to active duty from the Reserves.

Upon graduation, he was assigned to the newly formed 3rd Marine Division at Camp Pendleton, California. The 3rd soon left Camp Pendleton for Okubo, Japan, but first Bill was temporarily assigned to the Navy Hospital at Corona (near Riverside), CA, where he met his future wife Betty Thompson. While with the 3rd Division, Bill served the 3rd Signal Battalion and the 3rd Engineer Battalion. En route to Okubo, once a kamikaze training site, the division disembarked at

Kobe, a city still in ruins seven years after the end of WWII. After 15 months in Japan, he was due for transfer and requested orders to San Diego in order to be near his sweetheart. Curiously, a friend from Chaplain School was being transferred at the same time, having requested duty on the east coast. You guessed it, Bill got the east coast assignment and his friend went to San Diego! Bill was assigned to the Service School Command at Bainbridge, Maryland, where he and Betty were married and had their first child. Shore duty assignments at that time ran 20-22 months while sea duty assignments lasted 26-28 months.

Following his tour at Bainbridge, Bill was assigned to the USS Ajax, a repair ship with a crew of over 1000 men that split its time between San Diego and Sasebo, Japan. Then it was back to Naval Training Center, San Diego, followed by an assignment to the Navy Hospital on Guam, and then Mare Island Naval Shipyard north of San Francisco. Bill served in Vietnam intermittently from 1965 to 1970.

The Navy supplied the Marines with chaplains, doctors, dentists, and corpsmen. I often wondered how many Navy corpsmen were convinced that they had it made, that they were going to live the life of Riley until they suddenly discovered one day that they had orders to a Marine unit. The mortality rate among corpsmen assigned to Marine units was exceptionally high.

In 1965, I was assigned to the LPD USS Vancouver, a landing platform dock whose first mission was to take the Marine's 7th Engineer Battalion to Vietnam. There the 7th was expected to extend the airstrip at Da Nang. We loaded everything except the troops from the beach at Camp Pendleton, and among the equipment we loaded onto the LPD was a rock crusher. They brought it out on an LCM, short for landing craft medium, and tried to load it onto the well deck of the LPD, and we almost lost it. The crusher nearly fell into the sea when one of the cables broke as the LCM backed away from our tailgate. So, they took the rock crusher back to shore and loaded it on a MIKE boat, an amphibious equipment transport. Then they brought the MIKE boat, rock crusher and all, right onto the LPD and set sail for Vietnam.

After a few days at sea, the seamen discovered that a bird, probably a meadowlark, had a nest in the rock crusher. So, for the entire trip over to WESTPAC, they kept that bird fed so it would live and could feed its young, too. Otherwise, a land bird like that would never have survived at sea.

We were in a hurry to get to Vietnam so we took the Great Circle Route [Bill laughs]. We had fog and icebergs, but fortunately, we didn't hit any of them. We stopped in Yokosuka, Japan, long enough to refuel and then went on to Vietnam. There we offloaded the engineers and their equipment at Da Nang.

From there, we got orders to go to Subic Bay in the Philippines. The Navy had shipped a bunch of MIKE boats from Yokosuka to Subic Bay for further transportation to Da Nang where the River Command was going to use them as patrol boats.

During WWII, the Navy had two kinds of landing craft: the PAPA boats, which just carried troops, and the MIKE boats, which were larger and could carry vehicles. The folks in Yokosuka were supposed to have rehabbed these MIKE boats and gotten them into good condition, but they must have run out of time. All the way from Subic to the Mekong River near Saigon, the gunner's mates were busy getting the .50 caliber machineguns into condition, and the engineers were busy getting the engines on the boats working again.

Next, we went up to Okinawa, loaded a battalion of Marines, and came down to one of the islands south of Luzon for a practice landing. Then we went back over to Vietnam and offloaded them at Da Nang. Finally they let us head back to the states. What should have been at most a three-week deployment ended up almost three months.

After being back in San Diego for a short period, we headed out to WESTPAC again with an LSD and a helicopter carrier called, the Iwo Jima. We took a battalion of Marines with us from Camp Pendleton and again went to this island south of Luzon for a practice landing. Then we'd go up and down the coast of Vietnam, wherever Intelligence told us Charlie was working, and make a landing to try to destroy as much of Charlie as we could. We did this a few times and then loaded them back aboard ship, took them down to Da Nang where we offloaded them and left them there. Then, it was back to Okinawa to pick up another battalion and start the whole drill again.

We didn't lose many Marines in combat, but we always lost some. They were mostly Marines who had just come out of boot camp and schools, so they were green troops. I'm sure that always contributed to the losses we had.

When we returned to San Diego my tour of duty was up and I was assigned to the Marine Corps Recruit Depot in San Diego. I had one of the recruit battalions for about a year and then went over to the School Command, also for about a year. Besides conducting services every Sunday in the theater, I also led a class of lay leaders. We'd try to teach them how to conduct a worship service and what materials they would need. The boys who participated, all volunteers, were dedicated Christians themselves.

While I was at the Marine Recruit Depot, I had a clerk who had been at the Marine Corps base at Khe Sanh. He had been wounded three times and Marine Corps policy was that anyone who had been wounded three times got to leave Vietnam—he had bought his ticket home. He was never seriously wounded, but a wound was a wound was a wound. Why they sent Marines to Khe Sanh I don't know. He told me about some of his experiences. He said, *All you did was dig in and pray that you'd survive the next mortar or artillery barrage.* It got to the point where the C-131s transport planes would not land there. They'd come in low, drop their rear door, and just parachute the equipment and supplies to the ground. One day a chopper landed to pick up mail and troops that were leaving. Just as they were ready to take off, a mortar exploded right next to the chopper, killing everybody aboard.

I was at the Marine Recruit Depot for about 20 months when I got orders to Vietnam and ended up over there with the Force Logistics Command in Da Nang. I was assigned to an ammo company, which was located just across the road from the Marine Ammo Dump and the Air Force Ammo Dump. I also had responsibility for the military police battalion and the 3rd Marine Division brig, both of which were located near us, and the R&R Center down at the airstrip, probably ¾ of a mile away. The latter wasn't very demanding. Primarily, I'd go down there before the boys would go out on their R&R tour.

We got one week of R&R to Singapore, Hong Kong, wherever we wanted to go. When it was my turn, I met Betty in Hawaii, but we were short-changed. My plane took off from Vietnam and stopped in Guam to refuel. As we took off again, number four engine caught on fire, so we circled and landed again. We had to sit there for 24 hours while they flew another engine in from Hawaii. As a result, we were about 36 hours late getting to Hawaii and meeting Betty. I requested an extension of my R&R but the Navy said negative, so I just ended up with less time with my frau.

We had USO groups that came to Vietnam fairly regularly from Australia and the states. One year at Christmas, Ozzie Hoffman came over. They had a gathering for him in an area of the Air Force base in Da Nang. The command was worried sick because when you gather that many people in one place, you're inviting a mortar barrage. Fortunately, there was no attack.

While I was assigned to the Force Logistics Command, the trash detail would gather up refuse everyday and dump their collections just south of the Air Force Ammo Dump. Then the locals would come up and fish through the piles for any salvageable materials they could find. After that, the trash detail put a match to whatever was left. One Sunday the wind was blowing pretty hard and when they burned, some papers blew across the road into the grass where the Air Force ammo dump was located. The grass there looked green but underneath it was dry as it could be, and that stuff started burning. It was just a hoot and a holler from there to where a group of civilians from Crane Ammunition Company were rehabbing mortar rounds.

I was conducting a service in the nearby MP Battalion Chapel when we heard these booms go off. That wasn't at all unusual for Vietnam, so we didn't pay much attention to it. But finally, the colonel got up and walked outside. Pretty soon, he came back in and said, "Chaplain, you'd better secure the service. We've got a fire going across the street."

So I did and headed back across the road to my own unit. By this time, the fire was totally out of control. As the fire advanced to a berm where ammo was stored, it eventually got hot enough to explode the ammunition inside. The fire just kept advancing from berm to berm. After a couple of berms of ammo had gone off, the camp CO decided we needed to get out of there, so we abandoned our camp and went north. Whenever a berm would go up, you could always tell it. You could feel the heat from a ¼ mile away. When you heard the explosion and felt that heat, you knew you'd better get down on your belly or the ensuing concussion would blow you down.

We had to take a road around to the 7th Communications Battalion who were further away from the dump, a ½ mile as opposed to a ¼. The reason we couldn't move further away than that was because then we'd have been outside the compound and in even greater danger from Charlie than we were from the explosions at the dump. The CO told me to get my driver, go over there, and tell the skipper that we were all coming over to join him. I got my driver, Fred, and we drove over. As we were going in the front gate, an 81mm mortar round was lying not more that eight or ten feet from the guardhouse, and here was the guard with a fire extinguisher, one of the little portable kind. He was out there spraying that round, trying to keep it cool so it wouldn't blow. I thought to myself, man if that thing blows, he's gone and we're gone, too. But it didn't blow. That round had been propelled over there when a berm had blown ½ mile away!

I got hold of the CO and told him he was getting visitors. Finally, trucks brought all our people over and we set up on a concrete slab behind a building so we'd be out of the line of fire from the ammo dump. All night long, those berms blew. Every once in a while, we'd hear a whirring noise, a 250-pound bomb flying over us. The next morning when it got daylight, we could look around and see these 250-pound bombs lying all over the place. None of them ever went off! If they had, it would have been devastating, or if one had hit the building we were hiding behind, we'd probably have been wiped out.

It was amazing. The only casualty we had that night was a Marine who was walking perimeter guard carrying his M-16 rifle. A piece of shrapnel came down, knocked the butt off his weapon, and also hit his arm. It was as if someone had taken a real sharp knife and had just gone along the back of his forearm peeling off the skin. It went wrist to elbow, shearing off all the skin, but didn't break a bone. They called for a helo to take him to the Navy hospital, but the helos weren't flying and they weren't about to operate in that blast area. We were very lucky that was the only casualty we had.

On the other side of the Marine Corps Ammo Dump was a Navy Shore Party Battalion. They had one casualty, too. A young kid was sitting inside a bunker when a mortar round flew in the entrance and decapitated him.

After the ammo dump incident ended, there wasn't a building standing back at our camp except the chapel, one of the closest buildings to the blast area. Our hooch, where the officers were quartered, was right beside the chapel and it had burned to the ground. The chapel had been built by the SEABEES at some point prior to my arrival in Vietnam, and they had put up a brick crown behind the altar. On the altar was the standard Navy cross. One of the blasts had knocked that brick crown down and it had taken that three-foot metal cross and bent the top of it over, as if by giant hands. I took the cross and presented it to the senior chaplain.

I used to go down to the Naval hospital, which was a cluster of elephant Quonsets all sandbagged up to try to protect the staff and patients. Charlie never paid much attention to the Geneva Convention and they were good with their mortars. Before I got to Da Nang, they mortared the camp where I ended up. A mortar round had hit the top of the chapel and sprayed shrapnel all through the roof. There were still little, black metal fragments all over the pews when I got there.

Anyway, I'd go down to the hospital once a week to conduct a Lutheran communion service. When I went down, I'd usually stop by the chaplain's office to pay my respects and let him know that I was there. There were casualties who had just been brought in, members of our company. A tanker truck had hit a land mine and exploded. Over the intercom came a page requesting the chaplain report to the Emergency Room. He was already busy out at the triage center, so I went over to the ER to cover for him. They had two boys lying out on wooden tables. The gas tanks on the truck had caught fire and two boys were burned to where their skin was just like cinders. I said a prayer with them, although I'm not at all sure that they had any consciousness at all of what I was doing.

A few days later, I ended up holding memorial services for both of these boys. I went through each boy's personnel file as I prepared for the services. It was only then that I became aware that one boy was white and the other was black. When I had seen them stretched out on the tables earlier, there was just no way to tell, they were so badly injured.

I often conducted memorial services as a result of some strange occurrences. For example, we had a section of our ammo company who had a separate ammo dump and they had some of those ammo carriers, mules I think they were called. They were sort of like a jeep, only they had no passenger compartment. They were just a motorized platform for hauling ammo, with a place in one corner for the driver to sit. I had to hold a memorial service for some turkey who played with one of those mules, driving wild and wooly, when the thing rolled over and killed him.

Not long after that I got transferred over to the office of the senior chaplain. We had a Catholic chaplain, the first chaplain, and myself. There were two things that were never burned or thrown away: One was the Styrofoam casings from ammo containers because it could be used as insulating materiel, and the other was the parachutes that flares were attached to. When you shot a flare, to keep that flare in the air longer, it had a chute on it so the flare would float slowly back down to the ground and keep the area illuminated longer. We used the chutes to hold the Styrofoam in place along the walls and ceilings of our building. We had air conditioning in the hooch where our office was and the Styrofoam helped keep it cooler. You used anything you could—you learned to be resourceful.

When I was aboard ship off the coast of Vietnam, I'd ride a helo to shore and abscond with as many copies of *Stars & Stripes* as I could lay my hands on because we didn't get any aboard ship. That's where I learned how to supply myself. You might go through official channels and wait 10 years to get the material, but with the Marines I learned that you took what you could get wherever you could get it.

The Army was a good source of supply. I learned all I knew from a gunnery sergeant who had been a POW during WWII. He'd start out in the morning with a six-by-six truck, and he'd go out and visit Army camps. He'd come back with that big truck absolutely loaded with paint, tools, or whatever he needed. He never had a single requisition. That's how I learned how to survive.

I was at the 7th Division HQ for eight or 10 months, and then got orders to leave. That was in 1970. Word evidently had come down for the division to prepare to leave Vietnam. In one of my last jobs there I went around and determined how many cubic feet of space we would need to embark all of our gear and equipment. Fortunately, I wasn't there when they actually did it. I was glad to leave—I didn't leave anything behind [Bill laughs].

From there, I got orders to the 1st Training Regiment at Camp Lejeune, North Carolina. We got Marines when they graduated from boot camp. Those who were going to be grunts came to the 1st Regiment for eight weeks of additional training, while those who were scheduled to go to another school came to the 1st for only four weeks. The chapel seated 450 men and we had troops seated up in the chancel area, in the passageways, everywhere. Afterward, I'd walk through the empty chapel, and here and there would be puddles of water where some fellow couldn't hold it anymore.

We knew that these men were possibly headed for Vietnam. It was one of the most rewarding periods that I had in the service because there was an excellent opportunity to share the gospel message with them. Those guys were receptive!

Back during the Korean War, on the troop ships that took the Marines to Korea, our worship services were always packed. On the troop ships that brought the Marines back to the states from Korea, services were very lightly attended. The same things happened when we shuttled troops to and from Vietnam.

The 1st Regiment was broken down into three battalions. Two of the battalions were mainside, and the third was out in the bush commanded by a guy with an Italian name, and that name escapes me. He had stepped on an anti-personnel mine in Vietnam and lost a foot. They fitted him with an artificial one and he fought like everything to stay on active duty, so they let him. He was a lieutenant colonel at that time and he was good. At eight o'clock every Sunday morning, I had a service out there in the bush with that third battalion and then I'd come mainside for the other service.

One night, I got a call from sickbay asking me to come quickly. I went up there, and there was a Seabee sitting on a chair and on a stretcher next to him, covered up with a blanket, was another Seabee, dead. The one who was alive had shot the other Seabee, a good buddy of his, because they had been smoking pot. The pot in Vietnam was potent. They had gotten into an argument over who would be first to avail themselves of the services of a prostitute they had met. The argument reached the point where one of them pulled a .45 and shot the other one dead.

So, whenever I read or hear that pot is a harmless narcotic, drug, or whatever you want to call it, I just shake my head.

The marijuana in Vietnam was grown locally and the Vietnamese knew that the GIs and the Marines would buy it from them. I'm sure one of the reasons this happened was that they wanted to forget the realities of where they were and what they had to do.

War is still war and to me it's tragic that we lost as many men as we did for a cause that I feel was not worth it. The Vietnam Army was poorly led, poorly trained, and poorly motivated. I think the average Vietnamese couldn't have cared less who was telling him where he could live, and what he could do and not do. When we left, you know what happened: they just plain folded.

To me, Vietnam was a waste of manpower and money because we were not in there to win that war. I couldn't say anything at the time—especially being an officer—I had to keep my mouth shut. Nothing has happened since then to change my opinion. But I'd do it again. One of the most difficult periods of time that I had was during Desert Storm knowing that I wasn't going to get to go along.

In 1970, Bill Ude went to Camp Lejeune for duty. Upon retirement from there in 1972, he and his family moved to Greeley, CO, where he attended graduate school, acquiring a master's degree in psychology and counseling. He then served Grace Lutheran Church in Killeen, Texas, from 1975 to 1989. In 1989, he retired from the ministry but occasionally filled pastoral vacancies in nearby congregations. In 1995, he and his family moved to North Carolina where he still answers the call to fill pastoral vacancies in neighboring congregations.

CHAPTER 7
NAVY LIEUTENANT WALT WALTER

Fixed Wing Pilot

There were revetments just down from Operations and I pulled into an opening and parked. Another guy from my squadron, an Air Force captain, was parked a couple of spaces down from me. The bullets were flying and I could see the tracers flying all over the place. There were young Air Force officers with me. One of them said, "Sir, what are we going to do?" I said, "Well, let's find a foxhole and dig it deeper!"

*H*oward *"Walt" Walter grew up in Buffalo, New York, graduating from Buffalo Technical High School. From there he went to Purdue University and then into the Navy. He took pilot training in Pensacola, Florida, as a Naval aviation cadet, earning his wings in December 1954. Walt served intermittently in Vietnam 1961-64.*

The first time I went to Vietnam in 1961, I was a lieutenant. The last time I left there in 1964, I was a commander.

My tour in the Philippines ran from 1961-1963 and included frequent trips to Vietnam. Our admiral had jurisdiction over one of the commands in Vietnam, an administrative unit that took care of in and out personnel processing. In those days there weren't but a few advisors over there, so it wasn't that much of deal. The first time I flew into Vietnam, I was part of a team escorting four Army Mohawks across the South China Sea, about a 600-mile trip each way. I flew a C-47 attached to Sangly Point Naval Station. That was my first actual mission in-country where we did something for the war effort. Other times we were just escorting the admiral on inspections and things like that.

We had 40 advisors over there; some were in the field and some were Seabees. The Seabees had five or six people out in the countryside. They had one medical corpsman with them and they were doing civil liaison with the Vietnamese civilians, teaching them such things as how to dig wells and irrigate their crops. The medical guy would try to help them with minor afflictions and teach them things like boiling water in order to avoid diseases. The Seabees were trying to bring civilization, or at least a higher form of it, to the civilians, all this in an effort to get the people on our side. The other advisors over there were there to help the ARVN aviation folks fly and maintain their F-8F Bearcats. We had some Army troops up there, also in an advisory capacity.

Once, we took the admiral to Jakarta, Indonesia, and were intercepted by a MiG. They forced us to land, whereupon they had a big civil demonstration against us, saying that we had cameras on our airplane and that we were taking pictures of their military bases. We did and we were! We had cameras and we were taking pictures, but you couldn't tell because we had ports that slid open and closed to conceal the cameras.

That night, they burned the British Embassy right across the street from where we were staying, I guess just to impress us. All this was when Sukharno was head of the country and they were trying to throw him out. There was a lot of civil disobedience and civil discontent with Sukharno. Shortly after that, Suharto led a military coup and took over Indonesia.

During those two years in the Philippines, I didn't have much to do with Vietnam other than taking the admiral back and forth occasionally, and that one Mohawk escort mission. There was a place called the Iron Triangle, which is up northwest of Saigon. It really was loaded with VC, and that's where the Elephant Factory was located, about 20 miles inside the Iron Triangle.

The Elephant Factory made porcelain elephants that could be used as end tables or coffee tables. We had people who drove up there to buy elephants at the factory. They took their lives in their hands but they probably didn't know it. Those were senior Navy officers, captains and above, who should have known better. At about this time, 1963, the VC were putting a price on the heads of US military officers. The going price on lieutenants and below was $25; lieutenant commanders and above were worth $40.

I had another mission, in Laos (I'm probably one of the few people to fly into Laos), to help dismantle the military advisory group in Vientiane.

Later I participated in Project Handclasp. What we did, openly, was collect sample drugs and library books and package them up. In those days, the military would deliver those items to towns that might need a library or medicine. I delivered some of that stuff.

I also delivered some huge crates that had the Project Handclasp symbol on them, but you've got to understand that this project was a CIA cover, also. They claimed there were library books in those crates. I tore one of the cases open once and it was actually filled with rocket pods that were used on their T-28 aircraft to fight the communist bloc that was in Laos at that time.

Once, while stationed in the Philippines, I got a phone call advising me that we were going to have an intelligence briefing on Cambodia the next day. A guy walks into the briefing wearing a lieutenant commander's uniform.

We started asking him questions, like, *What do you do?*

"I'm a reserve on my two weeks active duty."

Bullshit!

What do you do in life?

"I work with AID."

When he said AID, that's the same thing as saying Project Handclasp. The CIA was involved. He was in Cambodia as a civilian but he came to the Philippines in uniform and gave us a briefing on Cambodia. While there, the CIA came in and debriefed him, passed him additional information, and then he went back to Cambodia. That's what it was about.

There were three factions in Cambodia at that time: one side favorable to the US, one to the communists, and a third faction that was fighting both of those groups. Brothers headed the latter two groups, that is, one man headed the communists and his brother headed the third faction. The third faction, led by Major Kong Lee, wanted to throw both of the other groups out of the country. We weren't sure if Major Lee would have been favorable to the US if he had gained power. He wasn't part of the government but he wasn't a communist either. We were supplying the government with T-28s and other equipment as part of Project Handclasp, but we tried to curry favor with Lee, too, just in case he did win.

In 1963, Walt went back to the States and got assigned to the aircraft carrier USS Independence. Soon, his eyes weakened requiring him to wear corrective lenses. Wearing glasses disqualified him from taking off and landing on a carrier, so Walt found himself attached to the Air Force and assigned to Sewart Air Force Base in Smyrna, Tennessee, flying C-130 cargo planes.

When I flew off the carriers, I flew a Skyraider, a single-engine attack bomber. Regarding flying to and from a carrier, I have to agree with Doctor Laura: It's easy taking off—it's the landing that's hard! I didn't fly many bombing runs in Vietnam because there wasn't much going on back then. We didn't do much close air support, mostly alfa strikes against, targets like schools, churches, and hospitals [Walt laughs]. I'm kidding of course, but they (the VC) were always accusing our pilots of doing just that. All the electrical substations were usually right next door so, whenever you bombed a substation, the collateral damage was always to a school, church, or hospital. Likewise, there were always Russian ships in the harbor and we had orders not to bomb the Russian ships, just the adjacent warehouses. The guys would bomb the warehouses all right, but they always made sure that the run was *toward* the Russian ships so that anything that exploded would splatter onto the Russian ships. The Canadians had ships there during the war, too, and they got damaged occasionally in the same way although we tried to avoid that.

There was a recent case of some Air Force F-16 fighter pilots who accidentally wiped out some Canadian troops training on the ground in Afghanistan. It turns out the pilots were on amphetamines, supposedly a standard and approved practice so that they could stay alert during the long flights to and from the targets. I think that anybody who would take drugs and then fly a high performance aircraft is a fool! Anything that takes away from your concentration is not worth it. You'll be putting your life on the line every time. We certainly didn't do it.

The Air Force operated under a different set of rules than the Navy. The Navy had a ship, a carrier air group, and a squadron commander. The orders came down from the fleet commander and he'd say, "These are going to be your targets," or "This is going to be your mission." From there, it was up to the CAG and the squadrons to plan the mission and fly it. The CAG was usually out there leading the bunch, right on the scene. So, if there was any question and one of his pilots says, "I've got a target and I've identified it as such-and-such. Do I have permission to fire?" The CAG is only about two miles away and makes the decision on the spot.

The Air Force didn't have anybody right there. They had to call the AWACS, and the AWACS called back to the headquarters where the wing planning took place to ask them if they could give permission to fire on the target. The word had to come from the HQ, back to the AWACS, and then back to the pilot. In one such case, a pilot was taking fire that appeared to be directed toward him. In the dark, it's one-dimensional— your depth perception doesn't tell you whether such fire is coming at you or going away from you. It's hard to distinguish.

That's the difference in how the Air Force and the Navy operated. The Air Force pilot could over-fly the target or be shot down before he can get permission to fire himself. In the Navy, the guy who did the planning was right there on the mission. He could even be leading the mission and could say yes or no right then; he didn't need to involve anyone else in the decision.

The CAG would tell the flyers, "You're going to provide such-and-such for the mission." The flyers would go back and plan it, even down to the final details. The squadron commander would talk to his operations officer and ask, "Who's going to fly this mission?" The operations officer would say, "We'll have the planes ready for them when they get up to the flight deck."

In the Air Force, the squadron had to call into the wing and say, "Pete, Jones, and Smitty are going to fly two days from now and they're going to fly tail numbers 125, 126, and 127." They provided the plane numbers and put out the schedule. When the mission came up, that's what had to go. If that pilot or that airplane was unavailable, they scratched the mission. They couldn't substitute.

The Navy didn't do that. If Pete got sick, Bill, who was sitting in on the briefing, was usually on the ready airplane. He just sat there and waited. If one of the mission planes failed, then the ready plane was launched to avoid scrubbing the mission or flying one plane short. There could have been as many as one ready plane for every two mission aircraft, but the normal ratio was one for four.

The Air Force didn't use the ready plane concept so, if one of their mission aircraft or pilots was unavailable, they had to scrap the mission or fly a plane short. I think the Navy was more flexible in that respect. The people down on a lower level knew what was going on because they'd been in on the planning.

Another difference: Let's say we had just come off a mission where we'd bombed a petroleum factory. Someone might call up and ask if any Navy guys are on this radio frequency, and we'd acknowledge that we were. Then he might say, "We're under attack. Have you got any ordnance that you could use to give us some support?" If so, we'd ask where they were and to send up a flare so we could tell their exact location. Then they might ask us to come in from the southwest so as to shoot over the top of them at the target. We'd occasionally ask why they didn't ask the Air Force for support. The answer was usually something like, "We called them, and they said they'd put us on the schedule for tomorrow!"

True stories. All planning in the Air Force was done at such a high level. The wing commanders did the planning. The second time over there [in Vietnam], I flew with the Air Force so I know whereof I speak.

Sometimes we flew out of Tan Son Nhut and sometimes we flew out of Da Nang. We flew to such exotic places as Phan Rang, Quy Nhon, Cam Ranh Bay, and a few other places further south. One time I flew into Quy Nhon and took fire on our approach to the airfield. They blew out the number-four engine on my C-130. The field itself was under attack when I landed.

The Skyraiders were actually taking off with their ordnance, leaving the gear down, making a turn of about 30 degrees and at the end and just to the left of the runway was a huge mound. I won't call it a mountain—it was a mound 600-700 feet high. On the backside of this mound were VC who were lobbing mortars over the mound onto the airfield.

We were parked over next to the fence watching the Skyraiders take off, drop their ordnance, turn down-wind and land, taxi up, take on more ordnance, and take off again. It was like a five-minute flight.

When the fighting died down, I went over and talked to the operations officer. I told him, "I've got to get this plane out of here and get it fixed. Where's the best place to go to go to get it fixed?" He replied that Clark was the closest place, about a 600-mile hop.

But the Air Force had rules that you couldn't fly without first getting permission from the duty officer. I called him, and you've got to remember where the duty officer was. He was in Smyrna, Tennessee! I called him on my high frequency radio and told him I was going to make a three-engine take-off.

He said, "You can't do that!"

"I know I can't. You're supposed to give me permission."

He said, "I can't give you permission."

"Why not?" I asked.

"It's too dangerous," he said.

We went on and on until finally I said, "Look, I'm going to take off anyway; it's either that or lose this airplane because this field is under attack. There are mortar rounds in-coming and they're bombing all over the place. The only way is to get this airplane out of here so I'm going to take off on three engines."

"Oh," he said, "then it's your responsibility, commander. I'm not taking responsibility for that. You're doing it on your own."

I said, "Yeah, I'm doing it on my own."

Then he tried to tell me how to fly the airplane, which was ridiculous. This guy is 10,000 miles away trying to tell me how to fly this airplane! I guess that, because of the bad engine, he thought I needed additional instruction.

I took off on three engines. Quy Nhon had only about a 5300-foot airstrip so I had to use a special technique. I got on the left side of the runway and lined up to run off the right side of the runway about halfway down. So, as I added power to the aircraft, I started feeding in the number-one engine, which gave me a swerve to the left. By the time I got halfway down, I was on the right edge of the runway. But the power I fed the number-one engine, which is on the right wing, caused the plane to arc to the left. As a result, I got airborne at the left edge of the runway by doing a big arc from left side of the runway to the right, and then back to left again. I couldn't control the plane with full power on three engines—it would have just pulled off to the left. I fed the number-one engine in as I gained speed and, since I was pointed to the right, it compensated by pulling to the left.

I got it airborne and climbed out of there. I don't remember who was controlling airspace at that time, but I radioed them that I was switching to Clark Air Base since that's where I was going to get the engine fixed. I called Clark and told them I was coming in on three engines.

They said, "We're going to launch search-and-rescue."

I said, "Don't bother; I took off with three engines."

They couldn't believe that. They were all unglued that I didn't want search-and-rescue to come get me.

I landed at Clark and got the plane fixed.

About three months later, I got back to Smyrna, Tennessee, and the same guy had the duty that I had talked to when taking off on three engines. As soon as I walked in, he saw my name on my uniform and said, "Now don't get mad, commander. I put you in for an air medal." He thought that would make me less of a violent person with him.

That is just an example of what was so frustrating about the way the Air Force operated. You were so restricted because everything you did had to be by the book. If the book wouldn't let you do something, you had to call the duty officer. Aboard ship, on the other hand, you just called the CAG, who is right next door. You told him what you wanted to do and he'd probably say, "Go do it."

That might have been about the most exciting time I had in Vietnam.

Another time, I came under attack in Da Nang. We had flown in during the middle of the night. Anybody who was ever in Da Nang will tell you that they never did clear out the VC from the south end of the runway. They were always shooting at us when we came in to land and the Marines, who were in charge of base security, would start shooting back.

We got to Da Nang, but that particular night the VC were on *both* sides of the runway instead of just off the end. They were shooting across the runway at us, lobbing in mortars, and stuff like that. There were revetments just down from operations and I pulled into an opening and parked. Another guy from my squadron, an Air Force captain, was parked a couple of spaces down from me. The bullets are flying and I could see the tracers flying all over the place. There were young Air Force officers with me. One of them said, "Sir, what are we going to do?"

I said, "Well, let's find a foxhole and dig it deeper!"

We found a foxhole between the revetments and the taxiway, and jumped in behind the sandbags. The Navy had given me a .38 and I always carried it, so I pulled it out. The Air Force would never issue me a sidearm. I also had a box of ammo in my pocket—50 rounds.

These kids looked at me and said, "Sir, what are we going to do if we're overrun?"

I said, "We're going to be in trouble. Where are your pistols?'

"We don't have any," they replied.

What do you mean, you don't have any pistols?

"We've never had any pistol training."

I said, "That's too bad but, if we're overrun, I'll try to shoot as many of them as I can and take them with me, but that's about all we can do."

They dug the foxhole a little deeper.

All this took place in the space of 5-10 minutes. The next thing I heard was a C-130 starting up and I'm wondering what the hell was going on. I stuck my head up out of the foxhole and looked over to see that Captain Studley had started up his airplane. He taxied out to the end of the runway, turned out all his lights, and took off. I'm watching all the tracers. As soon as he started up his plane, they started shooting at him. All the tracers are going toward him.

I hated to see Studley do this but, on the other hand, what a nice guy to take all the fire away from us!

About that time, a mortar went off and blew up an F-4 that was parked between my plane and where Studley's had been. The Marines finally got out there and chased the VC away—I don't know if they got too many of them but they made them leave. It calmed down and we got back to our normal routine.

The next day, I went down to Phan Rang and there was Studley. I walked over to him and I said, "Studley, what were you thinking about last night up at Da Nang?"

He said, "I really didn't know what to do. I was scared to death and I thought that the only thing I could do was get out of there."

I said well, you know my crew wants to thank you for taking all the fire and we really appreciate it. How many bullet-holes did you wind up with in your airplane?

"I think they only found 11."

I said, "You asshole! One of those could have been for you. Now tell me, you got a DFC for that, right?"

"How did you know?" he smiled.

The squadron put him in for a DFC for saving that airplane, for doing something stupid, really stupid.

I asked the kids who were with me if they wanted to go to lunch and invited Studley to go along. So, we jumped in the back of a pickup truck and a guy handed each of us an M-1 carbine and some ammunition. I loaded mine but the kids with me were saying, "Sir, we don't know how to load this thing. We've never even touched one."

Jeez!

Studley asked an Air Force sergeant, "What do we need guns for? We're just going to the mess hall."

It was about six miles to the mess hall.

The sergeant replied, "There are VC on the road between here and the mess hall."

"Here's your M-1 carbine back," said Studley. "I'm not hungry!"

You talk about small arms training, these kids had nothing. I'd fired all kinds of weapons in my life: .50-caliber machineguns, M-1s, M-60s, you name it. I had some working knowledge so an M-1 carbine was nothing to me. But those kids hardly knew what a bullet was and they were military officers. When they got back to Smyrna, Tennessee, you should have seen their sudden interest in getting small arms-qualified. They were peaked.

I got assigned as a flight instructor in Meridian, Mississippi, after returning from Nam. I went from flying C-130s back to flying single-engine jets. I could always fly single-engine but I couldn't fly on a carrier because I had to wear glasses. John McCain, now a US senator from Arizona, was a flight instructor in the same squadron with me just before he got shipped out to Nam. I remember some of the guys in the squadron were still talking about it and said that the war would be over in two weeks because John would talk them out of it [Walt laughs]. Shortly thereafter, I think within two years, he got shot down.

When I first went to Vietnam, I was very naïve about it. I believed that our government was doing everything right. I felt that the government was running the war, that they were behind us, and that they were doing the right thing. I really didn't know for sure.

But when I got out of it, I found out that we weren't doing it right at all, that we were really screwed up. It wasn't the military. It was the government that screwed it up. I really became perturbed about that. It was ridiculous. My cousin Colin and his brother were both pilots, one flew a Phantom and the other flew a Crusader. Colin was a photoreconnaissance pilot. I never talked to Colin much during the war, but afterward we had a family get-together at another cousin's place. Colin and I were in the backyard talking and he started talking about things.

He said, "Here's what was happening. We'd take the pictures and then transmit them back to Washington. President Johnson, Robert McNamara or Clark Clifford (secretaries of defense), and one other guy who escapes my memory would go down in the basement of the White House. They'd look at the photos and decide what our targets were going to be for the next day or the day after that. Then they'd send a message out to the fleet saying which targets to attack."

I said, "You've got to be kidding me! You mean to tell me that the President of the United States was involved in picking the targets we were bombing?"

"You're damn right he was!" said Colin. "That's exactly what was happening."

My whole opinion of the war changed because Colin put me onto two books [*The Ten Thousand Day War: Vietnam, 1945-1975* by Michael Maclear and *Vietnam: A History* by Stanley Karnow], which I still have. He said, "Read those two books and they'll tell you the true story of what really was happening."

After the war, I became knowledgeable about what was really going on. I hadn't been really involved in the planning and in what was going on in the transmission of data and how things were going. Some of the things I knew were happening but was not involved in directly. If you'll remember, we had a number of cease-fires and stop-the-bombing campaigns. The guys out on the ships just hated that because they had just bombed like hell for three or four days while the NVA had thrown up everything they had at them. They'd shot SAMs, they'd shot 137mm, and all that crap at us. And after about three days, they'd get a puff here and a puff there, and that'd be about it. They (the NVA) didn't have much left.

Our guys would say, "Oh man, we're home free now."

Then they'd get orders to stop the bombing. The photo recon pilots, like my cousin Colin, would fly over and take pictures while there was no bombing going on. He'd come back and report that all the trails looked like they were covered with little ants. It was the NVA carrying shells to re-supply all those anti-aircraft and SAMs sites.

Then, five or six days or a week later, the President would make a decision to start bombing again. All the people in the Ready Room would groan, "Oh my God, not again!"

The first day, the NVA would throw everything but the kitchen sink at them again. What a demoralizing thing for the troops. I didn't get involved with it that much because I wasn't out there. I was back in Washington for part of that time. It was stupid when you had the Commander in Chief, the Secretary of Defense, and advisors at the White House making decisions on what targets you were going to bomb in Vietnam when the Fleet Commander or the Commander in Chief, Pacific, should have been making that decision.

In addition, they'd put restrictions on us, like we couldn't bomb up near the Red River because we'd wipe out the rice crops—they didn't want to starve the people. That's BS! If you want to win the war, you do whatever you have to do to win it.

You may remember John Walker, the Lieutenant Commander who got arrested for spying in 1985. He had a cohort, a chief petty officer who was a communications guy. They were stealing the codes and giving it to the communists and Chinese.

People just kind of pooh-poohed that and said, "Oh, nobody was hurt."

Well, we don't *know* how many people were hurt or died because of what those two did. I personally had an experience where I could have been one of the casualties of that particular thing. I came down through the straits between Hainan Island off the Chinese coast and the Philippines. I was flying a C-130 and talking to a communications station, supposedly in the Philippines. They gave me a clearance to change altitude.

Well, I'd been listening to radio traffic pretty closely and I knew that there was another plane at that altitude coming from the other direction. So, I called them back and asked them for an authentication code, the stuff Walker was giving to the communists. I gave them the code to authenticate this challenge, and they came back and authenticated with a code that was two days old. So, I gave them a second chance, challenging them again. They came back again with old codes. I called back and advised them I was disregarding their last clearance.

I was pretty sure that it was a Chinese or NVA communist, speaking good English, talking on my frequency, and trying to run me into that other airplane.

Like I say, some folks think Walker was a great guy, that he was a spy who didn't do much damage. Well, that's BS! How many people were killed that we don't know about? If I hadn't been paying attention, I could have run right into that other C-130 and had a midair collision. Whose fault would it have been? The Navy might have decided that it was either my fault or the air controller's, but Walker would have been the real culprit because he gave the secret codes to the communists.

I went to school with a South Vietnamese naval officer. He and I were good friends, so I already had an insight into what was going on. When I'd go to Saigon, he and I would get together for dinner. I'd studied about Vietnam before I got there when I was at the Naval Post-Graduate School in Monterrey, California. I don't think it was required, but I took a course on the countries of southeast Asia because I knew I was going over there.

I'd been in the Philippines for two years and other places around the world just like it, so Vietnam was no different except there was a war going on. If you've been to Singapore, for example, it's quite a metropolis and people live fairly well. There are nice homes and nice buildings. Of course, you still have slums and poor areas. It's not like Saigon, which is very small and most of it's poor-looking.

Regarding morale in my unit, they were fat, dumb, and happy. The planes were flying, nobody was getting killed, and they didn't know people were shooting at them for real. Take Captain Studley, for example. Those bullets didn't mean anything to him. He didn't fully comprehend that someone was trying to *kill* him.

Let me do a little namedropping here: I knew Pappy Boyington. I used to drink with him back in the days when he was a professional wrestling referee. He'd come into the Officer's Club on Tuesday afternoons.

I've got to tell you another story, a real doozie. It'll give you a feeling for what the military was like in those days, particularly the Navy.

I was at the fighter club on Miramar Naval Air Station, California, just outside San Diego. We'd been out on the range teaching combat pistol shooting to some of the Naval aviators. After we got done, we went across the road to the Air Station Officer's Club. We were sitting there drinking a few beers and there was a lieutenant standing at the bar near us. He started talking and his group was close enough that I could hear their conversation (I didn't have hearing aids in those days!). They started talking about combat fatigue. They were flying off one of the carriers or a cruiser. Anyway, he was a helicopter pilot.

He said, "Oh yeah, we had to send my crewman back because of battle fatigue."

The guys he was talking to said, "Oh yeah, what happened?"

"Our job was to fly over and rake the junks that were cruising along the coast," he explained. "We had to see whether they had contraband onboard. Anyway, we came into a hover and flew along with a junk, which was going about five or six miles and hour. They started shooting at us! My crewman had a Garand and he started shooting back, killing a couple of guys on the junk. That's why he had battle fatigue, because he'd killed somebody, and we had to send him back to the states."

And then he made the most stupid statement a military person has ever made. He said, "We really didn't want to kill them. We only were trying to get them to jump off the junk."

I said to myself, *Walt, sit down, don't say anything, bite your tongue, and mind your own business.* I grabbed my glass, sipped my beer, and tried to ignore this kid.

Well, the crowd changed. Twenty minutes later, the kid tells the same story and when he comes to the final punch line, "Yeah, we weren't trying to kill them. We were only trying to get them to jump off the junk," I jumped up and got in his face.

I just couldn't take it anymore. I said, "You know something lieutenant? You're absolutely right. You were trying to get them to jump off the junk and they were shooting at you to get you to jump out of that helicopter."

I didn't say that they were trying to kill him, but I implied it.

I turned around and sat back down before he had a chance to answer me.

He stood there for 15-20 minutes, not saying much. I had my back to him and I could hear other people.

Finally, he walked over to me and he said, "Commander, you know, those bastards were trying to kill us, weren't they?"

I said, "You stupid asshole! You were out there for six to eight months raking junks, they shot at you, and you didn't even know that you were in a war? That they were trying to kill you? You could have come back in a body bag, but your whole attitude toward the war is that it was all a big joke."

My point was that, if you're in a war, people are going to try to kill you so you'd better kill them first. It took this kid 20 minutes to absorb that. That was the attitude of the guys in my Air Force C-130 squadron, too.

I've got to tell you, my attitude was a little different from some others. I was what you'd call a lifer. I'd been in the military a while, I'd seen people killed, and I'd seen plenty of action. To me it was just another job. If I bought it, I bought it. If I didn't, I didn't. When you fly, every flight is an experience and you could get it at any time. No, it's not like being a grunt where you're out in the field and people are shooting at you every minute of the day. I felt sorry for those guys because they were under constant pressure. We weren't. We had time to relax, drink a beer, and have a steak. It wasn't that kind of pressure with us.

Regarding civilian antiwar demonstrators, when I was stationed at Quincy Point, Rhode Island, in about 1969, there were daily protests at the gate to the installation. Our base had a gate that was set about ¾ of a mile from the main road. Fences ran along both sides of the road. There wasn't much clearance between the road and the fences. The protestors would get in the road and dare you to hit them. I never slowed down, holding my speed at 50 mph. They knew my car by about the second day, so they would get out of my way. I never hit one, but most people would stop for them and that's what they wanted. It didn't last too long. A few weeks after I was there, the protests kind of petered out and we didn't hear much about it anymore.

Walt got out of the Navy in November 1974 and went back to college and got two more degrees, one in education and one in geology. He taught high school for two years in Holland, New York, not far from Buffalo. Then he worked as an independent contractor, consulting for Trico Corporation, the folks who make windshield wiper blades, setting up all their technical training. When that job petered out, he went to work for Aero Corporation in western New York where he worked on government contracts supporting the SR-71, the U-2, the TR-3, and some Navy equipment. His expertise in government contracts and regulations came in handy.

He retired completely in 1989 and moved to North Carolina. Walt has published a book about the Navy hurricane hunters, and helped other folks by providing similar information for their books and articles. He also had a part in a show on the History Channel about hurricanes, a story called "Suicide Missions." An upcoming book of his is a novel involving Navy flyers and UFOs. He says his next book will be about military intelligence in Southeast Asia. He's on the NRA board of directors and owns eight national rifle-shooting records.

CHAPTER 8
ARMY SPECIALIST FOUR LARRY TOUCHSTONE
Infantry

I wondered why there were so many M-16s just lying around and it dawned on me that many of the owners were now dead. When I finally found mine there was a little piece of something lying next to it. It was black, about an inch square, and looked like Velcro. I thought, *What's that doing here?* I picked it up to see what it was. It was gray on the bottom, a piece from the top of my buddy's skull.

*L*arry Touchstone grew up on a farm near Rome, Georgia. After completing high school he earned an Associate's Degree in Electronics from Massey Technical Institute in Jacksonville, Florida. Upon graduation he lost his deferment. The draft was going strong but the lottery had not yet been implemented. Employers were very reluctant to hire people for meaningful jobs if they were still subject to the draft. Larry could have been drafted for two years but decided to enlist for three, believing he'd have more control over his destiny. If he had to go into the service, Larry wanted to come out with some useful training, a marketable skill. Ironically, when the lottery came into existence a few months later, his number would have been 366, the very last to be drafted. Larry served in Vietnam 1969-70.

I went to Basic Training at Fort Benning, Georgia. Almost no one got to Basic in the middle of the day, always late in the afternoon. It's intended that way. The first thing they gave us at in-processing was our serial number and told us to memorize it immediately. Within a few hours of arrival they asked us to recite our serial numbers. Our serial numbers had a two-letter prefix, NG for National Guard, ER for Emergency Relief (for some reason that prefix pertained mostly to Puerto Rican nationals), US for draftee, and RA for Regular Army. Mine was an RA number. When the Drill Sergeant asked us for our serial numbers, there was a difference in the way he treated us if we were RA, as opposed to some of the others. RA normally meant we had enlisted and wanted to be in the Army. Later, while I was in Vietnam, they changed our serial numbers to our Social Security Numbers.

In-processing took quite a while and we didn't get to bed until very late that night. The next morning they rolled us out around 4am, something that continued throughout Basic. We all took a battery of tests to determine our knowledge and aptitudes. I graded out in Group One, the tops. I figured I had it made—no way would I end up in the Infantry—not with my test scores. At that particular time there was a project called "McNamara's 100,000." The Army was desperate for troops and had already inducted just about every available man. Up to that point they'd only been inducting men in Groups One, Two, and Three. Group Four they considered un-trainable, but that changed with this project. The idea was that the Army could help these poor, dumb people by providing them a skill.

Thus, the folks who were inducted at that time ranged from really brilliant people, some with college degrees, to folks who couldn't tie their own shoes. All these folks were in the same barracks and training platoons. That was something!

We had one guy in Basic that I called a "PX Hero." He was a draftee and a lady's man. He went to the PX and bought sergeant's stripes and a ton of ribbons. He wasn't authorized to wear any of this stuff nor did he pin it on according to regulations. He just put the ribbons where he thought they looked nice!

He kept that uniform hidden in his locker but, as soon as he graduated from Basic, he put on that uniform and went off post to impress the girls. He'd been in the Army for all of eight weeks but he was decked out like a 20-year man. If he'd ever been caught in that uniform, he'd have been court-martialed. It wasn't illegal to buy the stripes and ribbons, but you weren't supposed to wear them unless you had earned them. There's probably someone like that in every platoon, someone who likes to show off.

Up until that time only people with a four-year college degree were accepted into OCS, but the pool of folks with those qualifications had run dry and the Army desperately needed more officers. Since I had good test scores and a two-year degree, they offered me OCS. I figured this was another way of controlling my own destiny, so I agreed. At that point

I was 19 years old and never realized that those folks would *lie* to you about such things. But they would! They'd tell you anything to get your signature on the dotted line. I told them I wanted to be in electronics and they assured me I'd end up in the Signal Corps when I completed OCS.

Of the men in my Basic Training company I would guess about half went to Vietnam, but I only remember seeing one man from Basic over there. Going through OCS delayed my arrival in Nam until much later. Basic training back then was eight weeks, shortened from 12, and we were assigned our MOSs upon completion.

Before going on to OCS I had to complete AIT. My MOS was Infantry and they ordered me to Fort Polk, Louisiana. They loaded us on a bus at Fort Benning and took us straight to Fort Polk, no time to go home or anything. That was an 800- or 900-mile drive.

AIT was a little easier than Basic because we were treated more like humans. After AIT I had to wait for an opening at OCS. By then it was about the middle of December and about half of the guys who'd completed AIT with me got orders for Vietnam. Those guys went through Basic, AIT, and straight to Vietnam without a break. That was really tough on some of those guys who'd never been away from home before. They didn't even get to go home for Christmas. It would have torn me up, too.

I had already signed a contract for a school, but when I finished AIT they told me my school had no openings at that time. I figured some Congressman must have pulled a few strings to get his son into that school, taking my slot, or the folks I talked to were just lying through their teeth. They told me that all Signal Corps officers had to go through Infantry OCS first, and then go to Signal Corps training. That was all garbage!

When they told me Signal School I'd signed up for had no openings, I could have gotten out of my contract right then and there. The Army had broken their end of the bargain. I could have gone home, but I decided to stay on at OCS.

I didn't get my opening for OCS until March. OCS was 183 days long, back at Fort Benning. Most people think that their basic training was worse than normal but the real shock was when I got to OCS. Basic, compared to OCS, was about like kindergarten compared to college.

In Basic I'd hear guys crying at night, but OCS was *really* tough. When we saw what was going on, about half the class wanted out immediately. But once you walked in the door and signed in, you could not get out for seven weeks, no matter how badly you wanted to leave. There was no way out—you belonged to them!

OCS was tough! For example, there was a small moat around our barracks. They had men out there picking rocks out of the moat, washing them, and putting them back in the moat. Everything was absolutely spotless. We didn't want to walk on the floors for fear of messing them up, in which case we'd have to polish them again.

That was quite a shock for a country boy, but the real shocker was the people. I'd never been around Yankees before. Probably a third of the platoon was from New Jersey, New York, or some place like that. They all talked funny [Larry laughs]. I'd never known those kinds of people. Most of those guys did not know how to drive, but someone had to drive the trucks needed to transport troops from one training site to another. As a driver I didn't have to pull KP. I did have to get up two hours before everyone else in order to go to the motor pool and wash the vehicle, fuel it up and so forth, but that beat KP all to pieces.

There were DIs and Tac Officers who could do anything they wanted to you anytime of the day or night. We had to have our boots spit-shined and standing under our bunk at night. One of the Tac Officers had it in for the guy in the bunk below mine, so one night I got awakened from a sound sleep by the Tac Officer chewing out this guy for having dust in the nail holes of one of his boots. If a Tac Officer wanted to give you a tough time, he could always find something wrong and give you a demerit.

Anytime you got a demerit, you had to pull a "punishment tour." We only had Sunday afternoons off—that was it. The guys who had earned demerits walked punishment tours on Sunday afternoons, which amounted to marching back and forth in front of the barracks. A punishment tour was two hours for each demerit. Some of the troops pulled punishment tours the whole time they were in OCS, even though they weren't that bad. The Tac Officers just recognized that some of these guys were a little weak and were hard on them, trying to whip them into shape or drive them out of OCS.

During that time period quite a few officers graduated who never should have made it, like LT Calley of My Lai infamy. He wasn't in my class but graduated somewhere around that time.

I went to OCS with visions of being an officer in the Signal Corps, as promised. Pretty soon I realized that wasn't going to happen. What they'd told me wasn't the way it was. But that was in the summer of '69 and we'd been hearing rumors about troop pullouts. I thought if I could just hang around there and kill a little more time I wouldn't have to go to Vietnam. I convinced myself that's what I needed to do.

OCS was a six-month course and after five months I quit. If I had stayed and graduated, I'd have had to sign a contract extending my tour another year. Me quitting made the Army mad and I immediately got orders for Vietnam.

I didn't know it at the time but officers only spent six months in combat, whereas enlistees had to stay a year. The Army wanted as many officers with combat experience as possible, so they cycled them in and out of the field in six months. They stayed in Vietnam a year but spent half that time at a desk job in the rear area. If I had known that earlier, I might have stayed in OCS.

Airborne School was also at Fort Benning. It was a three-week course and anyone could sign up for it at anytime, which I did. I passed the physical, got accepted, and that would have killed another three weeks. But they had a backlog and, before I could get in, my orders to Vietnam came due, so I missed Airborne School.

For pay purposes they promoted us to SP-5 in OCS. When I quit they dropped me back to SP-4. Most people arrived in Vietnam as an E-2 or E-3, but I got there as an E-4 and made E-5 again before leaving. I had a year of schooling with a whole lot of tax dollars spent on me. Thus, I was better trained than most troops arriving there. I knew more about what was going on than the average soldier. I went to Vietnam the first week of September and came home a year later, September 1970.

Another thing that helped me in Vietnam was rifle marksmanship. The Army used to have huge bulls-eye targets to shoot at, but by the time I got there they had human silhouettes that popped up. The targets were set up at 50-meter intervals at various ranges from 50 to 350 meters. When it popped up, that's when you fired at it. If you hit it, the target fell back down and you knew you'd made a good shot.

This target procedure conditioned the shooter to fire as quickly as possible when the target appeared, but accuracy was important, too. Typically, you'd get five or six rounds with which to hit five targets at various distances. If you missed one, you could fire again until you hit it but that meant you probably wouldn't have enough ammo to complete the course.

This training made quite a difference to soldiers the first time they encountered and fired at a live enemy soldier. From what I've read, this training caused first-time hits to rise from 25 percent to around 85 or 90, as compared to the old bulls-eye method. Speaking from personal experience, the first time I fired at an enemy it was an automatic reflex, just like in practice.

I trained with an M-14 in Basic because there weren't enough M-16s to go around. Then they pulled me and some other guys out of training and took us over to where we could use M-16s. We figured for sure we were the guys who were going to Vietnam [Larry laughs]. In OCS I went back to using an M-14.

The course of fire when qualifying with a rifle was 81 rounds. If you had 60 hits, you were declared an Expert. I shot a 59 the first try. I knew I was better than that and never shot less than 70 after that. I just had a bad day that first time. In OCS I out-shot everybody else in my class, about 280 people. My daddy wasn't a hunter or shooter, so I wasn't either, but I caught on pretty fast. Maybe I didn't have any bad habits to unlearn. I beat everyone else in the classroom, too.

After leaving OCS I'd been in the Army about a year and had accumulated 30 days leave, so I got to go home. From there I reported to Fort Dix, New Jersey. I'd never been north of Tennessee, so that was quite a shock to me. The guy in the bunk above me at Dix also went to Vietnam and we stayed together the whole time. Being September, New Jersey seemed very cool, temperature-wise, compared to what I was used to down south.

We got on an airplane and our next stop was Anchorage, Alaska. It was cool there, too. Then we flew to Okinawa for another fuel stop before finally landing in Vietnam. Each leg of the flight was seven or eight hours, so it took about 24 hours to get all the way over there. We flew on a civilian aircraft contracted by the Army. That means we were on a regular commercial plane with stewardesses and everything. Sorry, no alcoholic beverages available.

My first stop in Vietnam was Bien Hoa in September 1969. We'd been aboard an aircraft in a climate-controlled environment for 24 hours.

When we walked off the plane the heat hit us in the face and we just about passed out. Sweat popped out of us instantly. "Whoa," I said, "I've got to do this for a year?"

It took about a day for us to in-process and I got assigned to the 1st Cavalry Division. We went through three or four days of training right then and there, presumably to see what everyone could do. All the new troops had come from many different training sites, so they had to do a little screening. They issued me a rifle, but not a new one. It had been reconditioned and there was nothing wrong with it, but I was expecting a brand new one. We went to the range to zero our rifles and become familiar with them, but weren't yet issued any ammo to keep.

In 1968 the minimum civilian wage was $1.25, so working a 40-hour week you could make just over $200 per month. In the Army at that time Private/E-2 monthly pay was $92. This was not as bad as it seems because you could spend all of it the first day of the month and you still had a place to stay, food, clothing and medical care. I think PFC/E-3 pay was $120, SP4/E-4 about $180 and SGT/E-5 was $226. If I remember correctly, combat pay was an extra $68 per month. In the infantry there were not many places to spend your money so most of the men would keep about $50 per month and send the rest home. I saved enough to buy a new car.

Everyone in Vietnam had to have a ration card to buy anything in the PX. I only got to the PX about three times in the whole year I was there. The grunts thought of this as a joke because we had no money and carried everything we owned on our back. The Army must have issued ration cards to keep the men in the rear from making a profit. With no tax they might have bought cameras or electronics cheaply, and sent them home to resell at much higher prices.

When I arrived, our division HQ was in the process of moving from Phuoc Vinh to Quan Loi, which was further north and closer to the Cambodian border. First Cav originally went to Vietnam in 1965 as part of I Corps, up north near the DMZ. III Corps pretty much took care of the Cambodian border and Saigon, and that's where the division was assigned when I arrived. The only time I left the III Corps area while in Vietnam was during the Cambodian invasion.

If you hear someone talking trash, saying they were all over the place, they're lying! They were never in Vietnam. A division worked in certain places and that's where they stayed. They would move a unit but a soldier stayed with his unit. He did not go all over the place. I work in the new car business now so I know a liar when I hear one [Larry laughs].

Everyone who went to Vietnam immediately got himself a calendar and started marking off the days until he could go back to the World. Almost everyone carried something for luck. If you look at photos of combat troops in Vietnam, you'll see many of them had some kind of religious item on a chain around their necks. Or it could be almost anything in their helmet bands or in their wallets. I personally did not believe in this but I did carry a two-dollar bill that an old man, a neighbor back home, had given me when I got out of school. Whatever seemed to be working, I did not want to take a chance.

When our division moved they left a few guys behind, short-timers. That's all that was left of the division. So there I was, the guy I'd met at Fort Dix and come over with, and two old vets in the rear area. Division couldn't be bothered with new guys during the move. Later, the vets called the division on the radio, asking what to do with us new guys. The response was to bring us up on a convoy. That scared me to death! Here I was, brand new in-country, and I could just see the convoy getting attacked in the middle of nowhere. Then we got word that there was a C-7 aircraft, a little twin-engine plane called a Caribou, scheduled to fly to the new division area. We got on the plane and flew up to Quan Loi.

The first thing I saw when we landed was a C-130 that had landed there a day or two earlier. Just as it touched down an NVA rocket hit one of the engines. Shrapnel killed one man inside the plane. I'm thinking, *Whoa! I'm flying into this mess?* That C-130 sat there for about four months waiting for parts to arrive. Lockheed Aircraft Corporation eventually sent a crew from Marietta, Georgia, to rebuild the wing of that aircraft and fly it out of there.

I knew little about Vietnam before I got there and, thus, had no opinion on the war. I did feel sorry for the people there and wished we could have done more for them.

Division issued us our gear and then had to get us out to our company in the bush. The division firebases were set up so that their artillery could cover each other, that is their fields of fire overlapped so that nothing was out of range. One battalion operated each firebase. I was assigned to C

Company, 1ˢᵗ Battalion, 5ᵗʰ Cavalry Regiment (Charlie, 1/5), 1ˢᵗ Cavalry Division, III Corps. I spent most of my year in the northwestern area of III Corps, around Quan Loi and An Loc. We had contact with both NVA and VC.

We choppered out to LZ Ann, the name of the 1ˢᵗ Battalion firebase. As we flew I could see B-52s flying at 30,000 feet near the Cambodian border. I got to LZ Ann in the rainy season, which in Vietnam ran from around May through September. The rest of the year it was dry, very dry. Dust would be a foot deep in the winter.

There were four infantry companies in the battalion, which rotated in and out of the field. Three of the companies would be out in the jungle working and one would be on base defense. A company would spend three weeks in the field, then one week on base defense before going back into the bush. For artillery support the battalion had a battery of six 105mm howitzers, a battery of six 155mm howitzers, and the 81mm mortar platoon of whichever company was not in the field. The company not in the field secured the borders of the LZ.

I still hadn't met any of the people I'd be working with because they were out in the field. I had to wait until "log day" to join them. I was on the firebase about two days before the log bird was scheduled to go out. We got some incoming mortar rounds the first night I was there. I said to myself, *This is real!*

When I got out to the field and got off the bird, the guys in the bush went wild trying to get their mail. I ran into a guy I didn't know too well but someone I'd gone to school with at Massey Tech. He'd gotten drafted as soon as he left school. He was almost ready to leave and I'd just gotten there! All this while I was in OCS and other schools.

I met the company commander, CPT Vowell, and 1LT Miller, my platoon leader. I sent Miller a picture of himself recently from when he was in Nam. He's now an LTC in the Reserves and his daughter is in the Army, too. When she saw the picture she chewed him out for looking so grungy. We got that way in the bush.

In the bush we'd set up an FOB each night. We'd place trip flares and Claymore mines all around the perimeter as added security. We also put out three listening posts 100 yards or more out in front of everybody else. If there was an attack, the guys manning the listening posts were more or less expendable. Listening post was the first job a new guy got because he was *not going to fall sleep*! He'd be so nervous he couldn't sleep. Steven Drappola, another new troop, and I were assigned LP the first night we were in camp.

We set out our trip flares and Claymores in front of us and then got down into a small depression so that, if the Claymores were set off, the blast would blow over the top of us. We had radios but had to maintain radio silence, even if we heard or saw something. Every hour we'd get a call for a SitRep. If everything was okay, we keyed the transmit button twice without speaking. That caused the receiver at the other end to bark static twice. Any response other than that, or a total lack of response, indicated we had a problem.

It was the rainy season. Everything went smoothly our first night on LP until about 4am. A trip flare went off between our LP and the FOB. The pucker factor goes way up in a situation like that! We were all spooked, not knowing what was going on. Were the NVA between our unit and us? But apparently an animal had run into the wire and set off the flare. We were quite happy to get through our first night in the bush.

The next day we were marching through the jungle in what we called "ranger file," in a straight line, one behind the other. We'd rotate walking point. If my platoon walked point one day, we'd move to the rear the next day, and be in the middle the day after that. My platoon was bringing up the rear that day. I was new so they didn't put me at the very back. An old hand was at the tail end but I wasn't far ahead of him.

If we found an enemy trail, we never used it. Instead, we'd cross it, go up a ways, and then cross it again. Every time we crossed a trail we'd look both ways looking for enemy soldiers.

We crossed an enemy trail and I had just gotten about 50 yards past it. The guy in the rear spotted a dink as he was crossing the trail and at the same time the enemy spotted him. The enemy soldier pulled up his AK-47 and made a sweep across the trail, firing on full auto, but didn't hit anybody. Some of our guys fired off a few rounds but he was gone. I don't think I got a round off in that instance, just the guys in the very rear.

A guy from one of the other units told me a story about his company being in the woods when they spotted a lone NVA. They followed him, hoping he'd lead them back to his unit. He did alright, right into an ambush. Twenty-six guys were killed and this guy lived!

It was late and about 500 yards further we stopped for the night. We got our perimeter set up and were eating when I had my first experience with close air support. We were not told in advance and there is no way to describe it so that someone else could understand the sounds that we heard many times after that, but here's my try: Suddenly we heard a very loud whine of turbine engines, the slap of rotor blades, and a Cobra whizzed by above us. The Cobra fired several pairs of rockets in rapid succession, and they exploded on the ground nearby in the general vicinity of where we'd spotted the dink.

I never knew if the CO had called in the fire mission or if the pilot himself had seen something on the ground. The next morning we went to check the area that had been fired upon and found several bunkers, but no sign of people. We threw grenades into each bunker and left. Whenever we found an enemy bunker, we never tried to go into it. We'd frag the thing and then throw CS grenades in to keep the enemy from using the bunker later.

The frags we used weren't the old "pineapples" they used in WW-II and Korea. We used smaller, baseball-size things that were much easier to throw. The outer surface was wire-wrapped and the wire had cuts in it so that, when the explosives inside went off, the outer shell would come apart sending small metal shards everywhere. They weren't quite as deadly as the pineapples but they were capable of injuring many more enemy soldiers.

During that first week or two, our job was to slow down the flow of supplies from across the Cambodian border. The enemy stockpiled supplies in Cambodia and had dozens of trails across which to carry them. Every day we'd set an ambush on at least one of those trails, and we'd get some action maybe twice a week.

You may have heard about new troops having buck fever or a reluctance to shoot another person. In my case it was easy. Whenever we'd set up an ambush and catch dinks coming down the trail, there'd be 12 to 15 other guys shooting along with me. I'd get the enemy in my sights and squeeze the trigger but never really knew if I'd done any damage. Chances are most of us hit him. Not knowing for sure sort of conditioned me and after that it was never a problem.

Whenever we shot a dink, we'd check him for papers or any other intelligence that might tell us what he and his comrades were up to, or what unit he was from. If the guy had a pistol, one of us kept it as a souvenir. Most of our enemy contact was small, usually just one or two men.

We didn't ever salute an officer while in the bush or he might have hurt us. The bad guys are looking to shoot radiomen to disrupt our communications, or the highest-ranking officer they could find. Saluting gave away an officer's identity.

Each company had three infantry platoons and a mortar platoon. Generally, the mortar platoon stayed on the firebase because they couldn't move very fast in the bush with all their heavy weapons.

In the rainy season we'd often have to cross small rivers. Usually the water was swift and deep, and to cross with all our gear we'd stretch a rope tight to the other side so we could pull ourselves across one at a time. Occasionally someone would lose his grip on the rope and fall into the swift-moving stream. With all their gear weighing them down, they'd go under and possibly drown.

My platoon had the point one day and I was the first to get across one of those rivers. We secured the other side from possible enemy attack so the others could cross safely. I heard some noise in the water behind me but had to keep my eyes toward the jungle, looking for enemy soldiers. I learned later that a man had fallen from the rope into the swift water with all his gear and was drowning. Another man from my squad, Randy Rhoades, saw this and without hesitation jumped in and pulled the man to shallow water where he could get his feet on the bottom. I do not know who put him in for it but a month later Rhoades got The Soldiers Medal, an award for heroic action during combat activities not involving enemy fire.

There were three guys, one from Florida named Benny "Gator" Gerell, Skip Shirks and Rhodes. All three got the Soldier's Medal for doing things like that. Those three guys at different times threw off their packs, jumped in, and saved their buddies. Gator was a good swimmer and did it more than once.

I feel very lucky to have known personally many real heroes. The highest military award is the Medal of Honor but I never met a recipient. The next highest is the Distinguished Service Cross (DSC) and I know two guys who got that. After that comes the Silver Star and I know more than 20 winners. Next comes the Bronze Star, which can be given for heroism or for meritorious service. If the Bronze Star has a V on it, V for valor, it's for heroism. I had two Bronze Stars awarded for valor, the second signified by an oak leaf cluster. So, officially, I have a Bronze Star with V-device and oak leaf cluster.

Later that month we were on base defense duty at a firebase named LZ Vivian. We were on bunker guard one day when a group of VIPs came over near our bunker. An officer that I did not know asked if there was an M79 in the area. For those who have never seen one, it is a grenade launcher that looks like a short shotgun. It has a 40mm barrel and fires a half-pound grenade. Someone handed him one and he gave it to another man in jungle fatigues.

At first I did not recognize him—people just don't look the same in person as they do on TV. The other man was Ron Ely, who played Tarzan in the TV series. He wanted to fire a grenade, so everyone watched him do it and he seemed to enjoy himself. After that he shook hands and talked to each of us. In the year I was there he was the only visitor from show business who came out to see us—all the others stayed in the rear where it was safe.

The men liked our CO, CPT Vowell. He would not ask us to do anything that he would not do himself. He was tall and very strong. On several occasions, when we had been humping through the jungle for a long time, the men would be begging for a break. Captain Vowell would eventually give in and say, "Okay, take five." We would all sit down and have some water, but I would see him standing there with his pack on, leaning on his rifle, waiting for us to finish resting.

One day we were almost to where we were to camp for the night. My platoon was in the rear that day and I looked to the right and saw a man with an AK-47 about 75 yards out in the woods. I yelled out, "Any friendlies on the right?" The answer came back no friendlies on the right. I already had my rifle up and had him in my sights. About the time I fired four other men did, too. The target dropped out of sight, so we moved up to check out the area and found nothing. We could not believe we all had missed. I swear my round must have hit a twig and deflected because *I just didn't miss shots like that!*

The enemy soldiers wore uniforms much like ours, and the AK-47 didn't mean much either. Many of our troops carried captured AKs, hoping it would cause the enemy to hesitate, not knowing if we were friend or foe. That small moment of indecision could make all the difference in the outcome of a firefight.

Late that day, we set up an FOB for the night. Everybody sat down to eat supper when an M-60 opened up. It was textbook shooting, six- or eight-round bursts, to avoid overheating the barrel. Then I heard people shouting. A guy named Steven "Sherman" Branham and his assistant gunner, a guy named Schwartz, had set up a position for the night near an enemy trail. Out of the corner of his eye Sherman had seen a couple of NVA sneaking up on them. Sherman had been in Nam about four months and he was cool as ice. He acted as though he hadn't seen them and let them get even closer. He was talking to Schwartz, letting him know what was going on. Sherman waited until just the right moment, then rolled over with his M-60 and opened up. Sherman had gotten all the NVA he'd seen. We then maneuvered around the area to see if there were any more, but apparently there were just the two enemy soldiers. The CO gave Sherman a three-day in-country R&R as a reward for what he'd done, getting them before they got us.

That wasn't the first or last time Sherman did something like that. That boy was good. Another time he single-handedly wiped out a whole enemy patrol and saved his platoon. A few of our guys were wounded but no one got killed. I wasn't there to see it, but Sherman eventually got a DSC for that incident. In the same incident, Schwartz had his leg blown off just above the knee. To this day Schwartz hardly remembers what happened. He ended up working for the Veterans Administration, fitting disabled vets with prosthetics. Schwartz is retired now but he really was good at what he did.

I remember the first time anyone shot at me. One day during my first week in Nam we were on patrol checking enemy trails. We crossed a trail and I was second to last man. I looked back and saw a lone NVA soldier. He turned and saw us. Instantly he fired a burst of about 10 rounds in our direction. Puffs of dirt sprayed up on both sides of me. The man behind me and I each fired a whole magazine in that direction after he'd gone out of sight. None of us were hit so we went back to check out the area where the NVA had been seen. We found no sign of him or any blood trails, so no one was hit on either side.

In a firefight we'd get tunnel vision. We could only see what affected us right then, what was going to hurt us; that's all we were focused on. It would have been hard not to be that way—that's just the way it happened. Therefore, three or four other guys who were right there in the same action could give three or four different accounts of what had happened. It didn't mean any one of them was wrong. They were just relating how it appeared to them.

We only used our flares when absolutely necessary. A parachute flare would burn for a couple of minutes and if something happened at night we wanted to have enough to keep the place lit up until our side got the situation under control.

One night about 4am we heard a Claymore go off about 400 yards away at one of our LPs. They immediately called for flares and we began shooting them off, one of the duties of the mortar platoon. We wore ourselves out shooting flares until daylight.

I found out several days later that a squad leader had accidentally set off the Claymore. They had their mines positioned with wires running back to the LP, klackers positioned so they'd know which one controlled which mine. He admitted to me that they hadn't seen anything. He'd gotten up for his turn on guard, a little sleepy, walked over and sat down on one of the klackers [Larry laughs]. I never did tell any of the other guys in the mortar platoon or they may have tried to whip him.

Vietnam being in the tropics I expected to see all kinds of animals. Surprisingly there were almost none. I did see a few bamboo vipers, some monkeys, and some birds. I think most of the other animals were driven away by all the artillery fire, gunship attacks, and B-52 strikes. There was a lot of gunfire every day even if there was no enemy contact. I think the constant noise and vibration drove the animals deeper into the jungle. We didn't go there very often because we were always checking out known or suspected enemy areas, and the enemy didn't go into the deeper jungle either. I remember that we all felt good when we went into a place and saw or heard monkeys swinging through the trees. Wild monkeys did not stay around people so we felt safer knowing there probably weren't any enemies in the area.

Although the animals didn't bother us much, the insects did. Leaches were everywhere and the only two ways to remove them was to burn them with a cigarette or Army-issue bug juice. You'd see the latter in the helmet band of almost every infantryman in Vietnam. The leaches always seemed to get into places that you could not reach, forcing you to have help removing them.

I had a painful experience with another insect. Late one night we stopped and I put my poncho down intending to sleep on it. I didn't notice that I'd placed it on some kind of anthill. A few minutes after lying down, I jumped up feeling as though I'd been stung by a thousand bees. The next morning I found that the ants had eaten my poncho to shreds.

When we were in the bush we never wore underwear. In the constant heat and dampness, tight clothing would hold the moisture next to our skin. Sometimes we didn't get a chance to change clothes for many days or even weeks. The dampness could cause jungle rot, and in the wrong place it could be very painful and hard to cure. That didn't sound right [not wearing underwear] the first time I heard it. I've had people pull my leg before, but within three days I buried my underwear beside the trail. After that I listened very carefully whenever someone with more time in the bush spoke.

There were two kinds of malaria in Vietnam so we took two kinds pills to combat it. One small white one we took every day and a large green one every Monday. Once, while in the rear area for a few days, I saw some men in the unit next to ours who had a pet dog. That was rare because the local population would eat any animal they could find. For some reason the men decided that, because they had to take malaria pills, the dog should take one too. They gave him one of the big pills and he was dead in a couple of hours.

Most of the areas we worked in were free-fire zones where we could shoot anything that moved. But around Quan Loi there was a huge rubber plantation owned by the French government. When we were working in the rubber trees we were not allowed to fire unless we were fired at first because the US had to pay Michelin $300 for every tree we destroyed. If a round hit a tree, the sap started running and the tree just bled out.

Being forced to wait until an enemy shoots before we could fire put us at a severe disadvantage. When we saw an enemy out there with a weapon, why should we give him the chance to fire the first shot? I had friends who got hurt because of that rule—they had to wait too long to begin shooting. Of course, who's to say the enemy didn't fire first [Larry laughs]?

When the shooting started, we didn't just knick a few trees, we cleared out an acre or two. That's big money! Maybe that's why tires are so expensive! When we had that many guys in danger, we didn't take any chances when the shooting started. We kept shooting until we were *sure*. We wiped out a lot of rubber trees. The only thing I've ever read that mentioned the Michelin Plantation is in the book *We Were Soldiers Once, and Young* [by LTC Harold Moore]. I will never in my life buy a Michelin tire!

Our rear area was in the middle of the plantation. Rubber trees are tall. If an artillery round came close and hit a rubber tree, there'd be shrapnel [tree splinters] all over the place. That spooked me. Fortunately, I never got hit.

While in the bush, on log days a chopper would fly food, ammo, and water out to us. They had three-, five-, and seven-day logs, depending on what we were doing and where we were. We liked the three-day logs because we only had to carry food and water to last three days. Every man had two quarts of water and three C-ration meals per day. The first thing we did was to dump everything we didn't want or need and burn it, so we wouldn't have so much to carry. It was rough when we had to carry seven days worth of supplies.

The standard load in the Cav was 400 rounds of ammo per man carrying an M-16, two fragmentation grenades, two to four smoke grenades, bayonet, gas mask, and 100 rounds for the machinegun [the machinegun crew couldn't carry enough ammo to support their weapon]. The only time I ever wore a gas mask in Vietnam was when my sleeping quarters were right next to a 155. It was winter and they were firing that howitzer all night long, full charges, and every time they'd fire dust flew up off the ground. I couldn't breath without that mask!

When we came in from a patrol we'd shoot up all our ammo and get new stuff because we wanted fresh ammo every time we went out. In fact, the brass of the round in the chamber would turn black after a day or two because of the humidity. If you fired the weapon, that round would probably seize and cause a jam, not a good thing in combat. So every day or two, if we hadn't been doing any shooting, we'd take the round out of the chamber, throw it away, and replace it with a fresh one.

The way the Cav worked was called Charlie-Alfa, phonetic for Combat Assault. When battalion got wind of a suspected enemy area, they'd insert an infantry company using helicopters. It took three lifts of five to seven aircraft each. The first lift to land needed to have enough men to secure the area for the next lift.

To confuse the enemy prior to insertion, the battalion howitzers would fire in about a dozen different directions, including the one where we were going. We didn't even know ourselves where we were going except maybe for the number one guy in the first aircraft. We didn't want that information to get out accidentally.

The 105s fired a 30-pound shell and the 155s fired a 100-pound shell. After firing in all directions for a while, those guns would then concentrate on the actual insertion area. They'd fire as fast as possible for about five minutes, prepping the area by destroying all the trees and anything else out there. The last artillery round would be a white phosphorous shell that emitted a lot of smoke, which told us that the artillery fire was over but also told the enemy the same thing. When it came time to land, the birds would come in right over the tops of the trees. The idea was to hit the LZ within a minute after the WP round.

When we went into an LZ we didn't know what we'd find. Each bird had two door-gunners manning M-60 machineguns and all the ammo in the world. They'd hose down the area even if they couldn't see any enemy. Maybe only one out of 10 LZs we went into was hot, but we just never knew. Maybe the howitzer and machinegun fire ran the enemy off, or maybe they weren't there in the first place.

I don't know how many times a bird went down during one of these assaults, either hit by enemy fire or had a mechanical failure. An OH-58 went down during one of our assaults. My platoon got the job of securing it. I believe the bird had a mechanical failure of some kind. The tail broke off on the way down and the thing rotated like mad, doing a lot of damage. We found it, pulled the radios out, packed the bird with incendiaries, and blew it to smithereens.

We tried to stay five meters apart as we walked through the bush. That way one round likely wouldn't get more than one of us. Very seldom did we get hit with anything big. If we took any fire, it was usually AK-47s or B-40s. That was bad enough.

Everyone eventually walked point, except for the machine-gunners, and when I'd been there awhile I got my turn. I must have done a good job because soon I "got" to do it every time my platoon led the pack.

One day I was walking point and the captain patted me on the back—he liked the way I was moving the company. Some point men were too cautious but we were moving pretty fast.

I could always sense when something wasn't right. We were zigzagging across an enemy trail and had been doing it all morning. Around lunchtime we crossed the trail again and decided to set up an ambush. We got everybody ready and had a squad of about a dozen guys on one side of the trail, watching in both directions. Placing men on opposite sides could endanger our own men when the shooting started.

Suddenly, eight or 10 AK-47s opened up not too far away, knocking leaves and limbs on top of us. The fire was going right over our heads. What we didn't know was that the trail we were watching forked, just past the last point we'd crossed. The enemy had seen us and set up his own ambush for us. If we'd kept walking, as point man I probably would have walked right into that ambush. When the enemy realized we weren't coming, they just shot their wad and took off. We never saw them. After things quieted down we investigated and saw where they'd been. Pure luck kept us out of a disaster.

In later times we'd set up automatic ambushes, using Claymore mines and tripwires. Whoever set up those ambushes had better be the guy who took them down. Several times I'd heard of other people taking down an ambush and being killed because they didn't know where all the wires were. You had to know exactly where everything was before you fooled around trying to take one down.

When an enemy soldier got killed his comrades just buried him right beside the trail. Whenever we found fresh dirt we'd dig up the body to see if we could get any intelligence. That was a nasty job. Most of the time we didn't find anything on the body but we had to do it. We never knew what they might have left behind. If they were already loaded down, they might have left something. Even if we didn't get intelligence, we had an increased body count. That didn't impress me much because 100 of them wasn't' worth one of us.

We never ran across any tiger traps or bouncing Betties, but we did see a few punji stakes. I can't remember anybody in my unit getting hurt by one of those booby traps. The places we were the enemy didn't do much with booby traps. I heard that some of the other units ran into them quite a bit.

As I mentioned earlier, some of our guys carried captured AK-47s. These rifles were not as good as our M-16s. They just weren't. The clearances on an AK were looser than on our rifles. Thus, an AK would function very well in wet or dirty conditions, although it wasn't nearly as accurate as an M-16. The AK-47 was first designed in 1947, so it was old compared to our rifle but carrying one gave us a psychological advantage.

We didn't have ammo for AKs, just whatever we'd captured. Sometimes the enemy would sabotage AK ammo by pulling the bullet, removing the powder and replacing it with C-4, and then replacing the bullet. Anyone unfortunate enough to fire one of those rounds had the rifle blow up in his face. That was a common thing.

Early in Nam the ammunition issued to our troops for their M-16s was dirty—the powder really fouled up the weapon and caused frequent jamming. They had that problem corrected by the time I got there, thank goodness!

Our platoon leader had only been with us about a week, a replacement. As I said, officers came and went every six months. When we got a couple of new EMs, the new officer told me to take the new guys out and show them some dead dinks, so that's what I did. They'd never seen one before.

When you're in the field, have contact with the enemy, and someone gets hit badly, the medevac comes in to get him and that's normally the last time you ever see him. He's gone, even if he survives, but most of the time you never even heard anything more about him. That was hard if he happened to be your friend.

I remember one exception, one time when we did hear what happened to a wounded soldier who'd been evacuated. This happened in 1968 in my company before I arrived. The company commander at the time was Captain Dan Terry, his time was up and he was due to start home that day. His replacement was to arrive on the Log bird in about an hour. Just about that time they had enemy contact and several men were wounded including CPT Terry. A man named George Longway, helped put him on the medevac bird. CPT Terry had about five bullets in him, and George was certain that he was dead.

As I talked about before, when we sent someone in like that, we almost never saw him again or heard what happened to him. Things like this happened often and you did not forget but you had to get back to the business of doing your job and staying alive for just one more day. George went home in 1969 still thinking CPT Terry was dead. I had not known either of these men or heard the story.

In 2004, while I was trying to locate the men from our company for a reunion, one of the other men wanted me to try to find George Longway. I found an address and called him, he was very excited and said he would be at the next 1st Cav reunion. Both Dan Terry and George came to the reunion but did not know who else was coming at that time. They just ran into each other in the meeting room at the motel. After 37 years they did not recognize each other immediately but then they saw the nametags. With lots of shouting and crying, George said, "CPT Terry! You're supposed to be dead." I think Dan said, "Well nobody told me so I just came to the reunion." Dan had recovered enough to stay in the Army, retired as a LTC, and lives near Fort Benning, Georgia.

Although I did not know either one of them, we have become good friends now and look forward to seeing each other at the reunion every year.

In the early days of the Vietnam War, long before my time, there was a medevac pilot who became famous because he would come in under fire and evacuate wounded. He used the radio nickname "Dustoff." Units in the field eventually began asking for a dustoff so it came to mean the same thing as medevac. I also remember that Dustoff was killed in action.

In November '69 a Huey came in and picked up CPT Vowell. We knew something was about to happen but they wouldn't tell us what it was. He came back later and we spent another night at that location. Up to that point we'd never, ever stayed two nights in one place.

The next morning the CPT said, "Are you ready to go?" Three lifts came in and extracted us from the bush. This was the first time I'd ever been on the back end of an extraction. My company had been on point the previous day so it was our turn to be in the rear. The most dangerous part of an extraction is at the very end because the enemy would wait until most of the people had already left and then hit. We were a little spooked at the possibilities. We took off with me on the last bird. The door-gunners opened up as we were leaving, just in case there were any NVA in the area.

They flew us back to the end of the airstrip at Quan Loi and dropped us off where that C-130 still sat with the broken wing. They still hadn't told us what it is we were going to be doing. The CPT knew but the rest of us didn't. Everything was hush-hush.

It seemed like we waited at the end of the airstrip all day, but it was probably only an hour or so. One of our guys said, "I've had enough of this—I ain't doing this no more—I'm going home now!" He put the barrel of his M-16 on his foot and pulled the trigger. Everybody jumped when the rifle went off. There was no blood coming from his boot and the guy was still standing. He walked around me, sat down, and took his boot off. The bullet had passed between his big toe and the one next to it. He had a burn on each toe but that was it! Nothing was ever said about the incident—nothing happened to him. He went with us and did his job.

The most nervous part of sitting there is that we knew something was happening and we figured it couldn't be good. Whenever we did one of those combat assaults we knew that somebody was going to die. We'd done a lot of Charlie-Alfas and up until then the only people who died were the enemy, but this time we figured it might be somebody we knew. As we sat there waiting we had nothing to do but look around and wonder who's going to be dead in the next hour or two.

While at the strip we were issued flechette rounds for our 90mm recoilless rifles. That scared us because we knew battalion was expecting something that we didn't want to see. We knew we were in for some hot and heavy action.

Eventually choppers came and picked us up in three lifts and took us away. All they'd told us was that where we were going was going to be hot, but we already knew that. We were headed for a place called Bu Dop, up near the Cambodian border. There was a Special Forces camp there and had been a firebase, called LZ Jerri, but it had been closed. Things were getting hot in that area and they wanted to put us in there to rebuild and reopen the LZ.

Statistics stated that the average lifespan of a helicopter crew in a hot LZ was 13 seconds. Therefore, the crews were always desperate to get in and out of an LZ in 10 seconds or less. The first lift of five birds hit the LZ, the troops jumped off, and the birds were out of there. Coming in on the second lift, I saw that one of the birds in the first lift had been hit on the way out and had caught fire. We saw the helicopter going down in flames as we were landing. The flames were in the cargo area, well behind the cockpit, and the door-gunners were being roasted alive. The bird was about 75 feet above the trees when the door-gunners jumped. The pilots stayed aboard and managed a controlled crash. They were badly burned but they lived. It wasn't until several days later when we were out on patrol that we found the bodies of the door-gunners.

By the time the whole company made it to the LZ, we were taking heavy fire from the wood-line. Battalion had sent a team of snipers with us and they were among the first to land. The enemy had planted a mine, but the snipers saw it and by the time I got there the mine had been disabled.

We knew more things were going to happen, so we were filling sandbags like mad, trying to rebuild some of the old bunkers in order to survive that first night. We got our bunker dug but only had one layer of sandbags over it. We wanted three or four, but nobody could shovel that fast so we did the best we could. The first thing our mortar platoon always did was to build a circle of sandbags, a pit for their gun and ammo, and then they'd build their living quarters.

It must have been near midnight and we were all still working hard. We heard mortar fire way off in the distance so we knew it was coming— it takes a long time for a mortar round to reach a target. Our side had deserted the LZ some time ago but the enemy had been in the area, so they knew how to hit just about anywhere they wanted.

One of the guys said he saw something on the trail and opened up with his M-60. When we were under night attack we'd shoot flares, which lit the place up like daylight. I never saw what he was shooting at, but there had been an enemy ground probe and the machinegun fire had chased them off. Soon it quieted down and the mortar rounds stopped coming. About 2:20am we again heard incoming mortar fire. We returned fire before the enemy rounds even landed. Our mortar platoon got hit the worst, two men killed and almost all of them wounded.

The TOE strength for an infantry company is around 160 to 180 men. Captain Vowell told me that the most he ever saw on our roster was 138. We constantly had guys killed or wounded, and people rotating home at the end of their year. There was always a lag in getting replacements and, thus, the personnel shortage. We were *always* short. We never knew when someone would get wounded and we'd lose a friend, or we'd have a leader that we liked and, *boom*, he'd be gone. The union people would have hated that kind of job [Larry laughs] because you had to know everybody else's job—you could be doing it instantly.

An infantry platoon is supposed to have four squads of 10 men each. My platoon usually had only two or three squads and even then they weren't always full. The mortar platoon didn't have a full compliment of men either. They were supposed to have enough men to run four mortar tubes and four 90mm recoilless rifles, but never had enough men to run more than two of each and never had an officer while I was there. An E-6 ran the platoon, filling the officer's slot.

A few days later we were setting up an FOB for the night and the next morning they told us to dig foxholes and fill some sandbags. After we got set up, we were smoking and joking, although I didn't smoke. The mortar platoon hadn't gotten all their bunkers built so a couple men were sleeping in the pit, the safest place they could find. I was in a rifle platoon, but we were right next to the mortar platoon. An incoming round hit right at the entrance to the mortar pit and the two men in there were wounded.

The mortar platoon leader came over to see why the guns weren't firing. One of the wounded guys was nicknamed "Sad Sack." Ronald Rodriguez was his real name. When the platoon leader asked how everyone was doing, Rodriguez responded, "I'm hit but I'm okay, Sergeant, but my buddy just got shot." And he had been, too, just ripped open. I went over and took care of him and he lived. Rodriguez didn't look like he was hurt badly, but he died on the medevac bird from a sucking chest wound nobody had seen. He was the only man killed that night. Months later, the platoon leader himself got hit, which is how I eventually ended up in the mortar platoon.

We got the incoming fire suppressed and everything settled down for the rest of the night. The next morning we patrolled the areas where the enemy ground probe had been the night before. There were satchel charges and all kinds of stuff out there. They were planning to hit us hard. I helped our demolition guy blow up the enemy ammo we'd captured. There must have been hundreds of pounds of the stuff. We were way out in the trees, away from our unit. We put the stuff in a depression along with some C-4, the latter on top so the explosion would be down, not up where it could scatter and cause injury. We didn't have any electrical detonators so we used an old-fashioned fuse. I lit the fuse and then we walked off. I'd been trained to never, ever run when moving away from explosives that are set to go off, because I could fall, hurt myself, and not be able to get away. I distinctly remember lighting that fuse and trying to be calm enough to walk away because there was going to be a *big bang*. And there was. It left quite a hole.

We were hit with mortar attacks every night we were at LZ Jerri. There was so much going on in our area that battalion attached a sniper team to our unit, and they were in the bunker next to mine. Battalion also sent us a jeep equipped with a quad-50 and a searchlight. A quad-50 is an old weapon originally intended for anti-aircraft, but in Nam we used it for anti-personnel.

The second morning we were there, I heard someone yell "Chui hoi," Vietnamese for "Don't shoot!" This time it wasn't an enemy, just an old man and a young boy coming out of the woods. They wanted safe passage and we gave it to them.

Battalion scolded us once for not taking any prisoners during our ambushes. They wanted to get some intelligence, so we had to go find them some prisoners. We finally got one or two, but we weren't happy. We didn't want to take chances trying to capture prisoners—battalion wasn't going to learn anything from them anyway.

Morale in my unit fluctuated quite a bit, depending on what was happening. There were quite a few rumors in '69 about units going home early or at least reducing their strength. When those plans didn't include our unit, morale dropped. The Big Red One and the 82nd Airborne Division left in the fall of '69. When they pulled out, the people who had been in Nam less than six months were transferred to other units and had to stay until their year was completed. We started getting new people, not really new to Vietnam but new to us.

On the morning of November 10th, 1969, our recon platoon was on their way back to the FOB. As they approached within 400 yards of the firebase, they ran into some occupied enemy bunkers. The enemy opened fire and every man in the recon platoon got hit, although no one was killed. The guy who had been walking point carried a pump shotgun, the only time I ever saw that weapon carried in Nam. A B-40 rocket hit the end of the shotgun and it blew off his arm.

They called us for help so our platoon ran out there. After cleaning out the bunkers and running off the enemy, killing two NVA, we used machetes to cut out an area for an OH-58 to land so the most seriously wounded recon guys could be medevaced. The rest of them were in good enough shape to walk back to the FOB. Once back at the compound we called in an air strike on the enemy bunkers and cratered the place to make sure they'd be of no further use. The F-4s could carry a dozen or so 750-pounders, and one or two of those was all we needed.

We'd go in after an air strike to do a bomb damage assessment. Sometimes we'd see dud bombs sticking up out of the ground. Some of the guys would be sitting around, taking pictures, and just fooling around, me among them. I didn't think anything of it, but I heard later that those bombs weren't duds. They had chemical time-delay fuses set to go off later, hoping to catch some NVAs trying to cannibalize the munitions for their own use. I didn't hang around unexploded bombs much after that [Larry laughs].

We did damage assessment after a B-52 strike once or twice, but there wasn't much to assess. No trees or anything. The stuff a B-52 strike drops, three aircraft with 84 bombs each, could wipe out about three grid squares leaving nothing but huge holes.

In the first two weeks of November we killed over 400 NVA. By *we* I mean my unit, the Special Forces, and ARVN. It was getting to smell badly because of all the bodies, so division flew in a bulldozer to bury them. They had a D-5 dozer that was small enough that it could be carried without disassembly by a CH-53 flying crane.

Our 105mm howitzers were extremely accurate. They're primarily indirect fire weapons, but if you sight them for direct fire they'll hit right where you put the crosshairs for up to 500m, just like a rifle. For several days we got some daytime fire from a sniper, but no one could ever see him until the guys on the 105 crew spotted him one day, up in a tree about 500m away. They acted calm and nonchalant, and then wheeled the 105 around like nothing special was happening. They fired a round and hit the tree right where the sniper was. *Was* is the operative word here.

Guys who smoked had it especially tough because they couldn't light up after dark. Otherwise the match, lighter, or glow of the ash would give away their position. *Bang!* Some guys really had it bad and had to have one, and the only way to smoke at night was with ponchos over their head. That had to be rough!

On the FOB we had what we called a "mad minute." At a random time, everybody on the base would get up and for one minute we fired every weapon we had. If an enemy force happened to be out there setting up for an attack, we hoped they'd be unnerved. We didn't have a mad minute every night but just often enough to keep the enemy off guard. We also used H&I every night, all night long.

We had a mad minute planned one night for 3am, but somebody must have slipped up and said something about it on the radio. Something must have leaked out because the enemy had to know about it. Just before three we began hearing mortars in the distance, heavy stuff, 4.2 inch, the enemy's version of our 120mm mortar.

I grew up during segregation in the south. I'm not prejudiced and never have been, but I'd never gone to school with a black person. They lived in town, not way out in the country where I was. Being in the Army and around black folks was something new to me. Until then I really didn't know any blacks except just to say "Hello."

One of the snipers, Charles Keitt, was from New York, a black guy. He and I hit it off somehow; we were definitely good friends. Waiting for the mad minute, we were sitting on top of my bunker talking about the kind of cars we were going to buy when we got back to the World. Wine, women, and cars—that's about all there was to talk about in Nam. I thought that was a little strange, Charles talking about buying a car, because I'd gotten the impression that the people from New York didn't drive. What I didn't understand is that New York is a big state, not just the big city. He didn't live in the city. I remember him saying he wanted to get a 440 Plymouth GTX. That was his dream car.

It was about five minutes before three when we heard the enemy mortars. We dove inside our bunkers, him in his and me in mine. There were already three people in my bunker and I couldn't get all the way in because it was too crowded. Both my legs were sticking out. Stuff started hitting very heavy and I felt something hit my foot, knocking it around. I didn't think much about it because it didn't hurt. Later I checked my boot and there was no blood, so I figured I was okay.

When the firing stopped, everybody came out of their bunkers and someone popped flares. Our guys fired back, expecting a heavy charge, but I couldn't find my rifle anywhere. I found *a* rifle and fired it. However, one of the incoming mortar rounds had landed near it, covering it with dust and dirt. After one round the rifle jammed. I picked up another rifle and the same thing happened. Finally, on the third or fourth try I got one that would fire more than one shot. We fired into the wood line, whether we saw NVA or not. We sent suppressing rifle fire in that direction, along with a few 90mm rifle rounds, and eventually ran off the enemy.

I wondered why there were so many M-16s just lying around and it dawned on me that many of the owners were now dead. When I finally found mine there was a little piece of something lying next to it. It was black, about an inch square, and looked like Velcro. I thought, *What's that doing here?* I picked it up to see what it was. It was gray on the bottom, a piece from the top of my buddy's skull.

One of those incoming mortar rounds had landed right in his bunker. The round had a delayed fuse and didn't go off until it had gone through the roof. From the outside you could hardly tell anything had happened. It just blew pieces of people out the door. There was one other sniper in the bunker with Charles.

I heard someone inside the snipers' bunker yell, "Medic!" With a direct hit I knew nobody could have survived in there, but what had happened was one of the snipers had gone into the bunker after the round had hit. He dove in there into a big puddle of blood and body parts. I never knew who that guy was, but I'm sure he's relived that nightmare many times.

A large quantity of blood has an odd smell to it, similar to the taste of copper if that makes any sense. I could smell blood outside the door of the snipers' bunker while that guy was in there screaming. I couldn't handle it. I couldn't help him so I just sat down and waited for someone else to come.

When they dug those guys out of the bunker, one white guy and one black guy, they separated the pieces by skin color. That's the only way they could tell them apart. A 120mm mortar round weighs over 30 pounds and this one landed right between the two men.

Another mortar round hit the bunker of our battalion photographer, Chuck Harris, blinding him. Years later a world-renowned eye surgeon took a personal interest in his case, performed an operation, and restored Harris' sight in one eye.

The jeep we'd just gotten with the searchlight and quad-50s had been hit and was totaled. I never saw another quad-50 after that. They were replaced with Mules, small flatbed vehicles with 7.62mm mini-guns mounted on them. Speaking of mini-guns, they were mounted in planes called Puff the Magic Dragon, commercial propeller-driven passenger planes that had been converted to gun-ships. The firepower of those things was awesome. When they shot you didn't hear a *bang*, it sounded more like a high-speed saw.

During the mad minute attack on LZ Jerri, I called out for a Medic because three of my friends had severe wounds. The attack had just started and mortar rounds were falling very heavily on our section of the perimeter. I expected my friend Clark Douglas to respond but another medic that I did not know came to help us.

Douglas was one of the most memorable people I met in Vietnam, though he wouldn't be well known to many other folks. He was the medic in my platoon. Being in the infantry in Vietnam was a strange situation. We had to eat, sleep, and work just a few feet apart, almost never out of eyesight, 24 hours a day for weeks and months at a time. We became very fast friends. Douglas had the ability to be where he should be almost before he was needed.

While he was on the way to help us, mortar round had hit very close to Douglas and killed him. I had heard talk of a medal for him but never knew for sure if it had been awarded until 30 years later. While reading a list of men who were awarded the Distinguished Service Cross, I found his name. I do not know what the citation said or what happened, but he had often risked everything to help a friend.

Douglas will never be forgotten at my house. He was a true friend and a great American who always did his job. I could not help but think that if I had not called for a medic until after we had fired back and stopped the attack that Douglas might still be alive.

The day before, November 10th, 1969, my platoon went to help another unit that was in contact with the enemy just outside the firebase. During that fight I got hit with several small pieces of shrapnel, all of them minor flesh wounds. The medic that bandaged me up was Clark Douglas, the same guy who got killed in the next attack less than 12 hours later, before he had time to write up my wounds. I had been hit 2 times in 12 hours but only medevaced once so I only got one Purple

Heart. The only reason I am telling you this is that I remember many men who got three Purple Hearts for minor wounds, but never heard of any like Senator John Kerry who went home as a result.

About an hour after the attack ended, my foot began to swell. Up to that point I certainly hadn't had time to take off my boot. When I did I saw a hole through the front and a hole in my ankle. There was no blood and, consequently, had been no squishiness in my boot. A small piece of shrapnel, not much bigger than a BB, had gone through my boot into the front of my ankle. It lodged between the two bones, just above the joint. It hit me hard enough to knock my leg around and was hot enough to cauterize the wound as it went in.

I realized that I needed to go to the aid station. There the medics treated me with antibiotics and said that I had to go back to Quan Loi for X-Ray. It was still dark and I lay on the ground at the aid station, along with several other wounded men and five dead ones. While we still had incoming fire, the medevacs came in and picked up the more seriously wounded, leaving the KIAs, another wounded guy, and myself for a later flight.

When it got light that morning the medics opened the body bags to collect dog tags and I saw Douglas' face for the last time. Then came the worst part: survivor's guilt. Many others know the feeling but do not understand it. Then, just for a split second, I had a very upsetting feeling that I was glad he was dead, but the truth is I was just glad that it was someone else in the bag and not me.

When the last bird came I got on, along with the other wounded man and five KIAs. They'd run out of body bags so the medics had to wrap one of the KIAs in a poncho. It was a short ride, less than 30 minutes, but it seemed like a day with all those thoughts going through my head.

At the battalion aid station in Quan Loi, they had a nice X-ray machine. They took a picture and showed me where the shrapnel had lodged, right between the bottom parts of my tibia and fibula, just above the ankle. They decided they'd do more damage trying to get it out than the shrapnel would cause if they just left it there, so that's what they did. They gave me more antibiotics. It took about a month to get over it. That piece of shrapnel is still in my ankle.

While I was in Quan Loi our mortar platoon leader, an E-6, was there, too recovering from several pieces of shrapnel in the chest. They were small pieces like mine and he was about ready to go back to the field. His platoon nearly had been wiped out. Of 16 men there were only four left alive, so he needed replacements. He needed people badly, but the pipeline for replacements was too slow. He needed them *now.*

While convalescing he'd looked through some of the personnel records and saw that I had mortar training while in OCS. He asked if I'd like to transfer to his platoon. That put me in a quandary. If I went to the mortar platoon, I'd have to go back to the field two or three weeks sooner but I wouldn't have to hump it through the bush, wouldn't have to go out on patrols. The mortar platoon normally stayed at the firebase because they couldn't lug those heavy mortars through the jungle.

The First Sergeant pushed me to go to the mortar platoon, too. Doing so would make him look better on paper since more men would be back working. He was a Hawaiian guy and he was something else!

Ray, the mortar platoon leader, went back to the field. I thought about the offer for two or three days before I gave an answer. It was a hard decision. If I went to the mortar platoon, I probably wouldn't be out in the jungle but, on the other hand, the platoon had just gotten wiped out! And occasionally they would take the mortars to the field whenever they had a situation that required it.

I think I did the right thing and went to the mortar platoon. By then the battalion was at a firebase called LZ Vivian. (I'm not sure how they came up with the names of these firebases but they weren't all named after women.) When I arrived at the platoon all the guys I'd known before were gone, either wounded or killed. They'd gotten a few replacements, including me, but they still didn't have enough. Some of the replacements had been transferred from the 1st or 82nd, and the rest were new in-country.

As an infantryman you carried everything you owned on your back. There was no place to store a thing. In that time period [the early 1970s] cassette tape players had just come on the market. Troops were making tapes of themselves talking and sending them back home, and the folks back home would reciprocate. But the guys in the infantry really couldn't do that, even though they were arguably the ones who needed it the most. They just couldn't carry that stuff in the bush.

Since I was now in the mortar platoon, one of my buddies, John Mike Rice, had a recorder but he was an infantryman. He asked me to keep it for him, planning to use it every three weeks when he came in from the field. I agreed to do that but never saw John again. He didn't make it. He and another guy named Vickery from up near Gatlinburg, Tennessee, were killed on January 8, 1970. I don't know how John's cohorts knew I had some of his personal items, but they got them from me, boxed them up, and mailed them home to his folks.

The mortar platoon performed base defense at the battalion firebase. At the division airstrip they needed a certain number of mortars around it, too. Every so often, on a rotating basis, we'd have to go back and defend the airstrip for a week or two. By the time it was our turn for a rotation back at division, we'd all learned the ropes of how things were done in a mortar platoon.

In February 1970 the Army came up with a new idea: pacification program. Our side tried to train old men and young boys in the villages, people who weren't already in the ARVN, to secure and protect their own people. Our company moved to LZ Granite and spent about three weeks training for that mission before they broke us up into platoons. Each platoon had an assigned village—I was the mortar man assigned to our platoon.

We stayed in the village of Tic Phim, training the locals on the pacification program. We also had a doctor with us and he took care of the sick. I hated being in a small unit that far away from the company and it made me nervous. I had no problems with the general population. They seemed like good people although it was hard to communicate with them. I felt sorry for them. While we were there they held an election and had us secure the place. I'm not sure if they were voting for President of South Vietnam or what. They'd never done anything like that before and I don't think they quite knew what to make of it.

While we were in that village we had some enemy contact one night and we killed a VC, one of those black pajama guys. He had been the barber in the village where we were. He was friendly by day but an enemy guerilla by night. A Claymore mine has 700 small ball bearings powered by C-4 explosive and can be deadly for up to 50m. One ball bearing hit the barber in the center of the chest but that's all it took. He had to be a considerable distance from the mine to be hit by only one pellet, but it just wasn't his lucky day! They dragged him back to the village and laid him out on the porch for everyone to see.

After a few weeks in the village, battalion decided that we needed to swap assignments with another platoon so we wouldn't get too chummy with the locals. We swapped on April 30. We were picked up by airlift and moved to a different village, while the platoon that had been there moved to our previous location. Now we had to learn how the new village worked.

We were sleeping that night and at 3am got an alert that we were moving out. We'd just gotten there! But it wasn't just our platoon; it was the whole division. They airlifted us to a place called Loc Ninh. The 1st Cav had about 900 helicopters and I believe every last one of them was in the air that night.

The next day we went into Cambodia, May 1, 1970. In one huge airlift we put the entire division in Cambodia. We were all ready and happy that this had finally happened. Until then we'd been dealing with stuff coming across the border but we weren't allowed to go to the source and stop it. Now we were going to clean it out and that took the NVA by surprise. They had no idea we were coming. They'd been just across the border for years and we hadn't messed with them.

On one patrol there we found over 20 vehicles, one of them a Willys Jeep. On another patrol we captured 900 SKS rifles and anybody in the company who wanted could have one. We couldn't bring home AK-47s because they could fire fully automatic, like a machinegun, but an SKS was okay. We had plenty of extras so every chopper pilot in III Corps came around trying to trade liquor or beer for an SKS. Everybody wanted one for a trophy.

The politicians saddled us with another silly rule, much like the "can't shoot first" rule on the rubber plantation. Officially, we weren't in Cambodia at all, yet we weren't allowed to stay there for more than 60 days or go more than 30 klicks beyond the border. Fortunately, that was enough to stop what the enemy was doing so the stupid rule really didn't hamper us.

Once we stopped the flow we had almost no enemy contact for a month at a time. If we had invaded Cambodia five years sooner, there's no telling how many lives would have been saved. We didn't have much in the way of enemy supplies and soldiers coming out of Cambodia after our invasion, and it took the NVA a year to get their supplies built back up by other means.

We had an LT named Francis Szczebak and he was a good guy, a really good officer. He was only with us a couple months. He'd been in the village with us, but when we moved to Cambodia they transferred him to Echo Recon. Battalion sent him out there, but the S3 couldn't tell him exactly where their campsite was. He eventually found it and when he arrived the Recon folks said, "Hey, you just walked through our automatic ambush!" After overcoming their shock, they went out to the AA to see what had happened. They wanted to find out why Szczebak hadn't been blown away. People just don't live through an AA—those things destroy *everything!* They shut it down and discovered that the AA hadn't worked because of a dead battery!

Szczebak wasn't with Echo Recon very long. One of his men got killed and Szczebak caught some shrapnel from a fragmentation grenade. He went home and never came back. He's now a lawyer in Arlington, Virginia, and has the dud battery and the piece of shrapnel sitting on the desk in his office.

We had a guy who was new to the company our first week in Cambodia, Michael Steven Tufts. I know I saw him because I was on the firebase when he came in, but I didn't want to get to know him and don't remember what he looked like. We just didn't want to get to know anybody in order to make it easier on ourselves in case something happened to him. He went to the field and got killed the second or third day out there. His unit called in and said, "We've got a KIA." When we asked who it was, nobody knew his name so they had to go check his dog tags.

The last place we went in Cambodia was called LZ David. We'd just gotten another new guy, John Hughes III from Houston, who was the replacement for a man who'd been killed in January. This was late June (see what I meant about replacement lag?). He had a premonition that he was going to die there, and he told me that several times. He had me all messed up. I just didn't want to hear things like that.

I was on the LZ and not in the bush with his platoon, but we were listening on the radio and they got into a pretty good battle. When they found John, he had one bullet wound in the chest and near him was an NVA who'd been shot in the head. We didn't know for sure, but it looked like those two happened to cross paths, fired one round apiece, and killed each other.

John's premonition was correct—he died June 23, 1970.

A week later we got two other guys, Mark Brantley and Richard Grieme. Grieme was a "shake and bake," having attended a crash course at Fort Benning that made him an instant NCO. He was a really good NCO and a pilot in civilian life. As we moved from place to place in Cambodia, we often flew in a Caribou. One day he walked up to the front of the plane and chatted with the pilot, before we even left the ground. When we got up in the air the pilot let him take the stick and fly the plane. He really enjoyed that.

Unfortunately, Grieme was killed about a week after that, the last man we lost in Cambodia. We were coming into a hot LZ one day and one of our door gunners accidentally shot him. He was one of two men I knew who were killed by friendly fire.

Sometime in June of 1970 we got into a firefight and a buddy of mine, Willie Harris, felt something explode next to his chest. After the fight was over and he had time to look, he saw what had happened. We all carried our rifle ammo in two bandoliers with seven magazines of 20 rounds each crisscrossed, shoulder to waist. During this fight an enemy bullet had passed between his chest and the bandolier, cutting open a magazine, and setting off some bullets inside, but he was not harmed. He saved that magazine with a bullet hole in it as a reminder of his close call until it was his time to go home.

When he processed out he wanted to take that magazine home with him. The empty magazine was cut almost in half and was nothing but a worthless piece of metal to anyone else, but some martinet told that he could not keep it because it was government property. So he had to give it up if he wanted to go home.

As if we didn't have enough to deal with, we sometimes had idiotic bureaucracy on top of it!

We had a really hot ground attack while at LZ David. We had to fire our mortars, but the thing about mortars is that 75m is the minimum range—even with minimum powder charge and maximum tube elevation. The enemy was so close that day that we had to fire across the compound in order to get enough range.

Aside from fighting, many folks don't realize how dangerous ordnance can be, just to handle. For example, a case of mortar rounds needs to be handled with care, especially after the box is opened. That many explosives in the open are very dangerous, but we had to have a large number of rounds ready to go at all times. An 81mm mortar round weighs about 10 pounds and has little sacks of gunpowder attached to the rear end.

One night one of our rounds misfired. It cleared the tube but stuck in the ground not far away. The projectile wouldn't have been armed until it had traveled a certain distance, but nobody wanted to go near it. We called in an EOD team. The team drove their jeep up to the round, looked it over, and then one of the guys just turned his head to the side as he picked it up. We said, "You're crazy!"

Mortars were a favorite for base defense because they could be fired much more quickly and more often than artillery or anything else. All we had to do was drop a round down the tube and, when that one fired, drop another one. If you kept it up, the tube would eventually overheat. Then you'd pour water on it and shoot some more.

While at Quan Loi we were shooting one day, not because of enemy action, just for practice. That was something we did all the time. One of our shooters got the next round up to the tube a little too fast and the round coming out of the tube knocked the one he was holding out of his hand. The unfired round fell to the ground a few feet away and we all beat feet a safe distance away.

A mortar round has a safety fuse that doesn't arm until the charge goes off and the round clears the tube by some distance. But in this situation we couldn't be sure what had happened. After a while nothing had happened so we came back, placed sandbags around the round, and then blew it up in place.

Again at Quan Loi we were conducting H&I fire all night long, 600 rounds a night out of one tube. We did that all night, every night. In the daytime we'd have to work four or five hours just opening ammo and pulling off powder bags to get ready for the next night. Each round had nine charge sacks on it, but we only needed one or two for the ranges we were shooting. As we plucked off the bags we'd toss them in a box to be burned later.

We'd just completed prepping over 500 rounds, nearly done for the day. One of the guys brought up more rounds and accidentally hit the end of a box with the primer on one of the rounds. It went *bang*, like a shotgun shell, and lit the powder bags attached. That wouldn't have hurt anyone but we had thousands of powder bags lying around 600 rounds of ammo, and the guy quickly dropped the round in the middle of the bags, setting them all afire. At 10 pounds apiece, 600 rounds amounted to three tons of explosives. That much ammo would make a *big* hole if the powder bag fire spread to the rounds themselves!

We all leaped the sandbags surrounding the mortar pit and took off running. We just knew there was no way we could get far enough away from that thing before the ammo blew. I know I remember thinking, *This is it*. Fortunately, nothing went off except the powder bags. However, we had to wait about eight hours before we went back into the pit. All the heat from the powder burning could easily have caused some of the rounds to cook off. All it would have taken was one, and then there'd have been a chain reaction and they all would have gone off.

When we left Cambodia and got back to Bien Hoa, we got off the plane and were waiting for a ride back to Quan Loi. We got a call on the intercom for Adam Collins, one of our guys. It was the Red Cross informing him that his mother had died. He didn't seem too upset at all and that surprised me. I learned later that it was his birth mother, but she immediately had given him up for adoption, so they weren't exactly close.

Most of the guys in Vietnam wanted to go to Australia or Hawaii for R&R. Some of the guys would have their wives meet them there and they'd spend a week having a second honeymoon. I wasn't married and didn't have a girlfriend at that time, so for me R&R was just a way to get away from combat for a while. The Army was paying for it so I figured I might as well take advantage of it. I didn't want to use up somebody's slot in Hawaii so I spent a week in Taiwan. That was in July 1970, about two months before my tour ended.

We had quite a few guys who got "Dear John" letters while I was in Vietnam. No one wanted to be around when that happened. People could get hurt because those guys went crazy.

One of the guys I knew was what you might call "addicted to sex." He would find himself a girl wherever we went. We were at Loc Ninh for about a month and he had a girl that he was with pretty much the whole time. He'd go see her every day or two. Thirty-some years later in California he saw a girl he thought he knew. He went up to her and said, "Hey, I know you!" Sure enough, it was the same girl he'd known in Loc Ninh. She'd come to California after the war.

Fragging wasn't common where I was, but I know of three incidents. The year 1969 was the worst for it, getting near the end of the war. Soldiers just wouldn't put up with a leader who'd put them at risk unnecessarily. Fragging happened occasionally, but only to people who were putting guys at risk just to make a name for themselves.

A major from battalion came into our company one night, just after we'd been under mortar attack. Several men had been killed and some hurt, so we were already a little tense. The major gave us a hard time and we didn't need that right then. As he started to leave one of the guys pulled up his M-16, flipped the switch to full auto, and was about to saw the guy in half as he walked away. A black guy said to him, "Hey, man, let him go. He'll get his."

The major carried a .45 pistol on his belt, locked and loaded. A few mornings later they found him in his bunk, shot with his own .45. The round entered just above his hip and angled up through his chest cavity. The official investigation determined cause of death to be the result of a defective weapon sear.

A man in my platoon had a very good-looking wife and she sent him some nude pictures of herself. He was very proud of them and one day he was showing them to some of the other men. One man looked at the pictures and asked him who took the pictures. Suddenly we saw that panicked, dear-in-the-headlights look on his face. He went home soon after that and we never found out the rest of the story.

In early 1970 on LZ Granite, I was in the mortar platoon when the rest of our company came in after being out in the field for a longer time than usual. I think they had been out for 51 days instead of the usual 21. Our men were a little restless or wild, but very happy to have a rest. About 1 or 2am, while I was on guard duty I heard an explosion near the headquarters bunker. There were many noises during any night in Vietnam and nothing else happened so I forgot about it. The next morning I found out that the officers' latrine had been blown up. We all laughed, but I never understood who blew it up or why and nobody would talk about it.

Our latrines in the field were primitive at best. We'd go into the bush, dig a hole, do our thing, and then fill the hole. It's not that we were eco-conscious—we just didn't want to leave any evidence that would tell the enemy we had been in the area. Back at the LZ, things were a little better but not much. We had half a 55-gallon barrel with some diesel fuel in the bottom of it. Across the barrel we'd set a board with a hole in it and that's where we sat to do our thing. Basically, it was just an outhouse without the house. We had no privacy whatever.

It seems there was an officer in headquarters that thought he was too good to sit out in the open like the rest of us and had a wooden structure built for his privacy.

I have not found out what they did, but some of our people had made him mad a couple of months earlier. That wasn't a good thing to do because he was in charge of the rotation schedule and he was the one responsible for making our company stay out in the bush so long. Thirty-five years later at one of our reunions I learned the rest of the story about the night of the exploding shitter. It was a simple case of revenge.

We didn't have much in the way of racial problems where I was. We certainly weren't using blacks for cannon fodder. The percentages of blacks and whites that got killed or wounded pretty well reflected their respective densities in the Army. And the blacks weren't all druggies—that was something that didn't happen.

If anybody was doing drugs, it was probably cooks or clerks or somebody like that. You didn't do drugs in the field. If you had someone who did drugs in the field, you got him out of there pronto because he was going to get people killed. I never saw drug use. I may have smelled some people smoking a little grass back in the rear area, but that didn't happen with combat troops. Too many lives were at stake for a man to do drugs while, say, on guard duty, and in the field everyone had guard duty every night. But in the rear area I think many troops probably did it.

Before my time in Vietnam, there was a 1st Sgt with C, 1/5, Robert Allen Fowler, who got killed on May 4th 1968. In the spring of 1970, his younger brother, James B. Fowler came to the 2nd platoon of C, 1/5. I was in the mortar platoon at that time and we were working with 2nd platoon, so I got to know him. Most of us were about 20 years old then but this man was 10 years older than us. We called him "Pop" Fowler. We learned that he had been an Alabama State Trooper. When he joined the Army, they promised him that he could go to Vietnam and serve in the same unit that his brother had been in. He said that he wanted to kill as many Commies as he could for his brother.

The reason I am thinking of this now is that, in the Birmingham Alabama news recently, James B Fowler was indicted for the 1965 killing of Jimmy Lee Jackson. That murder started all the civil rights marches in Alabama.

When I got close to the end of my tour, I didn't want to take any chances. I did anything I could to delay going back to the field. If I was back in the rear for some reason, I made sure I took as much time as possible. But First Sergeant Wong was hot on keeping us in the field. He gave me a hard time because I drug out getting my shots, which I needed before I could leave. I probably took an extra day or two, and he didn't like that. I thought he was singling me out, but I learned later that he was that way with everybody. Like I said, he was something else.

I prepared to go to Bien Hoa and process back to the World after being in Vietnam for a year. They gave me my SKS rifle but wouldn't give me any ammo for it. I raised a fit about that. Here I was going to be riding in a convoy and I've got a rifle with no ammo! But convoys in that area were nothing compared to the places I'd been. Nothing much happened down there but I didn't know that.

As my year came to a close I could not believe I had made it that long. When I got on the plane to leave with a bunch of other guys, nobody said a word. But when the plane cleared the runway everybody hollered.

We arrived in California late at night so I didn't see many protesters. I got off the plane and soldiers from Fort Ord gave me a uniform. That's all I had in the world, the uniform I was wearing and my SKS rifle. When I got to the Atlanta airport I had to walk to a distant gate to catch a commuter plane, which would take me to within 15 miles of my home. I picked up my rifle at baggage claim, and the case was torn up so I threw it away. So there I was, walking through the Atlanta airport carrying a rifle over my shoulder. I got on a small plane, holding about eight passengers. They didn't have baggage check so I boarded with a rifle in my hand! Don't try anything like that today.

When I finished my visit home, I had a year left on my enlistment and my new assignment was with the 1st Armored Division, Fort Hood, Texas. After I had been there a while we heard that the 1st Cav was coming home and would come to Fort Hood. In March of 1971 the Cav took the place of the 1st Armored and we all were part of the event. So I was back in the Cav, this time with Charlie 2/8.

The patch of the unit a soldier is currently serving in is worn on the left shoulder and the patch of the unit with whom he served in combat is worn on the right. The Cav patch is very large and, with one on each side, the men in my platoon called me a bologna sandwich. Of my three-year enlistment I spent almost two of them in the Cavalry.

Recently, several of us have talked about who had the most trouble adjusting when they came home. While this wasn't a scientific study we decided that the ones in our group who had the most problems had been released from the Army when they returned to California and went directly back into civilian life. In the last years of the war, when a man's year over there was done, the policy was that, if he had less than 6 months time left to serve on his enlistment or draft term, he would be released from the Army. This was quite a shock to be in combat one day and, in just the time it took to process and travel home, be back in civilian life. These men had a lot of trouble. Sherman is one of them. He has Post-Traumatic Stress Disorder and is on 100% disability.

I was different. With another year spent at Fort Hood, there was time to come back to normal slowly before going back to civilian life. The war was unpopular and in the '70's no one wanted to hear about it, so we went on with our lives like nothing had happened. I did not talk about it to anyone for any reason. That was hard, even for me, and two years later I joined a National Guard unit just to be around other men who knew what it was like to be in the military. I have been able to adjust but many have not.

Larry Touchstone received the National Defense Service Medal, Vietnamese Service Medal with two Bronze Service Stars, Republic of Vietnam Campaign Medal, Purple Heart, Combat Infantryman Badge, Army Commendation Medal with V Device, Air Medal, Sharpshooter (M-14), and Bronze Star with V Device and Oak Leaf Cluster.

Upon leaving the service Touchstone returned to electronic equipment repair, but in the early '80s TVs, radios, and such became throwaway items. He switched to the automotive field and is considered an expert on automotive computers. His biggest hobby is woodworking. He also builds flintlock rifles and does it just as they did 200 years ago. It takes him about a year of his spare time to complete one rifle.

Asked if he had it to do over again, would he go back to Vietnam, he answered YES *without hesitating.*

CHAPTER 9
MARINE STAFF SERGEANT TONY CHIRICO
Infantry

In Vietnam you had all the stuff you needed and, not only did you get to fire live ammo, but occasionally one of those little yellow bastards would fire back. It kind of pissed a lot of us off that they (the officers) thought of Vietnam as some sort of glorious training opportunity.

*T*ony Chirico (rhymes with Jericho) grew up in the New Jersey Meadowlands when there really were meadows and not ballparks in that area. It was utterly rural yet only a 20-minute drive from New York City. As an eighth-grader, Tony tried to join the Marines when the Korean War broke out. Although he was tall enough to pass for an adult, his age was soon discovered and his enlistment nullified. He graduated from Lyndhurst High School in 1955 and went to boot camp, having enlisted before graduation. His father could not understand Tony joining the service, feeling that was an option only for folks who weren't smart, were in trouble, or just couldn't get a decent job on the outside. One older brother had been a Marine stationed at Hickam Field in Hawaii when the Japanese bombed Pearl Harbor. Another older brother joined the Marines during WW-II and was killed on Okinawa. A younger brother also became a Marine, as did two of Tony's sons. His wife is ex-Navy. Tony served in Vietnam 1965-66.

I got orders to join the 9th Regiment of the 3rd Marine Division in Okinawa and, about two months after I arrived, the division got orders to deploy to Vietnam. We were one of the first units to go there officially.

There were Marine air wings there long before the infantry arrived—fighter planes, not helicopters. When we first arrived, choppers were used for wounded evacuation rather than as troop transports. I thought choppers used as troop transports were a detriment in that they were picking up troops from a secured area and moving them to another area that wasn't secured, but as soon as the troops arrived the gooks left! They knew we were coming and they'd just disappear into the jungle and we were standing there in a now-secure landing area. So, what did we prove?

Meanwhile, the gooks are probably now at the secure place we had just left and now *it's* no longer secure! So, all we did was hopscotch all over the place not proving a damn thing! Prior to Vietnam, when you made a beachhead, you landed someplace and secured the area you were in. As you advanced, everything behind you stayed secured. You never gave up land you had already conquered.

We had big-time stuff going on down south with the Army. They were getting their asses kicked, sometimes right in the middle of Saigon. They were about as far as they could get from North Vietnam, yet they got blasted all the time. They did not have a secure perimeter; they did not keep areas behind them secure as they advanced. They were using what seemed to be novice strategies. The only time you should give up ground is during a tactical retreat.

My regiment went to Vietnam ahead of the division. We had orders, "Do not cross the river." I was part of a group that went out to reconnoiter the area along the Da Nang River before the regiment moved there. When we pulled out of the gate at the airbase near Da Nang, there were 12 of us in three jeeps and trailers heading out into the countryside toward the shores of the Da Nang River, planning to stay for about two weeks. Talk about having your weenie hanging out!

I was a communications specialist—that was my primary MOS— but because of my experience as a drill instructor, the Marines considered me infantry-qualified, too. They assigned me to the regimental HQ. I'm not bragging on myself, but because I had as much time in as I did (10 years of service), the kids in my unit may as well have been my own kids. As long as they did what I told them, when I told them, they usually made out pretty well. If they didn't, then I slapped the shit out of them. They knew it was for their own benefit. Today they'd call it tough love and that's exactly what kept their asses alive.

I had a few troops wounded by snipers but I never had anyone killed. Maybe if I had been in infantry outfits my whole career, I wouldn't have been as tough. These situations came up infrequently and, fortunately, you had time to figure out what in hell you were going to do.

One thing bothered me a lot: It was almost as if the Marine Corps used Vietnam as the perfect training facility. We hadn't seen combat since Korea. We had some skirmishes here and there, but nothing as far as a real pitched battle. They treated it as the ultimate in training. We were in there with a bunch of little yellow gooks who were ill trained, ill equipped, etc. We could go in there and try all the crap [strategy and tactics] the Marines had come up with since Korea. When we took out a vehicle, we could really open it up, go as fast as we wanted. When we were at home base, we had governors for speed, governors for distance, and governors for length of time. But in Vietnam, those limits were gone.

When the division left Okinawa, we closed up the base, just turned it over to a skeleton outfit for custodial care. We took all the Table of Organization equipment with us. The TO authorized us to have specific quantities of certain equipment. And what was so foolish, when we stood inspections, God forbid you should have one more radio or other equipment than the TO said you could have. But the inspectors knew damn well we had twice that many stashed away someplace because we couldn't operate with just the stuff on our TO.

In Vietnam you had all the stuff you needed and, not only did you get to fire live ammo, but occasionally one of those little yellow bastards would fire back. It kind of pissed a lot of us off that they (the officers) thought of Vietnam as some sort of glorious training opportunity. They thought it was the epitome of a training situation, until the casualties started coming in. Then the attitude changed. I'm talking big-time!

Morale was good among the troops, except for the stupid "Rules of Engagement," such as not shooting across the river. That was the only thing that pissed off the young troops. These kids knew these restrictions were not really in their best interests. You've got to face it: We were in the business of warfare. Here you've trained these kids for years, and then you put them in a real combat situation, have them use all the things they've been trained for, except things like not being able to shoot back across the river. Nothing could change their morale, except that we had told them during training to do things one way and now they were in that position and we said, "Now you can't do what we told you to do."

I took out patrols to run commo landlines, and in doing so went into areas that nobody else was going into. I led a night patrol the night a tank unit down-river from us was hit by enemy mortar fire. From across the river, the gooks mortared our tank park, the 3rd Marine tank unit. Naturally, we didn't see them because they were in the jungle. I think they killed something like 12 of our guys and wounded quite a few others.

As soon as the shooting started, the lights went on. Our side sent up parachute flares all over the place to illuminate the area. All of the regimental support units were set up along the south shore of the Da Nang River. There were engineer units, tank units, infantry battalions, and you name it. There was a kid, a lance corporal, who climbed into his tank and located one of the mortars that was firing on his location. He was about to fire on the mortar with the tank's main gun when his lieutenant, the tank commander, hit the override button shutting down everything in the tank, including the main gun. This kid wanted to kill that lieutenant.

The next day, the kid went to the commanding officer of the tank battalion, wanting to bring the lieutenant up on charges. The CO told that kid, "You're lucky the lieutenant was there and did what he did because, had you fired, you would right now be in front of me facing a court marshal!"

How do you explain something like that to this kid? He's been shot at and maybe lost a couple of his buddies, and the LTC told the kid he couldn't shoot back. You do not re-motivate a Marine after something like that happens. His morale was permanently destroyed. This was the first real combat encounter we had since arriving in-country, and not being able to return fire was just devastating to our troops. The lance corporal was maybe 19 years old. Here he had an enemy gun in sight that's been knocking the shit out of his CP, and then has his lieutenant overrode his return fire and the LTC tells him that he (the lance corporal) nearly got himself court marshaled.

That was the first time I ever heard about something called "The Rules of Engagement." Not only did you have to get slapped in the face, but also you had to have at least one nostril bleeding before you could hit back. But then it became, you also had to have your ear hanging by a thread. And then you had to have your toes stepped on at the same time and, if your nose was bleeding, *then* you could return fire. It was okay for them to shoot at us but we couldn't shoot back. We were not to fire across that river, period!

We were probably in-country four weeks or more before they finally brought in a Marine recon outfit, a company-size unit of probably a couple hundred men. They were going to do some advance scouting before any of the rest of us went across the river. They ran into a hornet's nest and we had to send an infantry outfit over there from the 9th Regiment to pull their asses out of the fire.

I could see the political crap that was going on in Vietnam. Here we were with a big difference between our political and our military leaders. Part of that was, we had people who had spent 30 years studying warfare, studying military tactics, etc., and then some well-meaning (benefit of the doubt) guy from some backwater area who's been elected to the House of Representatives and he had the ability to dictate how that professional military guy was going to conduct a war. Amazing!

Everybody back here [the States] wanted to go to Vietnam on a fact-finding visit. They were going to check this and they were going to check that. Is this being done right, is that being done wrong, and who can we hang along the way? To me, that was just so stinking stupid but that's the way it was. That was probably the biggest thing that convinced me to leave the service. I was a career Marine up until that time.

We had people who had spent their entire lives learning tactics, methods, and military history. The military always tried to remove the politics from the battlefield. But then some punk son-of-a-bitch who's been elected for the first time in the House of Representatives had the right to go over on a fact-finding mission and dictate combat tactics to the military.

This is beyond us as a nation to put up with this crap, to have a bunch of ragtag sons-of-bitches (the VC) go on as long as they did. They stayed in the game for, what, 12 years? And that doesn't even count all the advisor stuff that went on before that. The first advisor went into Vietnam right after WW-II and the first casualty was in 1946, an Army major who went there as an advisor. A land mine killed him while he was helping the French.

While I was there, the gooks didn't really want to tangle with us. The North Vietnamese regulars avoided contact at all costs. The only thing we saw were Viet Cong—the North Vietnamese didn't start engaging until much later. There were skirmishes but as far as a real pitched battle is concerned, there just wasn't one. They'd snipe at us or lob mortar shells at us, but that was it. They did not want to mix it up with us. What happened after I left I can't say.

I remember the first VC we killed. The poor guy who killed him carted him around in a jeep trailer for four days trying to tell people where he killed him and how he killed him. Everybody came out and gawked at the body, but no one would say what to do with it.

While I was there, there was no case where the VC overran an American unit. There were cases where an American cadre of eight or 10 would go out with 200 ARVN, and those are the kind of units that got overrun. It wasn't until the first Tet Offensive, way after I left, that the VC really started getting serious about fighting. I don't want to demean anybody, but that was when drug use over there became rampant. Whether those two events coincided, or which was cause and which was effect, I couldn't tell you.

We always acquitted ourselves just fine. If the enemy wanted to stand toe-to-toe with us, you punch me and I punch you, we always made out well and that includes the Army, too. In a pitched battle, the VC never whipped our asses. They whipped us politically. They whipped assholes like Ted Kennedy, that's who they whipped. They did not whip the guys wearing the uniforms. That's about as strong as I can make it. Whenever the gooks heard us coming, they went someplace else. I don't care what anybody said or reported, they did not defeat the US military. They defeated US government tactics. Anybody who tells you differently is full of crap.

We did *not* get our asses kicked in Vietnam. Our own politicians kicked our asses. I got out of the service because of people like Teddy Kennedy. Here we took highly intelligent individuals and sent them to some of the best schools this country has, places like West Point and the Naval Academy. We gave them the benefit of all this history and training. We provided them with the absolute best equipment in the world. And then we elected some dirt-bag asshole from Who-Knows-Where, sent him to Washington, and that son-of-a-bitch told the guy who'd made a career of the military what to do? That's stupid! That is absolutely stupid.

Kennedy is a shitbird who is only where he is because of his family's money and his brothers. I'll tell you what, his fact-finding tours to Vietnam were a farce but he believed Ho Chi Minh was showing him exactly what was going on over there. That tells you he was serving *their* purposes.

Kennedy is just a shitbird, an out and out shitbird. He has never done anything. He's a lawyer, I guess, but never had a case. It's crap like that that was so frustrating. We had guys like that calling the shots. If he were anybody else, he'd be in jail or executed for murder by now for that girl he drowned, besides all the other crap that he's done. As an individual, he isn't worth the sweat off a private's ass. As far as being an American, he hasn't accomplished anything for America. That's just my own opinion, you understand.

Nowadays, we would be better off as long as we can curtail assholes like this wretched little worm from South Dakota, Senator Daschle [since defeated for re-election]. Somebody should just slap the dog shit out of him. As far as being a patriot is concerned, he's nothing.

Those kids that are wearing those uniforms, they can't be killed and they will tell you that. They may have buddies falling all around them, but they themselves can't be killed. That's why they go to battle. That's the difference between some asshole who tries to get 16 more votes from his district and the guys that are out there securing freedom for this country. That pisses me off.

You had guys like Calley [Lieutenant William, of My Lai infamy] who paid the price, and that's another crock. Do you know how many gooks were killed by somebody pulling that kind of crap? The others just didn't get caught. They didn't have some politician looking over their shoulder asking, "Did you have a right to shoot that guy? He was behind you. You're not supposed to shoot to the rear." Bullshit, that guy was trying to *kill* me and you want me to follow some silly rules?

Overall, we are probably the fairest as far as a world power is concerned. We treat our enemies better than any other world power would. If you're going to have an enemy, pick the US. You're going to make out just fine.

We were located on the outskirts of a little village and, naturally, in every one of those places there were VC sympathizers. Not that I hate little yellow people, but if there was a question in my mind, I assumed that son-of-a-bitch was the enemy. That's just the way I looked at it. Guys that I hung out with tried to say there were good Vietnamese and there were bad Vietnamese. That's fine and they never got into trouble until they trusted the wrong one. I never trusted any of them and, consequently, I never had any trouble.

Do you realize how many Americans were killed over there by women and children? The gooks had no more humanity than to take a five or six year-old kid, put a grenade in his hand, pull the pin, and say, "Go give this to the Americans." They didn't give a shit about that kid. If they could wound an American, they didn't care about killing a kid to do it. They knew that if they wounded an American, at least two more would be needed to carry him out. They did it exactly the way the Japs did it in WW-II.

[If I ran the country and] you wanted to badmouth America, your citizenship would be revoked—get the hell out of here! We wouldn't have all that ACLU crap going on where they say, "Ah, we have to be able to have abortions and we have to be able to do this and we have to be able to say that." Let those pacifist bastards go over and try to negotiate with somebody like the Taliban.

Until Vietnam came along, you had a period where people manned the military who had grown up during WW-II. They had a completely different outlook, but they were not the big numbers that went to Vietnam. I was in that interim period, in that I wasn't a WW-II or Korean War veteran. There were a lot of WW-II vets that ran the military at the beginning of the Vietnam War.

How did the '60s generation turn to shit as far as how they treated the military, and how did the government get the say as to what the military would do? I had brothers who came home from WW-II and knew what all that crap was all about. The attitude of veterans returning from WW-II was probably what set the stage for what happened after Korea and Vietnam, as well as some of the other more recent conflicts. Hopefully, we're getting back and I just hope that we don't have too many guys pay the price before we square the hell away.

Most Americans really have no idea how lucky they are to live in America. They should spend some time touring Europe, even England. Do you know why they all wear cardigan sweaters over there? It's because they don't have any heat. That's why they wear sweaters. Everybody over there drives little dinky cars because the cost of gas is astronomical. And France has some of the worst sanitary conditions in all of Europe.

The French, now there's a bunch of assholes! There were a lot of stucco buildings in Vietnam built by the French. They didn't have much in the way of windows, but there were plenty of fans and other ventilation devices. The architecture was more open to promote the flow of air.

The damn Frogs are just a bunch of pigs. That's just hearsay from people I know who have been to France. They left Vietnam after being there for hundreds of years and left absolutely nothing. Other than a few buildings, there were a couple of cement bunkers, cement telephone poles, some train facilities and bridges, but nothing in the way of road systems. They were there to *take*.

There were a lot of gems in Vietnam. There were rubies, sapphires, emeralds, and semi-precious stones like tiger's eyes. If you went to Da Nang, there'd be kids sitting along the street with big trays, and the trays would be full of compartments and each compartment held a different kind of gem. These kids would be lined up one right after the other.

Rubber was a big deal, too. Our famous General McArthur had many personal holdings in Vietnam. He had rubber plantations, banana plantations, and coffee plantations. Those are facts that you don't see in many of the history books. I don't know that McArthur had anything to do with getting us involved in Vietnam, but he certainly had a lot of holdings over there.

I had absolutely no opinion on the Vietnam War before I went over there. When I first heard about it in 1965, I had to go to the library just to find out where it was. There was hardly any detectable mood among the American civilian population regarding the war. Troop morale was good, until the "Rules of Engagement" bullshit.

I personally do not recall any drug use while I was over there. There were a couple of guys that maybe got hold of some grass but, other than that, there was no big-time drug use. There was little contact between the troops and the indigenous personnel. I'm sure that, going into town, you could get dope but as far as anything organized I don't believe it happened while I was there.

The worst thing that ever happened while I was there, as far as troops doing things that they weren't supposed to be doing, was that we had guys dealing in the black market. They were dealing in currency. A

$10-bill or larger was a big-time thing on the black market. The Russians were looking for greenbacks and they were paying over face value for the bill. The bigger the bill, the bigger the percentage they'd pay over face value. If you were talking about a $100-bill, you were talking about a big exchange rate, maybe as much as $150 in Vietnamese currency or scrip. When I first went over there, we were using scrip in lieu of greenbacks. Then that went completely out and we started using greenbacks. That's when the black market started.

I went to Okinawa on R&R. Big deal! Other services allowed their folks to take R&R in places like Hawaii or Australia, but the Marines never pulled any of that kind of bull. When you went overseas, it was an unaccompanied tour. There was no fooling around, no honeymoons in the middle, and that included the officers, too. It didn't matter if you were a general. The Corps didn't even give out three-day passes for in-country R&R the way other services did. In fact, when a group went to Da Nang on business, we had to have a certain number of staff NCOs whose duty was to ensure that nobody went into a bar. The NCOs went in, but only to ensure no troops were in there. No one stayed for a drink or anything else. If I was going to take a six-by-six with 12 or 14 guys into town, it was almost like I was looking out for them, kind of like MP duty.

I had a kid in my unit who was always impressed that I had been a drill instructor. He said he'd always wanted to punch a DI because they had given him such a tough time in boot camp. I'm six-foot-six and he didn't even come up to my chest, but he said, "One of these days we're going to have to go a round or two."

He was already in the unit when I got to Okinawa. His tour was nearly up, but he still went to Vietnam with us. He was probably there three months. Just before he went home, again he says, "We're going to have to get it on one of these days."

I told him, "Anytime you feel froggy, you just jump up here and give it your best shot."

One day, he got as far as grabbing me by the cartridge belt, which I had around my waist, and he said, "Sergeant Chirico, if you were just a little bit smaller...." While he's doing this, he has a buddy take a picture of us. That was a close as he ever came to punching a DI, that I know of anyway. He probably would have liked to do it, but he was just a little too smart to try.

The Marine Corps tried to give many of us battlefield commissions. I turned down warrant officer and lieutenant. Because of my MOSs, they offered me a choice. As a communications guy, they wanted me to accept a warrant officer appointment, but what they really wanted me to do was accept an appointment as a second lieutenant because of my infantry experience. I said, "No way." Guys who accepted commissions made captain almost immediately because they knew the tactics and the Marine Corps didn't give a shit about time in grade. They made company commanders out of them because they knew what was going on and had probably been to Nam twice, three times, or even four times.

After the war, some of them reverted back to their enlisted rank, although they were usually promoted to whatever grade they might have made had they remained enlisted the whole time. Most of these guys retired as sergeants major, but their pension was based on the highest pay grade held, usually an officer rank. A good friend of mine accepted a commission and eventually retired as an LTC.

The Marine Corps was entirely too small for the Vietnam War. You figure, we had three divisions: a division on the east coast, a division on the west coast, and a division in RVN. You can't have a one-year rotation for the troops and expect to maintain all three of those divisions. Some of my contemporaries had six tours of duty in Vietnam before it was all over. Some of them weren't in the states for more than a few months before they were sent back to Vietnam for another tour.

The young kids didn't think about that stuff, but I was in a different position. I was a staff sergeant, a career Marine. Not that I was better, I just had more experience. I'd gotten all that gung-ho shit out of my system. I was doing a job. I had a family back in the states, including four kids. That was my career and it was my ass that I had to cover, along with ass of everybody under me. I lost nobody, but there was always the possibility of getting our asses kicked if I didn't take care of them.

The Ontos [Greek for "the thing"] was a piece of equipment we had in Vietnam that only the Marine Corps had, although it didn't stay around very long. It was a small track vehicle with three recoilless rifles mounted on either side, six altogether, with 4.2-inch tubes I think. It had a .50 caliber spotting gun, used as an aiming device, and mounted on each of those tubes. They'd fire the .50 at a target and when they hit it then they'd fire the recoilless rifle. These weapons were really sub-artillery so their firepower was tremendous. They could be fired individually, all at once, or any combination in between. The vehicle had almost no armor on it, so it was very quick and maneuverable. Being built kind of like a small tank but without a turret, the loaders had to come up out of the chassis to load the rifles, and when they did they were completely vulnerable to enemy fire. Like I said, the Ontos wasn't around too long.

I graduated from Drill Instructor School in 1961with a class of 46. Our careers kind of paralleled each other, that is, we wound up at the same duty stations although possibly at different times. Many of us went from Parris Island where we were DIs to Quantico as OCS instructors. (I nearly had my younger brother in my unit when he was going through boot camp and I was a DI.) If you had a successful tour at Parris Island, they figured they were really going to stick it to you and have you train officers, too. By the time all that was over, we were all Staff Sergeants. Not to brag or anything, but that is what makes the Marine Corps, your staff NCOs, cadre, or whatever you want to call it.

My fellow DIs and I all went to Vietnam at least once. By the time I left the service, there were only 18 of us from the original class of 46 who were still alive, the rest having been killed in Vietnam. Of the 18, there were only a few who hadn't been hit at least once and there were probably a few others who bought the farm after I got out.

I had an officer who had been in WW-II and was still on active duty in Vietnam. He told me that he felt that the NCOs of the Vietnam period were probably the best-trained, best-motivated troops that he had ever encountered. And it was true. He based that on the fact that we, the NCOs, grew up during WW-II and Korea. We reaped the experience of hearing about those wars and we were naturally gung-ho. Guys who were WW-II vets provided all of our training, so that's how we were molded.

I never ran across any tiger traps or bouncing Betties while I was over there, but there were guys who did and have the scars to prove it. Some came home in boxes. Many of the guys who got busted up in Vietnam, but not killed, were discharged. Some of those guys were ruined. They figured as long as they were still able to walk, they should be in the Marine Corps yet they were discharged. I'm glad I wasn't in that position but I could empathize with them. They felt like they had been discarded. Some guys just went off and committed suicide. Some of them got over it and maybe realized they were better off out of the service.

The guys who'd been to Korea, some of those son-of-a-guns couldn't even read or write well. They came mostly from rural areas. They lived and breathed the Marine Corps. You take a guy like that and, if he got busted up to the point where the Marine Corps couldn't use him, he'd lost everything. That was one of the things that bothered me. I was very lucky. Some of those guys are still very bitter.

We had a Marine Corps Commandant who retired not too long ago and I remember that son-of-a-bitch when he was a candidate in OCS. He was in the platoon next to mine. His father had been a general so the OCS staff pointed him out to us. I talked to his father at Quantico and he was real people; he was WW-II; he was Korean War; he was a *real* general. His kid got into OCS because of his father.

Personally, I thought the kid was a little frigging worm as a candidate and he was still a little frigging worm when he became Commandant of the Marine Corps. One of the strongest things the Marine Corps had going for it was traditions that had been passed from generation to generation for hundreds of years. The Marine Corps still used nautical terminology because that's how it was in the beginning.

But now, they no longer serve aboard ship. Almost every man-o-war had at least a Marine detachment aboard, but this commandant decided that all this was pointless nonsense. He also decided that bulkheads were no longer bulkheads, they were walls. Likewise, decks became floors, ladders became stairs, overheads became ceilings, and heads became bathrooms. This terminology was one of the first things I learned in boot camp. This guy did away with all that tradition. He put women in wrong places and did a lot of other things to undermine loyalty and esprit de corps. In doing so, he discouraged longevity. This guy did more to undermine the traditions of the Corps than anyone else in history.

When we first went to Vietnam, those were good times in some parts of America. Many people were making money hand over fist. But a lot of the guys who went into the Marine Corps back then came from depressed cultures where things weren't going so well. They came from places like Tennessee, South Carolina, Georgia, and for many of them the Marines was the best that they could do. Otherwise, they'd be walking behind a mule's ass, chopping up the same ground that their fathers and grandfathers before them had chopped up. The Marines was an escape for these guys and they were some of the finest people I've ever come across.

I was older and in longer and had a completely different slant on the war than the kids who got drafted and went over there for one tour and then got out. For most of them, it was a lark, a high adventure thing. They did all sorts of things and never told anybody about it when they got back. They just did the sniveling, crying, wailing, gnashing of teeth because that's what was the accepted outlook of Vietnam veterans at the time. That pissed me off.

I will not be in the Vietnam Veterans Association because they are just a bunch of sniveling, crying, whining assholes. They talk one way now, but they did not act that way when they were in Nam. That does gripe me that they put on this façade, "Oh, poor Vietnam veteran." That's bullshit! That's why I cannot be a member of the VVA. I joined for something like six months but they're just not my kind of people. If you got them to sit around and have a couple beers, then a different side of them came out. You'd find out about some of the crap that they did and got involved in. I have some bad feelings about what came out of that war after I got back.

If I had it to do over again, I wouldn't hesitate to go to Vietnam. My only thought during the last days of my tour in Vietnam was: *How long am I going to be in the States before I get sent back over here?* I have no bitter feelings.

The Vietnam War was a losing situation. I could not understand how we could have people who had spent their entire adult life studying military tactics, but then have some asshole that had just been elected tell them what to do. I hate to keep coming back to it but I just do not understand it. We're the ones over there slopping around in the mud and doing all this crap, but here comes a guy on a four- or five-day whirlwind tour and then he got back on a plane to the clean, sterile USA again. And he told everybody back there exactly how it ain't! Why the American people put up with that shit, I'll never know.

Upon leaving Vietnam in 1966, Tony was assigned to Cherry Point, NC, got promoted to E-7 while there, and two years later left the service just before he was scheduled to return to Vietnam. He and his family moved back to Tony's hometown in New Jersey where he went to work for Western Electric. A few years later, he went into business for himself remodeling and building homes. He's now retired and lives in western North Carolina.

EPILOGUE

In my opinion an infantryman who went to Vietnam learned more about life in one year than most other people did in 10.—Larry Touchstone

There were five million people who served in the armed forces during the Vietnam War but only 2.6 million who served in-country. It took about 10 troops to support every infantryman in the field. That means there were only 260 thousand actual grunts. That's all there ever was. This country has 300 million people, so the odds of two actual combat veterans walking up to each other are greater than one in a thousand.

Eight million Americans claim to be Vietnam veterans! There are a lot of fakers out there. If you hear half a dozen guys sitting around telling each other, "I did this and I did that," you can just bet that every one of them is lying. Also, very few people pulled more than one tour over there, the exception being the lifers, the career soldiers. I do know a marine who'd pulled two tours and he got out after 10 years because they were planning to send him back again. Very few volunteered for multiple tours in Vietnam.

I've had folks ask me, "Didn't listening to all these stories get a little monotonous? Didn't you get tired of hearing the same things over and over?"

My answer was an emphatic NO! None of the incidents the vets related had any resemblance whatever to things others told me, not even the guys from 1st Cav, of which there were quite a few. I mentioned this phenomenon to Larry Touchstone and he said, "For every man that spent a year in Nam there are at least 365 stories. There is never a dull day in a combat zone."

I'm firmly convinced that he's correct.

Larry also observed, "Some men do not remember anything from Nam and I believe that's their minds' way of protecting itself. Everyone is different; I remember everything."

Fortunately, I ran across a number of guys with memories just as vivid as Larry's. I truly am honored that these incredible warriors allowed me to facilitate their always fascinating, occasionally humorous, and sometimes harrowing stories. I hope you've enjoyed reading them half as much as I've enjoyed telling them.

Ed Nielsen

APPENDIX
Enlisted and Officer Ranks
Unit Organization

ARMY ENLISTED
E-1   Private
E-2   Private
E-3   Private First Class
E-4   Corporal or Specialist Four
E-5   Sergeant or Specialist Five
E-6   Staff Sergeant
E-7   Sergeant First Class
E-8   Master Sergeant or First Sergeant
E-9   Sergeant Major

NAVY & COAST GUARD ENLISTED
E-1   Seaman Recruit
E-2   Seaman Apprentice
E-3   Seaman
E-4   Petty Officer 3rd Class
E-5   Petty Officer 2nd Class
E-6   Petty Officer 1st Class
E-7   Chief Petty Officer
E-8   Senior Chief Petty Officer
E-9   Master Chief Petty Officer

AIR FORCE ENLISTED
E-1   Airman Basic
E-2   Airman
E-3   Airman First Class
E-4   Senior Airman
E-5   Staff Sergeant

E-6   Technical Sergeant
E-7   Master Sergeant
E-8   Senior Master Sergeant
E-9   Chief Master Sergeant

MARINES ENLISTED
E-1   Private
E-2   Private First Class
E-3   Lance Corporal
E-4   Corporal
E-5   Sergeant
E-6   Staff Sergeant or Specialist Six
E-7   Gunnery Sergeant
E-8   Master Sergeant
E-9   Master Gunnery Sergeant

NAVY & COAST GUARD OFFICERS
O-1   Ensign
O-2   Lieutenant Junior Grade
O-3   Lieutenant
O-4   Lieutenant Commander
O-5   Commander
O-6   Captain
O-7   Commodore
O-8   Rear Admiral
O-9   Vice Admiral
O-10   Admiral

ALL OTHER SERVICE OFFICERS
O-1   Second Lieutenant
O-2   First Lieutenant
O-3   Captain
O-4   Major
O-5   Lieutenant Colonel
O-6   Colonel
O-7   Brigadier General